Mastering SentinelOne

- Table of Contents
- About This Edition
- Copyright
    - Trademark Notice
    - Disclaimer
- Dedication
- Foreword from the Author
- Preface
    - Why This Book Exists
    - Who This Book Is For
    - What This Book Assumes About You
    - How the Book Is Organized
    - How to Use This Book
    - About the Academic Edition
    - A Personal Note
- Acknowledgments
- About the Author
- How to Use This Book
    - For Instructors
    - Assessment Recommendations
    - Lab Environment Setup
    - For Students
    - A Final Note
- Chapter 1
    - The SentinelOne Command Console at a Glance
        - Learning Objectives

- **Chapter Opener**
- **1.0 Foundations: What This Book Assumes (and What You Need to Know)**
- **1.1 What SentinelOne Is and Where It Fits**
- **1.2 The MSSP Console Hierarchy: Global, Account, Site, Group**
- **1.3 A Walking Tour of the Left Navigation**
- **1.4 Policies, Exclusions, and Policy Overrides**
- **1.5 Locations, Notifications, and Audit Logging**
- **Chapter Summary**
- **Key Takeaways**
- **Hands-On Exercise**
- **What's Next**
- **Review Questions**
- **Discussion Questions**
- **Hands-On Lab Exercises**

- **Chapter 2**
  - **The Dashboard**
    - **Learning Objectives**
    - **Chapter Opener**
    - **2.1 What the Dashboard Is, and What It Is Not**
    - **2.2 Scope: The Most Important Filter in the Product**
    - **2.3 Scope at Scale: MSSP Tenants and Cross-Customer Views**
    - **2.4 The Core Widgets**
    - **2.5 Graph Types: Choose the Shape That Fits the Data**
    - **2.6 Customization Discipline and Team-Shareable Layouts**
    - **2.7 Dashboard Refresh and Cache Behavior**
    - **2.8 Situational Awareness Versus Actionable Detection**
    - **Chapter Summary**
    - **Key Takeaways**

    - **Hands-On Exercise**
    - **Review Questions**
    - **Discussion Questions**
    - **Hands-On Lab Exercises**
    - **What's Next**
- **Chapter 3**
  - **Ranger**
    - **Learning Objectives**
    - **Chapter Opener**
    - **3.1 What Ranger Is**
    - **3.2 The Four Device Classifications**
    - **3.3 How Ranger Discovers Devices**
    - **3.4 Reading the Ranger Dashboard**
    - **3.5 Finding Rogues and Gaps with Filtering**
    - **3.6 Tagging and Review Workflows**
    - **3.7 Configuring Ranger for Your Environment**
    - **3.8 Common Pitfalls and How to Avoid Them**
    - **Chapter Summary**
    - **Key Takeaways**
    - **Hands-On Exercise**
    - **Review Questions**
    - **Discussion Questions**
    - **Hands-On Lab Exercises**
    - **What's Next**
- **Chapter 4**
  - **Sentinels: Endpoint Fleet Management**
    - **Learning Objectives**
    - **Chapter Opener**
    - **4.1 The Endpoint List: What You Are Looking At**
    - **4.2 Reading the Columns: Status, Health, and Activity**

- 4.3 Filtering: Finding What You Need
- 4.4 Tags and Customer Identifiers: Organizing Your Fleet
- 4.5 The Device Detail Page: Everything About One Machine
- 4.6 Remote Shell, File Fetch, and Remote Actions
- 4.7 Bulk Actions: Working at Scale
- 4.8 Status Interpretation: What "Online" Really Means
- 4.9 Field-Team Workflows: Getting Work Done
- Chapter Summary
- Key Takeaways
- Hands-On Exercise
- Review Questions
- Discussion Questions
- Hands-On Lab Exercises
- What's Next

- **Chapter 5**
  - **Sentinels: Remediation and Lifecycle**
    - Learning Objectives
    - Chapter Opener
    - 5.1 The Four Core Remediation Actions
    - 5.2 Disconnect vs. Isolate: The Key Distinction
    - 5.3 The Isolate Workflow End-to-End
    - 5.4 Decommissioning Endpoints: Keeping the Console Clean
    - 5.5 Agent Uninstall, Passphrase, and Re-Enrollment
    - 5.6 Agent Upgrade and Maintenance Windows
    - 5.7 Telemetry and Forensics When an Endpoint Goes Offline
    - 5.8 Case Studies: When to Use Which Action
    - Chapter Summary
    - Key Takeaways
    - Hands-On Exercise
    - Review Questions

        - **Discussion Questions**
        - **Hands-On Lab Exercises**
        - **What’s Next**

- **Chapter 6**
    - **Incidents: Triage, Investigation, and Response**
        - **Learning Objectives**
        - **Chapter Opener**
        - **6.1 The Incidents Queue and Filtering**
        - **6.2 The Storyline View**
        - **6.3 Thread Details and Threat Indicators**
        - **6.4 Manual Mitigation Actions**
        - **6.5 Analysis Verdict and Incident Status**
        - **6.6 Notes and Collaboration**
        - **6.7 Threat Hunting and Sweep Across the Fleet**
        - **6.8 VirusTotal Integration and External Intelligence**
        - **6.9 Closing Procedures and Handoff**
        - **6.10 The Daily Analyst Workflow**
        - **6.11 Worked Example: Triage of a Suspected False Positive**
        - **Chapter Summary**
        - **Key Takeaways**
        - **Hands-On Exercise**
        - **Review Questions**
        - **Discussion Questions**
        - **Hands-On Lab Exercises**
        - **What's Next**

- **Chapter 7**
    - **Applications: Software Inventory for Security Operations**
        - **Learning Objectives**
        - **Chapter Opener**
        - **7.1 Understanding the Applications Inventory**

    - **7.2 Reading the Vulnerability Data: CVSS Scores and Severity Bands**
    - **7.3 Filtering, Sorting, and Hunting**
    - **7.4 From Vulnerability to Remediation: The CVE Cross-Reference Workflow**
    - **7.5 Finding Unapproved Software and Shadow IT**
    - **7.6 Scope Awareness: Scanning Across Sites and Accounts**
    - **7.7 Integration with Vulnerability Management and Patch Workflows**
    - **7.8 License Compliance as a Side Benefit**
    - **7.9 Case Study: Coordinating a Cross-Endpoint Vulnerability Remediation**
    - **Chapter Summary**
    - **Key Takeaways**
    - **Hands-On Exercise**
    - **Review Questions**
    - **Discussion Questions**
    - **Hands-On Lab Exercises**
    - **What's Next**
- **Chapter 8**
  - **Activity Logs: Audit Trails and Operator Accountability**
    - **Learning Objectives**
    - **Chapter Opener**
    - **8.1 What the Activity Log Is and Why It Matters**
    - **8.2 The Activity Log Interface**
    - **8.3 Understanding Activity Categories: Administration, Operations, Malware, and More**
    - **8.4 Finding the Answer: Filtering by User, Action, and Date**
    - **8.5 Exporting Activity for Compliance and Incident Review**
    - **8.6 Activity Log Retention and Long-Term Integration**

- 8.7 Reading Activity Anomalies: The Insider Detection Pattern
- 8.8 What the Activity Log Does Not Track: The Blind Spots
- 8.9 Common Audit Questions the Activity Log Answers
- 8.10 Integrating Activity with SIEM and Log Aggregation
- Chapter Summary
- Key Takeaways
- Hands-On Exercise
- Review Questions
- Discussion Questions
- Hands-On Lab Exercises
- What's Next

- Chapter 9
  - Reports: Communicating Security Posture Upward
    - Learning Objectives
    - Chapter Opener
    - 9.1 The Five Core Report Types
    - 9.2 Scheduling Cadence: Daily, Weekly, Monthly
    - 9.3 Audience-Appropriate Customization
    - 9.4 Executive Reports vs. Analyst Reports
    - 9.5 Building a Metrics Narrative
    - 9.6 Avoiding Vanity Metrics
    - 9.7 Handling Bad News Reports
    - 9.8 Report Delivery and Distribution
    - 9.9 Archiving for Compliance
    - Chapter Summary
    - Key Takeaways
    - Hands-On Exercise
    - Review Questions
    - Discussion Questions

        - **Hands-On Lab Exercises**
        - **What's Next**
- **Chapter 10**
    - **Automation: STAR Rules and Response Playbooks**
        - **Learning Objectives**
        - **Chapter Opener**
        - **10.1 What STAR Is and Why It Matters**
        - **10.2 STAR Rule Anatomy**
        - **10.3 Writing Your First STAR Rule**
        - **10.4 Testing Automation Safely**
        - **10.5 Building a Response Playbook**
        - **10.6 Common Automations: Auto-Isolate, Auto-Quarantine, Auto-Tag**
        - **10.7 Guardrails: Preventing Runaway Automation**
        - **10.8 When Not to Automate**
        - **10.9 RemoteOps and Script-Driven Responses**
        - **Chapter Summary**
        - **Key Takeaways**
        - **Hands-On Exercise**
        - **Review Questions**
        - **Discussion Questions**
        - **Hands-On Lab Exercises**
        - **What's Next**
- **Chapter 11**
    - **Settings: Tenant Configuration, Policy, and Governance**
        - **Learning Objectives**
        - **Chapter Opener**
        - **11.1 Notifications: Email and Syslog**
        - **11.2 Email and Syslog Delivery**
        - **11.3 Site and Group Policy Hierarchy**

        - **11.4 Exclusions: Power and Peril**
        - **11.5 Users, Roles, and RBAC**
        - **11.6 Service Users and API Keys**
        - **11.7 Integrations: SMTP, Syslog, and Single Sign-On**
        - **11.8 Locations: Network-Aware Endpoint Groups**
        - **11.9 Sites and Account Management**
        - **11.10 Change Management and Console Governance**
        - **Chapter Summary**
        - **Closing: What You Have Built**
        - **Key Takeaways**
        - **Hands-On Exercise**
        - **Review Questions**
        - **Discussion Questions**
        - **Hands-On Lab Exercises**

- **Appendix A**
    - **Lab Setup Guide: Building a Three-Product Cybersecurity Lab**
    - **Introduction**
    - **Licensing Paths for Academic Programs**
        - **Path 1: Direct Vendor Partnership (SentinelOne Education Program)**
        - **Path 2: MSP/MSSP-Brokered Tenants (Most Common for Community Colleges)**
        - **Path 3: Free/Trial Tenants (Capstone Use Only)**
        - **What to Ask the Vendor: A Checklist**
    - **Hardware Bill of Materials: Starter Lab**
        - **Bill of Materials: Detailed Breakdown**
        - **What You Can Skip (If Budget Is Tight)**
        - **What to Upgrade (If Budget Allows)**
        - **Virtual vs. Physical Infrastructure Considerations**

- **Network Topology**
  - **Network Isolation: Validation and Testing**
  - **Network Access Options: Wired vs. Wireless**
  - **Remote Access to Lab Machines (For Hybrid or Online Classes)**
  - **Classroom Topology**
  - **Workstation and Network Specifications**
- **SentinelOne Tenant for Education**
  - **Multi-Tenant vs. Single-Tenant Lab Patterns**
  - **Recommended Tenant Structure**
  - **Sample Policy Hierarchy for Student-Safe Operations**
  - **Detection Engines and Baseline Configuration**
  - **Student Account Creation and RBAC**
  - **Lab Console Access Patterns**
  - **Provisioning Workflow and Console Navigation**
- **Tenable Nessus Lab Deployment**
  - **Nessus Architecture: Manager vs. Scanner**
  - **Lab Scanning Patterns**
  - **Vulnerability Remediation Workflow in the Lab**
  - **Integration with SentinelOne**
- **ServiceNow Integration**
  - **ServiceNow Incident Management Workflow**
  - **SentinelOne to ServiceNow Integration**
  - **Incident Lifecycle in the Lab**
- **Sample 16-Week Lab Schedule**
- **Day-1 Troubleshooting Playbook**
  - **Issue 1: Agent Install Fails on Windows (Error: "Unable to Open Log File" or Install Hangs)**
  - **Issue 2: Agent Install Fails on macOS (System Extension Not Approved)**

    - **Issue 3: Agent Install Fails on Linux (Missing Kernel Module Dependencies)**
    - **Issue 4: Agent Installs but Shows Offline in Console (Firewall/Proxy Blocking)**
    - **Issue 5: Console Login Fails (SSO Misconfiguration or MFA Lockout)**
    - **Issue 6: Ranger Shows Zero Devices (Not Discovering Anything)**
    - **Issue 7: Activity Logs Show No Recent Actions (Retention or Timezone Issues)**
    - **Issue 8: STAR Rules Not Firing (Rule Not Matching Threats)**
    - **Issue 9: Reports Show No Data (Date Range or Scope Filter Wrong)**
    - **Issue 10: API Token Returns 401 Unauthorized (Token Expired or Malformed)**
- **Lab Exercises by Chapter: A Cross-Reference**
    - **Using This Table to Plan Your Semester**
- **Capstone Lab: End-to-End Incident Scenario**
    - **Scenario Brief**
    - **Learning Objectives**
    - **Capstone Deliverables**
    - **Capstone Rubric**
    - **Role Assignments**
    - **Capstone Timeline**
    - **Grading and Feedback on the Capstone**
- **Faculty Notes: Common Pitfalls and Operational Tips**
    - **Pitfall 1: SentinelOne Tenant Gets Misconfigured**
    - **Pitfall 2: Student Machines Stop Checking In**
    - **Pitfall 3: Malware Simulation Does Not Trigger Detection**

        - **Pitfall 4: Students Forget Lab Credentials or Lock Themselves Out**
        - **Pitfall 5: Nessus Scan Takes Too Long or Overwhelms the Network**
        - **Pitfall 6: ServiceNow Developer Instance Expires**
    - **Maintenance and Updates**
        - **SentinelOne Product Updates**
        - **Chapter Updates and Curriculum Sync**
        - **Threat Landscape and Vulnerability Data**
        - **Seasonal Refresh**
        - **Documentation and Knowledge Sharing**
        - **Best Practices for Lab Sustainability**
    - **Lab Assessment and Learning Outcomes**
        - **Chapter-by-Chapter Learning Outcomes**
        - **Formative vs. Summative Assessment**
    - **Closing: The Journey Ahead**
- **Appendix B**
    - **MITRE ATT&CK Mapping for SentinelOne Operators**
        - **Why ATT&CK Matters for the Operator**
        - **How This Appendix Is Organized**
        - **ATT&CK Tactics Covered in This Book**
        - **Tactic-by-Tactic Mapping**
        - **Building an ATT&CK-Driven Detection Catalog**
        - **References for Further Study**
- **Appendix C**
    - **NIST Cybersecurity Framework 2.0 Mapping for SentinelOne Operations**
        - **Why NIST CSF 2.0 Matters**
        - **The Six Functions of NIST CSF 2.0**

        - **Function-by-Function Mapping**
        - **Implementation Tier Considerations**
        - **References**
- **Appendix D**
    - **CIS Critical Security Controls v8 Mapping**
        - **Why CIS Controls Matter**
        - **How This Appendix Is Organized**
        - **Control-by-Control Mapping**
        - **Common Mappings at a Glance**
        - **References**
- **Appendix E**
    - **ISO/IEC 27001:2022 Annex A Controls Mapping**
        - **Why ISO 27001 Matters**
        - **ISO 27001:2022 Annex A Structure**
        - **Theme-by-Theme Mapping**
        - **Compliance Considerations**
        - **References**
- **Appendix F**
    - **CLI and API Quick Reference**
        - **About This Reference**
        - **Section 1: Endpoint Agent CLI (Windows / macOS / Linux)**
        - **Section 2: Management Console REST API (v2.1)**
        - **Section 3: Common Automation Patterns (Python Examples)**
        - **Section 4: SIEM/SOAR Integration Quick Reference**
        - **Section 5: Troubleshooting Cheat Sheet**
        - **Section 6: Best Practices for Automation and Integration**
        - **Section 7: Quick Reference for Common Tasks**
        - **Key Takeaways**
        - **Section 8: Comprehensive sentinelctl and API Reference**

        - **A**
        - **B**
        - **C**
        - **D**
        - **E**
        - **F**
        - **G**
        - **H**
        - **I**
        - **K**
        - **L**
        - **M**
        - **N**
        - **O**
        - **P**
        - **Q**
        - **R**
        - **S**
        - **T**
        - **U**
        - **V**
        - **W**
        - **Z**
- **References**
    - **Citation Standard**
    - **Primary Industry Frameworks and Standards**
    - **Vendor Documentation**
    - **Foundational Texts in Cybersecurity Operations**
    - **Scholarly Articles and Research**
    - **Incident Response and Digital Forensics**

- **Endpoint Security and Detection and Response**
- **Government and Regulatory Resources**
- **Malware Analysis and Threat Intelligence**
- **Network and Application Security**
- **Automation and Orchestration in Security Operations**
- **Cloud and Container Security**
- **Active Directory and Identity Security**
- **Process and Memory Analysis**
- **Compliance and Audit**
- **Authentication and Access Control**

Table of Contents

Table of contents will be auto-generated when you open this in Word.

Mastering SentinelOne

A Complete Guide to Endpoint Detection and Response: From Console Operation to Automated Response

Kendrick Washington

Technology Interpreters, Inc.

First Edition

About This Edition

This is the first edition of Mastering SentinelOne. It reflects the author's hands-on experience with SentinelOne as an operator, instructor, and consultant as of late 2025 and early 2026.

Endpoint Detection and Response (EDR) platforms evolve rapidly. New detection engines are added, console layouts change, and operational best practices shift based on emerging threats and operator feedback. This book teaches foundational concepts and operational workflows that are built to last, but specific user interface details, menu paths, and feature names may differ from what you see in your current SentinelOne console.

If you encounter a step in this book that does not match your console exactly, two resources will help: (1) Use the in-console Help feature or the SentinelOne Knowledge Base to verify the current location of a feature. (2) Check the official SentinelOne documentation for your specific agent and console version. The core concepts, hierarchy, policy inheritance, incident triage, automation principles, remain consistent across versions. The UI details should not.

This academic edition is designed for a 14-16 week semester course and serves as the primary textbook for cybersecurity programs adopting SentinelOne in a hands-on lab environment. The structure of the book, including learning objectives, lab exercises, and review questions in each chapter, aligns to this standard academic schedule. An instructor's pacing guide is included in the "How to Use This Book" section.

Questions or feedback on this edition? Contact the author through Technology Interpreters at the website listed in the About the Author section.

Copyright

First Edition: 2026

Published by Technology Interpreters, Inc.

ISBN (Paperback): 979-8-9958831-0-4, placeholder, confirm before print

ISBN (Hardcover): 979-8-9958831-1-1, placeholder, confirm before print

Trademark Notice

SentinelOne®, Singularity™, and Ranger® are trademarks or registered trademarks of SentinelOne, Inc. Tenable® and Nessus® are trademarks of Tenable, Inc. ServiceNow® is a trademark of ServiceNow, Inc. MITRE ATT&CK® is a registered trademark of The MITRE Corporation. NIST and the NIST Cybersecurity Framework are products of the National Institute of Standards and Technology, an agency of the U.S. Department of Commerce. CIS®, CIS Controls®, and CIS Benchmarks® are registered trademarks of the Center for Internet Security, Inc. ISO® and ISO/IEC 27001 are registered trademarks of the International Organization for Standardization. All other trademarks belong to their respective owners. The author and publisher are independent and are not affiliated with, endorsed by, or sponsored by SentinelOne, Inc., Tenable, Inc., ServiceNow, Inc., The MITRE Corporation, the National Institute of Standards and Technology, the Center for Internet Security, Inc., the International Organization for Standardization, or any other organization referenced in this book. Use of trademarks is for descriptive and educational purposes under the doctrine of nominative fair use.

Disclaimer

The information in this book is provided "as-is" and reflects the author's experience as of the publication date. Software interfaces and capabilities change. Always verify against current vendor documentation. Neither the author nor the publisher shall be liable for damages arising from the use of this material.

Dedication

To the analysts who answer the alerts at 3 a.m., keep the networks running at 4 a.m., and find the time to mentor the next generation by 5 a.m. And to the students who will outlast and outthink us all.

Foreword from the Author

There is something to be said about knowing your worth.

I have over thirty years of experience in cybersecurity. I was doing this work before it was formally a field. While working on the help desk, I spent hours on the phone with McAfee dealing with viruses, trojans, and eventually rootkits, the kind for which there was no current detection and against which McAfee's antivirus simply did not work. McAfee occasionally provided me with internal tools, utilities that existed nowhere outside the company, to combat new generations of malware that the commercial product could not stop.

At the time, I did not understand that what I was doing was unusual. In fact, it was exceptional. I stood among a small number of people in the world who had that skill set, who fundamentally understood Windows internals at a level that allowed them to remove and unhook malware no scanner could touch. To me it was just a normal day at the help desk. The equivalent role today would place me among the most senior practitioners in the field, analysts who understand malware at a deep technical level. But I did not see myself that way. I just saw problems and went to work solving them.

In 2018, I formally transitioned into a cybersecurity role at the company where I had been since I was an intern in 1997 and a full-time employee since 2000. The cybersecurity team was newly created, and one of my senior co-workers in the networking department, Dan Smart, was promoted to be its director. I am thankful that Dan understood my value and the work I had been doing as a network engineer. He had mentored me through firewall administration and perimeter security in addition to the networking I already knew. I will never forget the day he casually mentioned, "We have a position on the cybersecurity team." That was his way of letting me know I should apply, and that there was a high likelihood I would get it. I am forever thankful to Dan for seeing my talent before I saw it in myself.

Around the same time, I was leading other things I also did not understand were unusual. Within three years of joining InfraGard I went from member to vice president to president. During my two to three years as president, I came to appreciate the platform the organization gave me, and I worked with an extraordinary board of directors to grow our chapter into one of the top chapters in the nation. I remember speaking in Dallas to a room full of InfraGard leaders and FBI coordinators about how we had built that success. During my time as president we partnered with Homeland Security to host IED-detection classes, ran active-shooter training with local police departments, and worked on church-safety initiatives. The following year, our FBI coordinator was recognized as FBI Coordinator of the Year. That, too, was not normal.

I never felt prepared for any of these positions. I have always treated life the way I treated my job in IT: I solve problems. I troubleshoot. And at the core, there is something in me that has always wanted to improve and innovate, that is never satisfied with the status quo.

I stayed at that company from 1997, first as an intern, through 2021. In 2021 I received an offer to join a cybersecurity startup composed of former Foundstone engineers. (Foundstone was the professional services arm of McAfee, eventually absorbed into Cylance, which was later acquired by BlackBerry.) I was at a pivotal moment. I could stay at the company that had been faithful to me for two decades and represented genuine stability, or take a leap of faith into a startup with all the uncertainty that implies. I thought about it, prayed about it, and pondered it for a long time. I made the move. I knew that if I did not, I would regret it.

Going to work for a managed security service provider is not an easy task. It is a tough job. But it is also one of the fastest ways to grow as a security professional. Within three months I began to identify opportunities for improvement and to implement them. The people skills I had built at the help desk, the ability to listen for the real problem behind the stated one, paid dividends. After a short stint, I found myself supporting up to forty cybersecurity client companies single-handedly. We deployed roughly sixteen different security solutions across that portfolio, and SentinelOne was among them. I learned what it takes to take a company from no security at all to fully secured. I scripted in PowerShell and shell scripting daily, a natural extension of my software engineering background. Years earlier, as an undergraduate, I had earned my degree in Software Engineering Technology from the University of Southern Mississippi. (Go Eagles. SMTTT, fellow Southern Miss alumni will know exactly what that means.)

I spent a great deal of time inside the SentinelOne console. I deployed remediations that often required me to drop into the SentinelOne remote shell and operate directly on the endpoint, fixing broken security agents, repairing other vendors' tooling, or pushing the actual remediation that closed a vulnerability. I came to appreciate how SentinelOne, compared to the other products I worked with, was unusually easy to learn and use while remaining genuinely effective at stopping malware.

The benefit of working at a startup is that you see every part of the process. As I worked deeper in SentinelOne, I realized that my own home computers were running only the built-in Windows protection. I knew that the McAfee-era tools were no longer adequate against the current generation of malware, and that EDR, endpoint detection and response, was now the standard of care. I wanted that level of protection at home, on machines that ran some enterprise-class software for my own work.

I reached out to Arete. The company name is taken from the ancient Greek word ἀρετή (aretē), meaning excellence, virtue, the highest quality a person or thing can achieve, the idea of fulfilling one's maximum potential through moral goodness, physical strength, and intellectual skill. Arete is more than a name; it is a philosophy. I explained to their business development representative, Paul Elias, that I wanted to use their SentinelOne offering on my YouTube channel so I could teach others how enterprise cybersecurity actually works using the actual tool. My channel was growing at the time and currently has fifty-three thousand subscribers. Paul took my request to leadership, and they agreed to provide me with an MSSP console offering full access to SentinelOne, equivalent to what I used every day at the day job, and in fact with a few features I did not have access to at work.

I deployed it fully in my own environment. I made YouTube videos. And in the process I discovered things about SentinelOne that many of my own teammates, and likely many people who use the product only at work, did not know, because I had a level of familiarity with the platform that comes only from running it as both an operator and an instructor at the same time. Those casual SentinelOne videos grew into the top SentinelOne content on YouTube. Today, if you search "SentinelOne" on YouTube, my videos are often the first results. Several rank as the number-one result for specific SentinelOne searches.

Making that content did not just grow my channel. It grew me as a professional. People stopped by the channel and left comments thanking me for the training because they could not find it anywhere else. Viewers asked if I would teach them directly. So I did. I taught and ran cohorts. The cohorts became a program, a structured cybersecurity mentorship that combined enterprise tools (SentinelOne, Tenable) with the core skills people lacked: networking, PowerShell, Windows command line. The program was successful, and it was profoundly motivating to watch graduates of major university cybersecurity programs and well-known boot camps arrive at our program after completing those credentials, because they had still never touched the actual tools and could not yet do the job.

That experience is why this book exists.

I have extracted what I have taught over many hours of YouTube videos and reduced it into this book in a form that can be read sequentially, returned to as a reference, and assigned as the curriculum text for cybersecurity programs that want their students to graduate ready for the work. I hope it does for you what those original videos did for the people who left those comments: get you ramped up on SentinelOne quickly so you can unlock the real potential of the product and, more importantly, of yourself.

, Kendrick Washington

Technology Interpreters, Inc.

Preface

Why This Book Exists

I wrote this book because there is a gap between two worlds, and students and working analysts fall into it every day. In one world, you can take a SentinelOne certification exam, pass it, and know what a policy override is. In the other world, you open the console on your first day as a tier-1 analyst or a student in a cyber lab, and you have no idea what to do or where to start. The vendor documentation tells you what each button does. It does not tell you why you would press it, when you are wrong to press it, or what breaks when you press it in the wrong order.

This book sits in that gap. It is written from the operator's chair, not from the vendor's perspective, and not from a general "how to do security" perspective. It is written by someone who has deployed SentinelOne at scale, who teaches it to mentees and students, who runs it in production for multiple customers, and who has had to explain to both security leaders and frontline analysts what actually matters when the alerts start firing at 2 a.m. on a Tuesday. You will find perspective here that you will not find in vendor docs or in academic papers.

Who This Book Is For

This book is written for six kinds of people, and you might be more than one: Tier-1 and tier-2 SOC analysts who are new to SentinelOne or EDR in general and need both depth and speed. IT generalists who are pivoting into security and need to understand how one of the leading EDR platforms actually works. Students in undergraduate and graduate cyber programs who are learning EDR as part of a structured course, especially students whose program is adopting SentinelOne in a hands-on lab environment. Managed Security Service Provider (MSSP) operators who need to support multiple customers' SentinelOne deployments and need to understand the multi-tenant hierarchy inside out. Security leaders and architects evaluating whether to deploy SentinelOne and needing to understand both its capabilities and its operational complexity. Instructors designing a cyber lab curriculum who want a textbook that maps directly to the tool their students will be using.

What This Book Assumes About You

I assume you have basic familiarity with Windows and Linux system administration. You do not need to be an expert; you just need to know what a process is, what a file system is, and roughly how a user can log into a machine. I assume you understand the fundamentals of TCP/IP networking and can visualize what happens when a machine opens an outbound connection to an external IP. I assume you have never used SentinelOne before, and you might have never used any EDR platform. I assume you want to understand not just how to click buttons, but why the architecture is designed the way it is and what operational problems the design solves. Everything else, I will teach you.

How the Book Is Organized

The book moves through three conceptual arcs, though they are not formally divided into parts in the table of contents. Part I is Foundations: You will learn the four-level SentinelOne hierarchy, the console navigation, and the mental model that makes everything else make sense. Part II is Daily Operations: You will work through incident investigation, threat remediation, reporting, and the day-to-day tasks that occupy a SOC analyst's time. Part III is Programmatic Defense: You will learn how to automate responses, write detection rules, integrate SentinelOne with your broader security stack, and build operational maturity over time.

Within each arc, chapters build on each other. Read them sequentially your first time through. After that, you can jump to individual chapters as a reference without losing context, each chapter stands alone.

How to Use This Book

If you are a student reading this as a course text, read every chapter in order and do every lab exercise. The labs are not optional; they are where learning happens. When an exercise tells you to log into a SentinelOne console and perform a task, do not skip it. Reading about how inheritance works is not the same as watching it behave on a real console with real data. When you have finished a chapter, attempt the review questions and the discussion questions, even if they are not assigned. They exist because they are the questions your classmates or colleagues will ask when you are explaining this material to them.

If you are a working analyst using this as a reference, you can cherry-pick chapters based on what you need right now. Chapter 3 is all about Ranger if you are debugging asset discovery. Chapter 6 is about incident investigation if a detection landed on your team's queue. But I encourage you to read the foundations chapters (Chapter 1 and Chapter 2) even if you think you already understand SentinelOne. Many analysts pick up the tool piecemeal and discover gaps in their mental model two years later when something unexpected happens. A solid foundation prevents that.

About the Academic Edition

This academic edition is structured for use as a course text at colleges, universities, and technical training programs. In addition to the core material, every chapter includes review questions designed to check comprehension of concepts; discussion questions that ask you to think beyond the text and apply ideas to real scenarios; hands-on lab exercises that map to a typical institution's cyber lab setup (featuring SentinelOne, Tenable, and ServiceNow integration); framework mappings (e.g., NIST, CIS, MITRE ATT&CK) that show where the chapter's material aligns with industry standards; and recommendations for pacing and assessment. The appendix contains a complete Lab Setup Guide designed specifically for instructors setting up a shared SentinelOne environment for a class, including multi-tenant Site configuration, Group structure, and sample policies that balance pedagogy with realistic complexity.

This academic edition is the curriculum text for cybersecurity programs adopting SentinelOne as a teaching platform, with the structure of the book aligning to a 14-16 week semester schedule mapped in Appendix A. Instructors can use the pacing guide provided in the "How to Use This Book" section to align lab exercises with weekly learning objectives. The combination of foundational chapters, hands-on labs, and framework mappings ensures that students graduate with both conceptual understanding and operational competency.

A Personal Note

For the past two years, I have taught cybersecurity to mentees in a structured mentorship program. Many of them came from non-traditional backgrounds, some changed careers from other fields, some were recent college graduates with no job-market traction yet, and some were working analysts who needed to level up. What I found is that every one of them was blocked by the same bottleneck: the gap between "I understand the concept" and "I can do this on the console." They would read a vendor white paper about endpoint detection, and it made perfect sense on paper. Then they would open SentinelOne for the first time, see the four-level hierarchy, and blank. Or they would read about policies and think they understood, then get confused by the difference between a policy, an exclusion, and a policy override.

This book exists because of those conversations. I would say, "Let me show you the console," and I would walk them through the left navigation, and something would click. Then I would say, "Now let me show you what happens when you change a policy at the Site level," and they would see the inheritance and understand why it mattered. The book is an attempt to codify that walk-through, to be the voice on your shoulder as you open the console for the first time and to explain not just what you are looking at, but why it is designed that way and what it means for your daily work.

Acknowledgments

I would like to thank the many people who have contributed to my career and to this book.

To Caesar Nduna, one of my first bosses and my early manager on the networking team: thank you for recognizing my skill and, especially, for fighting to bring me back into networking after I was transitioned to the help desk during a downsizing. Without your willingness to advocate for me, this story takes a very different turn.

To Dan Smart, my former coworker, mentor, and boss: you have always been willing to share knowledge and help others grow. You truly lived up to your last name. I was fortunate to work under you in the networking department and to be invited by you into cybersecurity.

To my cousin Corey White, who provided me with the opportunity to come and work for his startup: none of what followed would have been possible without that experience. Thank you for the door you opened.

To Daniel McKinney, Jr. and Allyson White, who were my ride-or-dies through some of the toughest seasons at the startup, and who remain lifelong friends today: Daniel was one of the first people I ever mentored in cybersecurity, and through mentoring him the cybersecurity mentorship program at technologyinterpreters.com took shape. To both of you, thank you for being there.

To Penelope Blair, who served as part of the leadership for the mentorship program: you are one of the most positive cheerleaders I have ever worked with. Your words of encouragement and affirmation are legendary, and the program was better because you were part of it.

To the founding mentees of the Cybersecurity Mentorship Program, Jabari Holt, Scottie Harris, Jr., and Pier Brown, thank you for trusting the process. All of you graduated and returned as alumni members to help mentor the next generation, and the program is stronger because of it.

To Dr. Natalie Foster Johnson and CyberMINDS Research Institute: thank you for partnering with Technology Interpreters to build a truly job-ready cybersecurity program at Palm Beach State College.

To Dean John Hadley at Palm Beach State College: thank you for being willing to work with us to give your students true hands-on enterprise experience. Your dedication to the students of Palm Beach County is exceptional, and your impact will outlast all of us.

To Daniel Akiva, who valued my work during my time as a consultant at the MSSP and who now serves as CISO at the company where I currently work: thank you for recognizing what I brought to the table.

To Samuel "Sam" Rodriguez, friend, coworker, and board member of Technology Interpreters: I am truly blessed to have a friend like you.

To my daughter Adaia Washington, President of Technology Interpreters: it is a profound blessing as a parent to watch your child grow into a capable adult and a strong leader. I am proud of who you are and look forward to who you will become. Never forget your superpower. I love you.

And finally, to my father Richard Washington and my mother Eva Washington: you have defined me, encouraged me, motivated me, and supported me without condition. I love you both more than I can put into a paragraph.

, Kendrick Washington

About the Author

Kendrick Washington is a cybersecurity engineer and founder of Technology Interpreters, Inc., an independent security operations and training firm. He has deployed and maintained SentinelOne across dozens of customer environments, ranging from small businesses to large enterprises, and has designed SOC workflows and detection strategies for organizations in finance, healthcare, retail, and technology sectors. His teaching via the Technology Interpreters YouTube channel has reached over 155,000 viewers, with the SentinelOne training material becoming a reference resource for practitioners learning the platform. He maintains an independent perspective, Technology Interpreters is not affiliated with SentinelOne, Tenable, ServiceNow, or any other vendor covered in this book. That independence shapes both what he teaches and how he teaches it.

In addition to his consulting and training work, Kendrick mentors cybersecurity students and career-changers through a structured mentorship program, helping them bridge the gap between academic knowledge and operational competency. He believes that security expertise is learned through a combination of solid mental models, hands-on practice, and relationships with experienced practitioners. This book reflects that belief.

When not working on security problems or teaching, Kendrick investigates how to make technical education accessible to people from non-traditional backgrounds and how to build learning environments where students can fail safely while learning.

How to Use This Book

For Instructors

This book is designed to support a 14-16 week semester course in Endpoint Detection and Response, with SentinelOne as the primary hands-on platform. A typical pacing guide follows.

Weeks 1-2: Foundations (Chapters 1-2)

Have students complete Lab 1.1 (hierarchy mapping) and Lab 1.2 (policy tracing) in their first lab session. By the end of week 2, every student should be able to explain the four-level hierarchy and work through the console without getting lost.

Weeks 3-4: Asset Discovery and Network Visibility (Chapter 3, Ranger)

Have students deploy Ranger in their lab group and watch it detect rogue devices on the test network. Discuss the NIST framework mappings (Asset Management, Detection).

Weeks 5-7: Endpoint Management and Detection (Chapters 4-5)

This is the densest part of the course. Have students build policies, create groups, apply detection engines, and practice policy inheritance. Use Lab 1.3 (threat vs. alert vs. exclusion) as a foundation, then advance to custom policy creation.

Weeks 8-10: Incident Response and Investigation (Chapter 6)

By week 8, students should be ready for incident investigation labs. Use test events or simulated malware (e.g., EICAR test files) to generate detections. Have students practice remediation, rollback, and evidence collection. Connect to your ServiceNow instance for ticket workflows.

Weeks 11-12: Vulnerability and Application Risk (Chapter 7)

Integrate Tenable or another vulnerability scanner. Have students compare what SentinelOne's Applications feature sees versus what a dedicated scanner reports. Discuss remediation priority and false-positive management.

Weeks 13-14: Automation, Reporting, and Operations (Chapters 8-11)

Introduce RemoteOps (Automation chapter) with safe, non-destructive examples first (e.g., collection scripts before remediation scripts). Have students build a custom report and schedule it. Discuss operational metrics and SLAs.

Weeks 15-16: Integration, Capstone, and Assessment

Have students complete a capstone exercise: design a detection strategy for a hypothetical customer, document it, and present it to the class. Assess based on technical correctness, understanding of the hierarchy, and ability to justify design choices.

Assessment Recommendations

Each chapter's review questions can be administered as a quiz (20-30 minutes, closed book or open notes depending on your preference). Discussion questions work well as writing assignments or classroom discussion. Labs should be graded on completion and correctness: Did the student do the exercise? Did they demonstrate understanding in their write-up? Peer review of capstone projects is valuable, have students critique each other's detection strategies using a rubric you provide.

Lab Environment Setup

The appendix (Lab Setup Guide for Instructors) contains step-by-step instructions for configuring a shared SentinelOne account for classroom use. Key points: (1) Create one Site per cohort or per student group, not one Site for all students, to preserve data isolation. (2) Within each Site, create at least two Groups, a Monitoring Only group and a Full Enforcement group, so students can see policy differences without accidentally remediating each other's test systems. (3) Populate test Groups with sample endpoints (physical or virtual machines in your lab network). (4) Configure one shared ServiceNow instance for ticket workflows, with read-only access for students. (5) Document the Site Key, default policies, and any existing exclusions so students know the baseline configuration.

For Students

Read the preface (above) and then work through the book chapter by chapter. Before each lab session, read the chapter and complete the review questions. During the lab, do the hands-on exercises. After the lab, discuss with classmates and review the discussion questions. Here is how to get the most out of this material:

Read with your console open.

Do not just read the text. When a chapter describes the Dashboard, open your SentinelOne console and look at it. When it explains the hierarchy, work through to the scope dropdown and trace it. Reading and seeing are two different things.

Do every lab exercise.

Labs are not homework. Labs are where understanding happens. You will learn more by spending 30 minutes creating a policy and watching it inherit down the hierarchy than by reading 10 pages about inheritance.

Take notes in two forms.

First, take procedural notes: the steps you took to accomplish something (e.g., "To create a group: Sentinels > Groups > New Group > Name: ..."). You will reference these notes on exams and in your first weeks on the job. Second, take conceptual notes: the deeper questions you are asking (e.g., "Why does SentinelOne require me to configure policy at the Site level instead of the Group level?"). These questions are what you will discuss with your instructor or bring to the study group.

Use the appendices.

The appendices contain reference tables (e.g., all the detection engines and what they do), a glossary, framework mappings, and a lab setup guide. When you encounter an unfamiliar term, check the glossary first. When you are designing a detection strategy and want to know where it aligns with NIST or MITRE ATT&CK, check the mappings.

When referencing this book in your own writing (papers, reports, presentations), use the citation below.

Washington, K. (2026). Mastering SentinelOne: A complete guide to endpoint detection and response (1st ed.). Technology Interpreters.

(This is APA 7th edition format. If your instructor requires a different format, adjust accordingly, but keep the core information: author, year, title, edition, and publisher.)

A Final Note

Security is not a solo sport. As you work through this book, engage with classmates, form study groups, and ask questions. If something in the text is confusing, ask your instructor or post in the course forum. If you discover that a lab exercise needs clarification, let your instructor know. And if you finish this book and find that you have more questions than you did when you started, that is a good sign. That is where real learning begins.

Mastering SentinelOne
Sample Expanded Chapter 1, Draft for Review
by Kendrick Washington, Technology Interpreters, Inc.

Chapter 1

The SentinelOne Command Console at a Glance

Learning Objectives

- Understand what Endpoint Detection and Response (EDR) is, how it differs from antivirus, and why behavioral detection matters.
- Explain the MSSP (Managed Security Service Provider) business model and why SentinelOne organizes data into Accounts, Sites, and Groups.
- Define the network fundamentals required for the rest of the book: subnets, IP/MAC addressing, DHCP, ARP, broadcast vs. multicast, and their role in security operations.
- Visualize the SentinelOne architecture: console, agent, data path, telemetry, and where Ranger fits into the picture.
- Describe SentinelOne's place in the EDR market and how it relates to adjacent products like CrowdStrike, Trend Micro, and Microsoft Defender for Endpoint.
- Work through the four-level MSSP console hierarchy: Global, Account, Site, Group.
- Identify every item in the left-navigation menu and understand what each capability does at a high level.
- Distinguish threats from alerts, and policies from exclusions from policy overrides.
- Recognize where scope is inherited down the hierarchy and where it can be broken by overrides at a lower level.

Chapter Opener

If you have been handed a SentinelOne console and told to run with it, the first thing that has to be right is the mental model. SentinelOne is not a single product; it is a platform organized around a specific hierarchy, a left-nav with roughly ten capability areas, and a layered policy system that works by inheritance. Get the mental model wrong and you will spend weeks fighting the interface. Get it right and everything that comes later in this book will make intuitive sense.

This chapter is the walking tour, not a deep dive into any single capability, but a complete map of what you are about to learn. By the end of the chapter you will not be able to configure a detection engine or run a live incident investigation, those come in later chapters, but you will know where every capability lives on the console, what it is called, and how it relates to everything else. That map is what makes every subsequent chapter land.

1.0 Foundations: What This Book Assumes (and What You Need to Know)

Before we walk the console, let's get on the same page about what Endpoint Detection and Response actually is, why SentinelOne organizes itself the way it does, and what happens when the agent talks to the cloud. If you're coming from a Help Desk background or transitioning from IT into security, you'll find a lot of acronyms and concepts in the chapters that follow. This section is your bridge. By the time you finish here, you'll understand the "why" behind SentinelOne's architecture, not just the "what."

Endpoint Detection and Response (EDR), in Plain English

You've probably heard of antivirus software. That's what Windows Defender or McAfee does: it sits on your machine, watches for files it recognizes as malware, and blocks them. EDR is related, but it's fundamentally different in scope and how it thinks about threats.

Antivirus says: 'I know what bad looks like, and I'm going to stop it.' It works by signatures, fingerprints of known malware. The problem is, by the time a signature exists, attackers have already moved on to variants the signature doesn't catch. Antivirus buys you time, but it's not a complete picture.

EDR says: 'I'm going to watch what this endpoint does, and I'm going to let you investigate.' This is the behavioral detection mindset. Instead of recognizing bad files, EDR records everything your endpoints do: processes running, files being read or written, network connections, user logins, scripts being executed. The endpoint agent, the tiny software running on your laptop or server, becomes a surveillance instrument. It sends that telemetry (the raw data of endpoint behavior) back to a central console, where AI engines analyze it in real time. Those engines look for patterns that look like attacks, not just known malware signatures.

Here's the practical difference. An antivirus might say: 'This EXE is signed by Microsoft, so it's safe.' An EDR agent will say: 'This legitimate EXE is creating network connections to a non-standard port, launching PowerShell scripts with obfuscated arguments, and reading the Windows SAM file. That's not normal for this process. Alert.' EDR catches the attack the antivirus would miss because the attack used legitimate tools. That's why EDR is called behavioral detection.

The telemetry that flows back to SentinelOne's cloud console includes process trees (what executable launched what), file operations (what files got created, modified, deleted), network connections (what IPs and ports are talking to your endpoint), registry changes (what configuration got altered), and user activity (who logged in, when, and from where). None of that is secret or private, it's the operational record of the endpoint. But it only becomes useful when you have a tool like SentinelOne that can ingest it, correlate it, and surface what matters.

Tip: Coming from Antivirus? Here's the Mindset Shift

Antivirus = "I recognize bad files and I block them." Success = zero files got through.

EDR = "I watched what happened, and here's the story of the endpoint's behavior." Success = I can tell you what happened, whether it was an attack, and what to do next.

If you've been working in antivirus, you're used to binary verdicts: infected or clean. EDR gives you context. A process might be suspicious, partially mitigated, escalating to malware, or benign depending on what else is happening. The job shifts from "block everything bad" to "investigate and decide."

The MSSP and Multi-Tenant Model

If you're a student at Palm Beach State College with 31 endpoints in a lab, you might think: 'Why do I need to understand the MSSP model? I'm not running a managed security service.' Good question. The answer is that SentinelOne's entire architecture is built around multi-tenancy, the ability to manage multiple customers, multiple business units, or multiple deployments from a single console instance. Even a 31-endpoint lab uses that same architecture. Understanding it now saves you weeks of confusion later.

Think of it like a hospital chain. A hospital corporation (Global) owns multiple hospitals (Accounts). Each hospital manages multiple departments (Sites). Each department has multiple teams (Groups). Policies set at the hospital level propagate to all departments. A department can override a hospital policy for their own needs. A team can override a department policy for specific cases. Everything flows downhill unless explicitly overridden.

In SentinelOne, it works the same way. Your 31-endpoint lab might live in a single Account (your school's deployment), a single Site (your lab environment), and maybe two or three Groups (workstations, servers, or a pilot group where you test policy changes). But the structure is identical to a real MSSP managing 500,000 endpoints across hundreds of customers. SentinelOne doesn't have one product for small labs and a different one for enterprises. It has one product that scales, and the MSSP hierarchy is how it scales.

Why does this matter? Because when Chapter 4 talks about applying a policy at the Site level, and Chapter 5 talks about overriding it at the Group level, you need to internalize that this is the same dance happening in a 31-endpoint classroom that happens in a 500,000-endpoint enterprise MSSP. The concepts are identical. The scale is different, but the mental model is identical. Get the mental model right, and you can work through both contexts without relearning anything fundamental.

In the MSSP world, Accounts and Sites also serve a privacy boundary. If you manage multiple customers, customer A cannot see customer B's data, endpoints, or detections. Sites enforce that boundary. In your lab, you might not care about boundaries yet, but the mechanism is the same. When you graduate and join an MSSP or an enterprise with subsidiaries, you'll appreciate why this structure exists.

The Network Fundamentals You Need

When we get to Ranger (Chapter 3), we'll talk about how SentinelOne discovers devices on your network. Ranger uses a mix of passive observation and active scanning to find unmanaged devices. To make sense of that, you need to know a few network concepts. Don't worry, you don't need to become a network engineer. But these terms will appear, and they'll make more sense if you've seen them before.

An IP address is a logical identifier for a device on a network, like a postal address for a computer. It's how packets find their way from machine to machine. A subnet is a group of IP addresses that belong together on the same network segment. If your network is 192.168.1.0/24, that means IP addresses from 192.168.1.1 to 192.168.1.254 are on the same segment. That matters because devices on the same subnet can talk to each other directly.

A MAC address (Media Access Control address) is a hardware identifier burned into every network card, how two machines on the same subnet actually find each other on the wire. IP addresses get you to the right network; MAC addresses get you to the right machine on that network. DHCP (Dynamic Host Configuration Protocol) is the mechanism that assigns IP addresses automatically when a device connects. When you plug a laptop into a network, DHCP hands it an IP address. When the laptop leaves, that IP goes back into the pool. ARP (Address Resolution Protocol) maps IP addresses to MAC addresses, it's how your laptop asks: 'Who has IP 192.168.1.1?' and the router answers: 'I do, my MAC is AA:BB:CC:DD:EE:FF.'

Broadcast means a message sent to everyone on the segment. Multicast means a message sent to a specific group. Unicast (which we use without naming it most of the time) means a message sent to one specific host. Why does this matter? Because Ranger watches for DHCP broadcasts, ARP requests, DNS queries, and multicast announcements to figure out what devices are on your network. The more you understand what these protocols do, the more Ranger's discovery patterns will make sense.

A Mental Model of the SentinelOne Architecture

Here's the simplest way to think about how SentinelOne actually works. You have a cloud console (SentinelOne's infrastructure, hosted by SentinelOne). You have endpoints (the laptops, servers, and Kubernetes nodes you want to protect). And you have an agent (a tiny piece of software running on each endpoint).

The agent is always on. It watches everything on the endpoint, processes, files, network, users, and ships that telemetry back to the console over encrypted connections. The console ingests that telemetry, runs it through detection engines (the AI that looks for suspicious patterns), and surfaces alerts and threats. When something suspicious happens, a few things can occur: the console can alert the SOC analyst (you), the agent can automatically remediate the threat (kill the process, quarantine the file, roll back the system), or both can happen.

The key insight is that there are two types of traffic flowing between endpoint and console. Management traffic goes from the console to the agent: 'Here's your policy,' 'Quarantine this file,' 'Run this script,' 'Update your agent version.' Telemetry traffic goes from the agent to the console: 'Here's what happened on the endpoint.' These two streams are separate, and both matter. If management traffic gets blocked, the agent keeps running but falls out of sync with policy changes. If telemetry gets blocked, the agent still runs locally, but the console goes blind.

Now, where does Ranger fit into this picture? Ranger isn't a separate product, it's a capability that lives inside the SentinelOne agent. Once you have agents deployed to your managed endpoints, those agents can see other devices on the network (via ARP, DHCP, DNS, multicast). Ranger correlates what all your agents see and builds a map of everything on your network, highlighting the devices without agents. That's how an MSSP discovers a rogue laptop or an unmanaged printer within minutes of it connecting.

Everything else in this book flows from this architecture: one agent, one console, telemetry flowing up, policy flowing down, detection engines firing on what they observe, and analysts investigating the results. When you open the console for the first time, you're looking at the ingestion point for millions of telemetry records per second from thousands of endpoints. The dashboard, the incident queue, the Ranger map, the reports, they're all different views into this telemetry stream. Understand the stream, and the rest is just filters and visualizations.

By the end of this chapter, you will know the SentinelOne console well enough to work through it and understand what each section does. By the end of this book, you will understand how to operate it, how to configure it, how to investigate detections, how to hunt for threats, and how to report results upward. The foundation you're building right now will support all of that.

1.1 What SentinelOne Is and Where It Fits

SentinelOne is one of the top Endpoint Detection and Response (EDR) platforms in the enterprise market, alongside CrowdStrike Falcon and Microsoft Defender for Endpoint. Industry analysts consistently place it in the Leaders quadrant for endpoint protection, and it powers some of the largest Managed Security Service Provider relationships in North America. If you have not heard of it outside of security circles, that is by design, EDR vendors sell upward into enterprise IT, not into consumer markets.

What you need to know at a category level is that SentinelOne does four things simultaneously. First, it runs an always-on agent on every endpoint (Windows, macOS, Linux, Kubernetes nodes, and several cloud workload types) that watches processes, file-system changes, network behavior, and user activity. Second, it applies AI-driven detection engines to that telemetry in real time, producing threats and alerts when something suspicious happens. Third, it gives the SOC or MSSP analyst a console through which they can investigate, remediate, roll back, and report. Fourth, it integrates with the rest of the security stack, SIEM, SOAR, ticketing, identity providers, so that findings flow into the team's workflow instead of trapping analysts inside yet another single-pane-of-glass.

The rest of this book is a deep dive into how to do each of those four things well. This chapter is about knowing what you are looking at before you start changing settings.

1.2 The MSSP Console Hierarchy: Global, Account, Site, Group

If you are at an MSSP, or you manage more than one business unit's security independently, you will live inside SentinelOne's four-level hierarchy every day. Understanding this hierarchy cold is not optional, every decision about who sees what, which detection engines apply where, and what happens when a threat fires gets made at one level of this hierarchy and inherits down from there.

Level 1 is Global. The Global level is the top of the pyramid. It represents the entity that has a direct contractual relationship with SentinelOne itself. Only the largest organizations, very large enterprises or the large MSSPs who resell SentinelOne to smaller providers, have Global access. If you are a small-to-midsize MSSP like Technology Interpreters, you are not Global. You are buying through a bigger provider who is Global. In our case, we buy through another provider who holds the Global relationship with SentinelOne; they then provision an Account for us. Everything above you rolls downhill: if your upstream provider publishes a policy or a RemoteOps script at Global, it propagates into your Account and down to your customers' Sites.

Level 2 is Account. The Account is your tenant. It belongs to your organization and, in an MSSP model, contains all of your customers. As the Account owner, you see everything below Account but nothing above it. You have the ability to see your Account's dashboards, your users, your policies, and your customer Sites. You do not see the Accounts of other MSSPs using the same upstream provider. Account is where your multi-tenant boundary sits.

Level 3 is Site. A Site is a customer, a business unit, or a deployment scope inside your Account. If you have twenty customers, you have twenty Sites. If you run SentinelOne for your own internal use across multiple regions or subsidiaries, you might have five or ten Sites instead. Sites are the primary boundary for separating one customer's data from another's. A Site has its own license consumption, its own policies, and its own Site Key, the unique identifier that agents use to register into the correct Site when they are installed.

Level 4 is Group. Below a Site are Groups. A Group is how you subdivide endpoints within a single Site. A common pattern is to have a Monitoring Only group where SentinelOne watches and alerts but does not take automatic action, and a Full Enforcement group where SentinelOne is enabled to kill, quarantine, remediate, and roll back on its own. You might additionally have groups for servers, workstations, critical executives' laptops, and a pilot group you use to stage policy changes before rolling them to everyone.

Understanding this is not just organizational trivia. Every decision, which detection engine applies to which endpoints, whether a workstation gets auto-remediation or just alerting, who gets notified when something fires, which reports get generated for which customer, is made at some level of this hierarchy, and it inherits downward unless explicitly overridden.

A practical mental model: policies at Global flow to all Accounts. Policies at Account flow to all your Sites. Policies at Site flow to all your Groups. Groups are the leaf level where real enforcement decisions land. When something is not behaving the way you expect, walk the inheritance chain before assuming the product is broken.

Operator's Checklist: The Policy Inheritance Check

Before you debug anything that looks like a SentinelOne misconfiguration, verify the inheritance chain.

At the affected endpoint's Group, read the effective policy. Then walk up to the Site, the Account, and (if you have visibility) the Global level.

Something along that chain is overriding what you expected. This three-minute check prevents hours of wasted investigation.

1.3 A Walking Tour of the Left Navigation

The left navigation of the SentinelOne console is your command center. When you open the platform you see a vertical column of icons. Each one opens a distinct capability. The map below lists each in the order you will encounter it, with just enough detail to know what each does. Every item here gets its own chapter or section later in the book.

Dashboard

The Dashboard is the landing page. It shows solved threats, unsolved threats, and mitigated threats at a glance, plus infected endpoints and healthy endpoints. When you log in in the morning, the Dashboard is your situational-awareness summary: how many incidents are open, how many endpoints need attention, and what the overall health of your environment looks like. It also surfaces the current scope of active detection engines, the AI engines enabled in your policies, and a breakdown of threats by type across categories like malware, potentially unwanted programs, suspicious behaviors, and several others. Chapter 2 covers Dashboard customization in depth.

Deep Visibility

Deep Visibility is SentinelOne's query-driven threat-hunting and investigation surface. It is where you run structured queries against endpoint telemetry, process trees, file activity, network connections, user actions, to follow up on something that has been detected or to proactively hunt for attacker behavior. Not every license tier includes Deep Visibility, and even when it is licensed, SentinelOne gates access behind a trained-user requirement: an untuned query can put real load on the platform's back end, and the vendor wants you to know what you are doing before you run one. Chapter 6 walks Deep Visibility end to end.

Ranger

Ranger is SentinelOne's network-asset-discovery product. It uses the endpoints you already have agents on to detect other devices on the network, printers, IoT devices, unmanaged laptops, rogue endpoints, and flags anything that does not have a SentinelOne agent installed. The classic Ranger scenario: someone plugs a personal laptop into a corporate network. Within minutes, Ranger identifies it, tells the security team there is a rogue on the network, and the IT team reaches out to either install the agent or remove the device. Ranger is how you answer the "what's on my network that I don't know about" question that keeps CISOs awake at night. Chapter 3 is entirely about Ranger.

Sentinels

Sentinels is the endpoint-management surface. This is where every device in your Site shows up, where you push policies, where you configure the detection engines, where you manage exclusions and block lists, where you configure network and device controls, and where you download the agent packages for installation. The Sentinels section contains the Site Key (which you use to bind agents to the correct Site at install time), the policies that control what the agent does, and the package repository for agent installs across Windows, macOS, Linux, and Kubernetes. Chapters 4 and 5 cover Sentinels end to end, Part A focuses on deployment and packages, Part B focuses on policies and detection engines.

Incidents

Incidents is where threats and alerts land after the detection engines fire. A threat is a detection produced by one of SentinelOne's AI engines, Static AI, Behavioral AI, Document AI, Script AI, Anti-Exploitation, Fileless, Intrusion Detection, and several others, and is the primary thing you investigate and act on. Alerts are different: they are conditions you proactively define, typically using a query language called PowerQuery, that fire when certain patterns appear in telemetry. Alerts are proactive detection layered on top of the AI engines. In day-to-day operations you will focus mostly on threats; alerts extend that coverage into organization-specific patterns. Chapter 6 walks the incident-response flow.

Identity

Identity covers SentinelOne's Active Directory and identity-protection capabilities: Ranger AD (detects indicators of compromise against AD), AD Secure EP (replaces real AD accounts and assets with deception targets so attackers waste time on fake objects), Ranger AD Protect (detects Kerberos-targeted attacks like Kerberoasting), Threat Strike (detects lateral movement), Detect or Deflect (raises alerts when untrusted endpoints access forbidden network resources), and Threat Path (shows attack paths an adversary could take through your environment). Identity is one of the most powerful parts of the platform and also one of the most frequently unlicensed. If it is not enabled in your deployment, that is a procurement question, not a technical one.

Applications

Applications turns the endpoint agent into a lightweight vulnerability scanner. Because the agent already knows every piece of software installed on the endpoint and what version it is, SentinelOne can cross-reference that against CVSS data and produce risk scores, critical, high, medium, low, and let you pivot from vulnerability to remediation workflow. For small organizations this can replace a dedicated vulnerability scanner like Tenable or Qualys; for larger organizations it complements them. Chapter 7 covers Applications in depth.

Activity

Activity is the audit log. Every meaningful action in the console, logins, policy changes, agent decommissioning, remote-shell sessions, manual scans, group changes, is written to Activity. This is your forensic record when you need to answer "who did what and when" after an incident. It is also what you hand to an auditor. Get in the habit of reviewing Activity weekly, not just during incidents; unexpected entries are sometimes the earliest indicator of a compromised admin account. Chapter 8 covers Activity.

Reports

Reports is the scheduled and ad-hoc PDF-generation surface. You build a report template that aggregates metrics, a filter that scopes it to certain Sites or Groups, and a schedule that delivers it on cadence to a mailing list. Reports are what goes to the customer CISO, the board, or the external auditor. Chapter 9 covers Reports.

Automation

Automation is where SentinelOne exposes its RemoteOps surface: PowerShell and shell scripts that you can run at scale across endpoints to remediate vulnerabilities, collect evidence, or take custom administrative action. In an MSSP environment, Automation is where a lot of the time-saving happens, deploying a one-off fix to five thousand endpoints in minutes instead of hours of manual work. Chapter 10 covers Automation.

Settings

Settings contains everything else. Notifications (email and Syslog), integrations (SMTP, Syslog, Single Sign-On via identity providers like Okta or Entra ID), policy overrides, users and RBAC, accounts and sites management, and locations (which let you group endpoints by network criteria like IP range, DNS resolution, and network interface type). Chapter 11 covers Settings.

1.4 Policies, Exclusions, and Policy Overrides

Three concepts in SentinelOne sit at different layers of specificity and solve different problems. Mixing them up causes real operational pain.

A policy is the default ruleset that a Group inherits. It defines which detection engines are enabled, whether SentinelOne takes automatic remediation action or only alerts, what behaviors to kill or quarantine, and so on. Policies live at the Site level and are assigned to Groups.

An exclusion is a narrow carve-out for a specific process, hash, file path, or executable that you do not want SentinelOne to inspect or act on. The common use case is a legitimate custom-developed application that SentinelOne keeps flagging as suspicious because its behavior looks malware-like. You exclude the executable by hash or by full path, and SentinelOne leaves it alone going forward. Exclusions are surgical at the object level.

A policy override goes one level deeper. When an exclusion does not work because the problematic behavior is pattern-based rather than file-based, you write a policy override, a declarative rule telling a specific detection engine not to act on a particular behavior pattern. This is more surgical than an exclusion and it is also more dangerous. A badly written policy override can blind the platform to real attacks. Treat overrides the way you treat privileged SQL statements: peer review, rollback plan, scoped blast radius, and tracked expiration.

The operational rule to hold in your head: reach for the narrowest control first. If an exclusion solves the problem, do not write an override. If adjusting a policy solves it without creating a rule exception at all, do not write an exclusion. Every exception is a piece of technical debt that has to be re-evaluated whenever your threat model changes, and exceptions pile up faster than you would think.

1.5 Locations, Notifications, and Audit Logging

Three final capabilities to register before closing the overview.

Locations let you define logical groupings of endpoints based on network criteria: IP address, DNS server configuration, DNS resolution behavior, network interface type (wired or wireless), registry keys, and connection state. Locations matter because SentinelOne can behave differently based on where an endpoint is. An endpoint connected to the corporate LAN might have a looser USB device-control policy, while the same endpoint on a public WiFi might lock USB devices down entirely. Chapter 11 covers Location design.

Notifications are how findings leave the console and reach the people who need to act. SentinelOne supports two primary delivery mechanisms: email (for human recipients) and Syslog (for machine recipients, SIEMs, SOARs, log aggregators like Splunk or Elastic). Both are configured at Site level, with recipient lists, severity thresholds, and category filters. Chapter 11 walks the Notification configuration.

Audit logging, via the Activity surface we touched on earlier, is your safety net. Every action, log in, log out, policy change, agent remote-shell session, manual scan initiation, decommission, is captured. When a customer asks whether someone made a change to their policy last Thursday, the answer lives in Activity. Get into the habit of reviewing Activity weekly, not just during incidents.

Chapter Summary

You have now walked the entire SentinelOne console at the capability level. The four-level hierarchy, Global, Account, Site, Group, is the structural backbone of the platform, and policies, notifications, and reporting all flow down this chain by inheritance. The left navigation surfaces roughly ten distinct capability areas: Dashboard, Deep Visibility, Ranger, Sentinels, Incidents, Identity, Applications, Activity, Reports, Automation, and Settings. Threats are detections from AI engines; alerts are proactive query-based triggers. Policies are the rules; exclusions carve narrow exceptions; policy overrides carve wider ones. Locations group endpoints by network criteria; Notifications deliver findings out of the console; Activity is the audit log.

Every remaining chapter of this book takes one piece of this map and goes deep.

Key Takeaways

- SentinelOne is a platform, not a product. Its four-level hierarchy (Global, Account, Site, Group) inherits top-down, and policy misconfigurations most often come from misreading what is inheriting from where.
- The left navigation covers roughly ten capability areas. You will spend most of your working time in Sentinels (endpoint management), Incidents (threat investigation), Reports, and Activity (audit log).
- Threats come from the AI engines. Alerts come from queries you define. Both land in Incidents.
- Policies are the ruleset. Exclusions are narrow exceptions. Policy overrides are surgical exceptions. Reach for the narrowest mechanism first, and never ship an override without peer review and a rollback plan.
- Ranger is for discovering what is on your network that should not be. Applications is for knowing what software is installed on your managed endpoints and where it is vulnerable.

Hands-On Exercise

Before you continue to Chapter 2, do the following in your SentinelOne tenant.

- Open the console and identify the level of the hierarchy you are currently viewing. Note the Account name, the Site name, and any Groups you can see beneath the Site.
- From the left navigation, click into each of the ten capability areas in order (Dashboard, Deep Visibility, Ranger, Sentinels, Incidents, Identity, Applications, Activity, Reports, Automation, Settings). For each, write down one question you do not yet know the answer to. You will be answering those questions in the chapters that follow.
- Go to Activity and scroll through the last seven days. Identify at least three entries whose meaning is not obvious to you. Record them, they are the beginning of your operational question list.

What's Next

Chapter 2 goes deep on the Dashboard: every widget, how the scope filter actually affects what you see, when to trust the visualization and when to go straight to the underlying query, and how to design a dashboard that surfaces the two or three things you actually need each morning.

Review Questions

- 1. What is the primary difference between a policy and an exclusion in SentinelOne? Why does the distinction matter operationally?
- 2. At which level of the SentinelOne hierarchy (Global, Account, Site, Group) are Sites primarily used as a multi-tenant boundary?
- 3. You are reviewing a detection on an endpoint that belongs to Group "Pilot." The policy applied is "Detect Only" (no remediation), but you would expect "Full Enforcement." Walk the inheritance chain: where might the issue lie?
- 4. True or False: A threat is the same as an alert. Explain your answer with an example.
- 5. When you enable a detection engine at the Account level, which Groups and endpoints will inherit that setting, and under what condition can the setting be overridden?

Answer Key: Review Questions

1. A policy is the default ruleset applied to a Group; an exclusion is a narrow carve-out for a specific file, hash, or path. Exclusions are surgical and do not affect the broader policy. Mixing them up leads to overly broad policy overrides when a simple exclusion would suffice, creating technical debt.

2. The Site level. Each Site represents a customer or deployment scope, and Sites are the primary boundary for separating one customer's data and license consumption from another's.

3. Walk from Group up to Site: check the Site-level policy for that Group. Then check the Account level: an Account-level policy override could affect all Sites below it. Finally check Global if you have visibility. Overrides at any level above the Group can change the inherited setting.

4. False. A threat is a detection produced by SentinelOne's AI engines (Static AI, Behavioral AI, etc.). An alert is a condition you define proactively using queries. Both land in Incidents, but they originate from different sources. Threats are automatic; alerts are custom.

5. All Groups and endpoints in the Sites below the Account will inherit the setting. The setting can be overridden at the Site level or the Group level, or a specific endpoint can have an exclusion or policy override applied.

Discussion Questions

- 1. Imagine you are a new SOC analyst joining an MSSP that manages 50 customers across 50 Sites. Your manager hands you the console and says, "Spend your first week learning the structure." How would you approach this task, and what three things would you prioritize learning first? Why?
- 2. Your security team is debating whether to enable automatic remediation globally (kill, quarantine, remediate) or to run in "alerts only" mode and have analysts manually review each detection. What are the operational trade-offs? Which mode would you recommend for a small team of two analysts covering 500 endpoints, and why?
- 3. Policy overrides are powerful but dangerous. Describe a scenario where a policy override would be justified. What safeguards should a team put in place before deploying an override to a production group?

Hands-On Lab Exercises

Lab 1.1: Work through and Map the Console Hierarchy

Objective: Map the complete hierarchy of your SentinelOne environment and document which level you have permissions to access.

You have access to a running SentinelOne test tenant (sandbox or lab account)

You have basic familiarity with web navigation and note-taking

Steps:

- Log into your SentinelOne console. In the top left or top center, locate the scope dropdown. Click it and note which levels are visible to you (Global, Account, Site, Group).
- If you have Account or Site access, work through to that level. For each level visible, record: the name, the number of child objects (Sites within an Account, Groups within a Site), and any special annotations (e.g., "MSSP Reseller Account" or "Test Customer Site").
- Work through to Settings > Users or Settings > Accounts to understand the multi-tenant structure. Count the number of Sites in your Account and note whether you can see any other Accounts.
- In the left navigation, click on each of the ten capability areas (Dashboard, Deep Visibility, Ranger, etc.). For each, take a screenshot or note the scope it is showing. Verify that the scope matches what you expect given your current hierarchy level.
- Return to the scope selector and change the scope to another Site (if available). Observe which console data changes and which remains the same.

Expected Outcome: You will have a one-page diagram or table showing your current position in the hierarchy, what you can see, and what you cannot. This mental map is foundational for all subsequent chapters.

Reflection: Based on this mapping, which policies or settings are inherited from above your current level? Where would you expect to find configuration for your current scope?

Lab 1.2: Trace a Policy Override Through the Hierarchy

Objective: Understand policy inheritance by identifying a single endpoint, reading its effective policy, and tracing where that policy originates in the hierarchy.

You have access to a Site with at least two Groups and multiple endpoints

You can work through to Sentinels and view endpoint details

Steps:

- In Sentinels, pick any endpoint and note its Group assignment.
- Click into the endpoint detail page and locate the Policies tab. Read the effective policy name that is currently applied to this endpoint.
- Work through to the Group that this endpoint belongs to. In the Group settings, find the policy assigned to this Group.
- Work through one level up to the Site level. Check the Site-level policies. Is the Group policy the same as the Site policy, or does the Group override the Site policy?
- If an override exists, note what changed (detection engines enabled/ disabled, remediation mode, exclusions). If no override, verify that the effective policy is indeed the Site-level default.
- Document your findings: "Endpoint [name] is in Group [group name]. Its effective policy is [policy name]. This policy originates at the [Site/ Group/Account] level, and no overrides are present" or "This policy originates at [level], and Group [group] overrides [specific settings]."

Expected Outcome: A written trace showing the exact policy inheritance path for one endpoint, demonstrating that you understand how policies flow down the hierarchy.

Reflection: If this endpoint were behaving unexpectedly, how would walking this inheritance chain help you debug the issue?

Lab 1.3: Distinguish Threat, Alert, Exclusion, and Policy in Practice

Objective: Observe real (or simulated) security events and correctly label each as a threat, alert, exclusion, or policy configuration.

You have access to Incidents, Sentinels, and Settings in the console

Your tenant has at least one threat or simulated detection (or you can review recent Activity logs)

Steps:

- Work through to Incidents. If there are any open threats, click on one. Note its name, classification (Malware, Ransomware, Suspicious, etc.), and which detection engine produced it. This is a THREAT.
- In the same threat detail, look for any linked Alert definitions. If alerts are in use, click into one. Alerts are user-defined conditions, often based on PowerQuery expressions. They appear alongside AI-based threats. Record the difference you observe.

- Work through to Sentinels. Find a Group and open its policy details. Within the policy, look for a section on exclusions or block lists. Create a note describing what exclusions do (they carve out specific files or hashes).
- In the same policy, note which detection engines are enabled or disabled. For example, "Behavioral AI: Enabled, Ransomware: Enabled." This is POLICY configuration.
- If your environment has any policy overrides, locate one and describe what it does. If no overrides exist, describe where you would create one (Settings > Policy Overrides or equivalent).

Expected Outcome: A one-page reference sheet with examples of a threat, an alert, an exclusion, and a policy override from your own environment. Include screenshots or descriptions of each.

Reflection: Which of these four (threat, alert, exclusion, policy) can you configure yourself as an operator, and which ones are produced automatically by the platform?

Mastering SentinelOne

Sample Expanded Chapter 2, Draft for Review

by Kendrick Washington, Technology Interpreters, Inc.

Chapter 2

The Dashboard

Learning Objectives

- Describe the role of the SentinelOne Dashboard in daily security operations and what it is (and is not) designed to surface.
- Use the Scope filter to drill from Global view down into individual Site data, manage multi-tenant MSSP views, and understand why most "my dashboard shows nothing" problems trace back to Scope.
- Identify the major widget categories and the visualization types each widget supports.
- Choose the right graph type for a given data shape, and avoid the common rendering mistakes that make dashboards look busy but read as empty.
- Understand dashboard refresh cadence, cache behavior, and why the Dashboard is situational awareness, not real-time alerting.
- Design a durable, team-shareable dashboard layout that a team can rely on for their morning check, including configuration export and version control practices.

Chapter Opener

Your shift starts at 8:00 AM. You open the SentinelOne console and land on the Dashboard. From that moment, you have ten seconds to know: do I have fires to fight today, or can I catch up on other work? For most operators, the Dashboard is the heartbeat monitor of the operation. It should answer four questions immediately: How many open threats do I have? Are my endpoints healthy? Which detection engines are talking? Do I have rogue or unmanaged devices on my network? The answers flow from what you see on that screen.

But here is where this gets tricky: the Dashboard shows nothing when you have done it wrong. No threats, no data, no colors,just empty widgets and blank rows. A common reaction from new operators is to panic and assume the system is down or that no detections are happening. In reality, the system is usually working fine. The Dashboard is just configured for a scope you are not looking at, or a time window that does not include your data, or it is showing you a Site where nothing is happening right now. Get Scope wrong and the most noisy network on earth looks barren.

This chapter walks through how the Dashboard is built, what every control does, and,most importantly,how to fix the nine-out-of-ten "empty dashboard" situations that are actually configuration problems, not product bugs. The underlying controls are simple: Scope, widget type, graph type, time window, and refresh cadence. The craft is in knowing how they interact with each other and in building a dashboard layout that your team can trust every single morning without having to learn it anew each time they log in.

By the end of this chapter, you will be able to spot a misconfigured dashboard in two seconds, know where to look first, and most importantly, you will design and lock a team dashboard that surfaces only the signal that matters and mutes the noise that clouds your judgment.

2.1 What the Dashboard Is, and What It Is Not

The Dashboard in SentinelOne is a configurable surface of widgets that aggregate counts, trends, and breakdowns across the scope you are currently viewing. When you land on it, you see solved threats, unsolved threats, mitigated threats, infected and healthy endpoint counts, detection-engine distributions, threat-by-type breakdowns, and, if you have Ranger enabled, rogue and managed-endpoint counts, plus Application risk-level summaries.

What the Dashboard is NOT: it is not where you work an incident, it is not where you configure a policy, and it is not where you audit actions. Each of those has its own surface, Incidents, Sentinels, and Activity respectively. Treating the Dashboard as the place where you do work is the single biggest reason new operators feel overwhelmed by the platform; the Dashboard is a status summary, not an operational surface.

The mental model to hold: the Dashboard answers four questions, and only four. How many open threats do I have? Which endpoints are currently unhealthy? Which detection engines are firing, and what are they catching? Are there any devices on my network that should not be there? Everything else belongs elsewhere.

2.2 Scope: The Most Important Filter in the Product

Nearly every "my dashboard shows nothing" problem traces back to the Scope filter, which is why it deserves its own section and not a footnote.

Scope lives at the top of the Dashboard. It lets you set the lens through which every widget below it reads. Three settings matter:

The first is Highest Level. This gives you the broadest view that your user permissions allow. If you are the Account owner, Highest Level shows you everything across all your Sites. If you are a Site-only user, Highest Level shows you that one Site. In an MSSP context, Highest Level at the Account tier is what a SOC manager wants on their morning review.

The second is Specific Scope. This lets you pin the Dashboard to a single Site, useful when you are spending your day focused on one customer, or when you want a dedicated monitor on a wall that surfaces one business unit at all times.

The third is Multi, which lets you select several Sites or Groups and aggregate them. This sounds attractive until you have a lot of tenants, at which point the widget rendering and the cognitive load both get out of hand. Use Multi sparingly and only for two-or-three-tenant comparisons you run intentionally.

The trap: Scope defaults matter. If your dashboard is showing zero detections when you know there are detections happening somewhere, the first thing to check is always the Scope. Usually the scope has been pinned to a Site where nothing is happening, or to a time window that excludes the detections you are trying to see. In that order: scope first, then time window. The two of them together account for well over half of all "the Dashboard is broken" tickets that turn out to be not-a-bug.

2.3 Scope at Scale: MSSP Tenants and Cross-Customer Views

In an MSSP environment, Scope behavior becomes operational. You manage dozens or hundreds of Sites, and the same Dashboard layout needs to work for morning reviews at Account level, for deep-dives into specific customer environments, and for comparative analysis across customer footprints.

Here is the pattern: Lock your Account-level Dashboard to Highest Level Scope. This shows you the aggregate view across all your customers. This is where you catch global trends,a spike in threats across the portfolio, a sudden jump in offline agents, unmanaged devices appearing at scale. From there, when you drill into a customer incident, you pin the Scope to that specific Site and open its dedicated dashboard (or create one on the fly).

In a multi-tenant environment, the Multi scope option becomes tempting. You might think: "Let me show threats from Customer A and Customer B side by side to compare." The problem: at three or four tenants, widget rendering slows down, labels get cramped, and the eye cannot parse it reliably. The better pattern is to keep Scope pinned to one Site at a time, and when you need a comparison, open two browser tabs. Pin one to Customer A at Highest Level, one to Customer B. Read both windows in parallel. This stays fast and readable.

The other trap: Scope permissions. Not every analyst has visibility into every customer. If you grant an analyst permission only at the Site level for Customer X, their Highest Level will show Customer X only, not the Account. This is by design,it is how you fence customer data. When an analyst seems surprised that their dashboard is empty, check their permission level before assuming the Dashboard is broken.

Operator's Checklist: The "Empty Dashboard" Triage

Before you escalate a "no data on the Dashboard" concern, work this checklist in order:

1. Scope: Is it set to the right level? Highest Level, Specific, or Multi? In MSSP, verify your user role has permission to see that level.
2. Time window: Most widgets default to last seven days or last thirty. Check the widget-level time filter.
3. Widget filters: The widget may be filtered (e.g., to only resolved threats, or only one detection engine).
4. Feature licensing: Some widgets (e.g., Deep Visibility, Identity-related) render empty when the tenant does not hold that license.
5. Agent health: If agents are offline en masse, you will not get recent data regardless of dashboard settings.
6. Dashboard cache refresh: Give the dashboard 30 seconds and refresh the page. Sometimes a slow back-end is showing you a stale render.

2.4 The Core Widgets

The default Dashboard ships with a curated widget set that Rapid7's product team, sorry, that SentinelOne's product team, believes most operators want on first login. Those defaults are a reasonable starting point, but they are not your dashboard. Treat the defaults as a template you will revise within your first week of running the tenant.

The widget categories worth knowing:

Threats Widgets

These surface open, resolved, and mitigated threat counts and break threats down by detection engine, analyst verdict, confidence level, or incident status. The single most valuable threats widget for morning review is a bar chart of threats-by-detection-engine over the last 7 days, it shows you at a glance whether the AI engines are behaving consistently or whether one of them is suddenly quiet.

Endpoint Health Widgets

Infected vs. healthy counts, plus segmented breakdowns by operating system, site, group, or agent version. The agent-version widget is underrated, it is how you catch fleet fragmentation before your change window closes on Friday.

Ranger Widgets

If you have Ranger enabled: endpoint Ranger status (enabled/disabled), endpoint Ranger versions, discovery method (neighbor scan, port scan, DNS, DHCP, mDNS, SSDP, SNMP, SMB), fingerprinting data (Mac addresses, OS version, manufacturer, host name), managed states (managed, unmanaged, unsupported, secured, unsecured, unknown), OS types, and rogues breakdown by operating system. Taken together, these widgets are how you answer "what is on my network, and which of it is not protected."

Applications Widgets

Risk-level distribution across your fleet: criticals, highs, mediums, lows, and false positives. This is the widget most useful for demonstrating vulnerability-remediation progress to a CISO, they want to see the critical-count line trend down week over week.

Threat Landscape

An information surface that shows a live feed of SentinelOne-published threat intelligence, typically as a stream of categorized links. The live feed is one-way: it teaches you about what SentinelOne's detection community is seeing. It does not yet accept external threat feeds.

2.5 Graph Types: Choose the Shape That Fits the Data

Every widget in the Dashboard supports several graph types, and picking the right one matters more than you might expect. A badly chosen graph type is how a widget with real data ends up looking like a widget with no data.

The options you have, and when to use each:

Horizontal Bar

The most versatile choice. Works for category counts of any size. Labels read naturally. Default for most of the shipped Dashboard widgets.

Vertical Bar

Equivalent data capacity, better for trend-style reads when the x-axis is ordered (e.g., by date). Avoid vertical bar with more than ten categories; labels get cramped.

Stack Bar

Two or more series shown on a single bar, stacked. Good for showing mitigated vs. unmitigated within each detection engine. Bad for reading individual series values, the eye cannot sum stacks reliably. If your goal is comparison across series, use grouped bars instead.

Pie Chart

Works for three or four categories with very different sizes. Breaks down immediately for more than six categories. Never use a pie chart to compare two series, that is what a bar chart is for.

Donut

Same use cases as a pie chart, with a hollow center. Note that a donut does not necessarily represent a full 100 percent. It is not the same as a pie chart with a hole, it is a different visualization for slightly different semantics (typically "progress toward a total" rather than "share of whole").

Word Cloud

Available in some widgets. Visually striking, analytically weak. Use only for non-critical categorical data where the storytelling value outweighs the lack of precision.

A quick rule: when a widget lets you pick the graph type, the default chosen by the platform is usually fine. If you find yourself switching graph types to try to make a widget “show something,” your problem is almost certainly Scope or time-window related, not graph-type related. Switch back and triage up the chain.

2.6 Customization Discipline and Team-Shareable Layouts

The Dashboard is intensely customizable, you can drag widgets around, add new ones, delete defaults, change titles and colors, and upload custom images. That freedom is a trap if you use it as a playground. The goal is not a maximally personalized dashboard; the goal is a dashboard the whole team can read without orientation every morning.

Here is the operational discipline that works in practice: lock the top two rows as your team's agreed “morning check” zone. These widgets do not move. These widgets do not change. Every analyst on the team sees the same four or five summaries when they land on the Dashboard. This means a new hire does not need a ten-minute tour. They read row one, and they know the shape of the day.

On those top rows, constrain yourself to three or four widget types: (1) open-threats summary, (2) endpoint-health summary, (3) Ranger rogue/unmanaged count if licensed, and (4) a seven-day threats-by-detection-engine trend. That is it. Anything more and the eye stops reliably scanning and starts skipping. The goal is data density without cognitive overload.

Everything below that second row is flexible. Put your investigational widgets there, your experimental views, your comparative summaries. If one of those lower-row widgets proves its worth over a month of daily use, promote it to the top two rows in your next team sync. If it does not, delete it. Do not let widgets accumulate like technical debt. A dashboard with fifteen widgets looks busy and reads as empty.

Most importantly: export and version-control your team's canonical dashboard layout. Use the download-dashboard feature (available in Dashboard settings) to export the configuration as a JSON file. Commit it to your operational runbooks repository. Document when you last audited it and who can authorize changes. When an analyst customizes past the team agreement, or when you onboard a new hire, you upload that canonical JSON and everything snaps back into place.

The Morning Dashboard Check (a team ritual worth building)

At the start of every shift, the analyst on duty performs a 60-second Dashboard scan. Not a deep dive, a scan:

Open threats, is the count the same as yesterday? If yes, move on. If higher, investigate why before anything else.

Unhealthy endpoints, same shape? Any cluster of new agents going offline?

Rogue count, any net-new rogues discovered in the last 24 hours? If yes, who owns them?

Seven-day threats-by-engine, is any engine suddenly quieter than usual? Silence can mean success (policies tuned) or failure (agent offline).

2.7 Dashboard Refresh and Cache Behavior

One of the more surprising behaviors new operators encounter is Dashboard staleness. You are watching a widget, a threat lands, and the widget does not update. You wait five seconds, ten seconds, and nothing changes. The first instinct is to assume the detection did not happen. The second is to assume the Dashboard is broken. Neither is true. You are looking at cached data.

By design, the Dashboard caches data at the back end and refreshes on a cadence rather than in real time. The default refresh interval is five to ten minutes. This is not laziness on SentinelOne's part; it is a scaling decision. Real-time dashboard updates for every threat across thousands of endpoints at an MSSP would require constant back-end computation and would make the system expensive to run. Instead, the platform trades freshness for performance. The Dashboard answers, "What is the situation right now, within the last five to ten minutes?" not "What is happening this second?"

This is why the Dashboard is a status surface and not an alerting surface. If you need to know about threats the moment they land, you do not watch the Dashboard. You set up Notifications in Settings to deliver alerts via email or Syslog. You integrate with your SIEM. You configure escalation to PagerDuty or Slack. The Dashboard is what you read after those alerts wake you up.

If you need a dashboard to refresh faster, you can adjust widget-level refresh settings in your settings (some tenants allow per-widget cadence override), but do not rely on sub-minute refresh. The back-end query will time out if you ask for too much too fast. The pattern that works: read the Dashboard for status and context, trust Notifications for alarms, and use Deep Visibility or Incidents when you need to drill into the details of something that has already been flagged.

2.8 Situational Awareness Versus Actionable Detection

The distinction between situational awareness and actionable detection is what separates operators who love their Dashboard from operators who ignore it.

Situational awareness is knowing the shape of your environment. Is it calm or busy? How many endpoints are healthy? How many open threads are sitting around? Are threats piling up or resolving? The Dashboard is designed to answer these questions at a glance. It should take sixty seconds. You read the numbers, you get a feel for the day, and you know whether to expect a normal flow of work or to clear your calendar.

Actionable detection is the opposite: I have a specific threat, I know its ID, and I need to take action on it right now. That is not a Dashboard moment. That is an Incidents moment. You go to Incidents, you filter to that specific threat, you read the file hash, you check if it is quarantined, you see what behavior triggered it, you decide whether to kill the process, and you document your decision. The Dashboard cannot and should not do that work. It is too high-level.

The mistake that kills productivity is trying to make the Dashboard do both jobs. Operators add so many widgets, filters, and drill-down options that the Dashboard becomes impossible to scan. They are trying to turn a status surface into an investigation surface. Instead, use the tools designed for their job. The Dashboard is for status. Incidents is for investigation. When you feel frustrated that the Dashboard does not show you what you need to work on a specific threat, you are in the wrong tool. Switch to Incidents.

The best operating teams build a Dashboard that answers one question in thirty seconds: "Is my environment okay, or do I have something to handle?" If the answer is "something to handle," they switch to Incidents and go deep. If the answer is "okay," they move on to their other work. A Dashboard that takes five minutes to read or that requires hunting through five levels of drill-down is a Dashboard that nobody uses.

Common Widget Misuse: What NOT to Put on Your Dashboard

Widget: Deep Visibility query results,Misuse: Using the Dashboard to run or display threat-hunt queries. The Incidents and Deep Visibility surfaces exist for this.

Widget: Per-endpoint detail tables,Misuse: Trying to see every endpoint and its status. This creates a massive, unscannable table. Use the Sentinels list for per-endpoint operations.

Widget: Filtered-down threat lists,Misuse: Showing only threats matching a specific criterion (e.g., "only hash X"). Incidents with filters does this better.

Widget: Real-time event stream,Misuse: Expecting sub-minute refresh. The Dashboard cache cannot support this. Use Syslog or email Notifications instead.

Widget: Custom calculated fields,Misuse: Building math-heavy summary rows (e.g., "threats per endpoint ratio"). These slow down Dashboard rendering and rarely drive decisions.

Chapter Summary

The Dashboard is the daily situational-awareness surface, a read-only status summary, not an operational workspace. The most important control on it is Scope, which determines what every widget shows, and in MSSP environments, Scope is where most configuration mistakes happen. Core widgets cover threats, endpoint health, Ranger discovery, Application risk, and the Threat Landscape feed. Graph types each have a correct use; the default is usually right. Customization is worth doing, but with discipline: lock a morning-check zone of three or four widgets on your top rows, constrain their types, export and version-control the configuration, and rely on team agreement to prevent drift.

The Dashboard is not real-time. It caches data on a five-to-ten-minute cadence by design, trading freshness for performance at scale. Do not watch the Dashboard for alarms; rely on Notifications for that. Use the Dashboard to answer one question in sixty seconds: is my environment calm or busy? If busy, switch to Incidents for the detailed investigation work. A Dashboard that tries to be both a status surface and an investigation surface ends up being neither, and nobody uses it.

In the next chapter we go deep on Ranger, SentinelOne's network-asset-discovery engine, and how to answer the question that keeps CISOs awake: what is on my network that I do not know about?

Key Takeaways

- The Dashboard is a status summary, not a workbench. Do your work on Sentinels, Incidents, and Activity, never on the Dashboard. It answers four questions and four questions only: open threats, endpoint health, detection engines, and rogue devices.
- Scope is the first place to check when the Dashboard seems empty. It accounts for more than half of "no data" tickets. In MSSP, verify your user role has permission at the level you are viewing.
- Scope at Account level shows you all customers. Scope at Site level shows you one customer. Multi-scope becomes unreadable above three tenants; use separate browser tabs instead.
- Pick graph types to match the data shape. Bar charts for categories, donuts for progress-to-total, pies only for small counts. The default is usually correct.
- Lock the top two rows of the Dashboard as a team-agreed morning-check zone. Constrain to three or four widgets: threats, health, rogues, engine trends. Export the configuration as JSON and treat it like production config.
- The Dashboard is not real-time; it caches on a five-to-ten-minute cadence. Use Notifications for alarms, Incidents for investigation, and the Dashboard for status.
- A 60-second morning Dashboard scan every day will catch most operational drift before it becomes an incident. If the scan takes longer, your Dashboard has too many widgets.

Hands-On Exercise

Before you move on to Chapter 3, do the following in your SentinelOne tenant:

- Open your Dashboard and write down, in one sentence each, what every top-row widget is telling you right now. If you cannot answer in one sentence, the widget is probably not pulling its weight. Mark it for deletion.

- Verify your Scope setting. If you are in an MSSP, pin to a specific Site and open Incidents. How many threats appear in Incidents that you do not see on the Dashboard? This teaches you about cache refresh lag.
- Build or audit the four-widget morning-check zone described in Section 2.6. Save the dashboard configuration. Export it as JSON using the download button in Dashboard settings. Commit that JSON file to your runbook repository with a timestamp and change notes.
- Set your refresh interval to the fastest available (usually five to ten minutes). Run a test: trigger a detection manually (or wait for a natural one to land), and time how long before it appears on the Dashboard. Document that delay. Now you know the Dashboard's actual refresh cadence.
- Write a one-paragraph "How to Read Our Dashboard" guide for your team. If you cannot fit it in one paragraph, the dashboard has too many widgets. Use that guide to audit whether your dashboard is optimal.

Review Questions

- 1. What is Scope in the Dashboard, and which three scope settings does SentinelOne offer?
- 2. Your dashboard is displaying zero threats, but your colleagues are seeing active detections. Before escalating, what should you check first?
- 3. Match each graph type to its best use case: - (a) Pie chart - (b) Bar chart - (c) Stacked bar - Uses: comparing individual values across many categories / showing two series side-by-side with a shared axis / showing three to four categories with very different proportions
- 4. True or False: It is acceptable to place experimental and investigational widgets in the same row as your core morning-check zone. Explain.
- 5. You want to monitor whether the Behavioral AI engine is catching the same number of threats week over week. Which widget type and graph type would you choose, and why?

Answer Key: Review Questions

1. Scope is the filter that determines which level of the hierarchy the Dashboard displays. The three options are: Highest Level (all Sites in your Account or all child Accounts if you are Global), Specific Scope (pin to one Site), and Multi (select several Sites or Groups for comparison).

2. Check the Scope filter first. This accounts for over half of "no data" problems. The scope might be pinned to a Site or time window where nothing is happening. Next, check the time window on individual widgets.

3. (a) Pie chart → showing three to four categories with very different proportions. (b) Bar chart → comparing individual values across many categories. (c) Stacked bar → showing two series side-by-side on a shared axis (although grouped bars are often better than stacked).

4. False. Lock the top two rows for your core morning-check zone and keep them consistent across all analysts. Place experimental widgets in a lower row. This maintains operational discipline and prevents the dashboard from becoming cluttered.

5. Threats widget with a vertical bar chart or line graph, showing 7-day or 30-day trend filtered by "Behavioral AI" engine. A trend visualization lets you spot whether the engine is consistently firing or has suddenly gone quiet, which could indicate configuration drift or agent issues.

Discussion Questions

- 1. A CISO asks your team to create a "single dashboard view of security posture" that can be displayed on a wall monitor in their office. The CISO wants to see "everything." How would you explain why a single all-in-one dashboard is a poor idea, and what would you recommend instead?
- 2. Your team uses Scope = Highest Level to see all customer data. One analyst mis-clicks a widget and changes its time window to "last 24 hours," then leaves for vacation. Other analysts spend hours wondering why threat counts dropped overnight. How would you design a process to prevent this?
- 3. Describe a scenario where the Applications Risk Level dashboard widget would be more valuable to your CISO than the Threats widget. When would you present each, and to whom?

Hands-On Lab Exercises

Lab 2.1: Build and Lock Your Morning-Check Dashboard

Objective: Design and configure a team-agreed dashboard with a locked top-row zone for daily situational awareness.

You have access to the SentinelOne Dashboard and can add, remove, and reorder widgets

Your team has agreed on the four core metrics you want to track each morning

Steps:

- Set your Dashboard Scope to "Highest Level" (or the level your team reviews each morning).
- Identify or add the four widgets your team wants in the morning-check zone: (a) Open threats count, (b) Endpoint health (infected vs. healthy), (c) Ranger rogue count (if licensed), (d) Threats by detection engine (7-day trend).
- Drag these widgets to the top two rows of the Dashboard and arrange them in a consistent order.
- For each widget, verify the time window (default 7 days or 30 days?). Document what the default is and whether your team wants to change it.
- For the "Threats by Detection Engine" widget, ensure it is set to a line or bar graph showing recent trend, not a pie chart or word cloud.
- Export your dashboard configuration. Go to Dashboard settings > Export Configuration. Save the JSON file.
- Create a team runbook called "How to Read Our Dashboard" (one page) that describes each of the four widgets, what values are expected, and what constitutes an anomaly (e.g., "Open threats count should stay stable day-to-day; a jump of 50+ in one day warrants investigation").

Expected Outcome: A locked morning-check zone with four agreed widgets, an exported configuration JSON, and a one-page runbook for new hires.

Reflection: How would this dashboard inform your shift priorities if open threats jumped from 12 to 67 overnight? What would your first action be?

Lab 2.2: Debug an "Empty Dashboard" Problem

Objective: Experience the "empty dashboard" triage workflow and verify you can work through Scope, time window, and filter controls.

Access to a Dashboard that shows zero or very few detections; ability to adjust Scope, time windows, and widget-level filters

Steps:

- Look at your current Dashboard. Note that it is showing very few or zero threats/detections. Do not be alarmed; this is intentional.
- Check the Scope selector at the top. Is it set to "Highest Level," "Specific Scope," or "Multi"? Write down what scope you are currently viewing.
- Click into one widget that should have data (e.g., "Threats" or "Endpoint Health"). Look for a time-window filter within the widget itself (usually top right of the widget). What time window is it set to? Change it to "Last 7 days" or "Last 30 days" and see if data appears.
- If data still does not appear, click the Scope selector again and change to a different scope (if available). Reobserve the widgets.
- If a widget remains empty, check whether it is filtered. Some widgets have category filters (e.g., "Show only resolved threats" or "Show only critical severity"). Look for a filter icon or legend and clear any active filters.
- Document which of the five triage steps (Scope, time window, widget filter, widget license, agent health) fixed your empty-dashboard problem, if any.

Expected Outcome: Confirmation that you know how to work through Scope, time windows, and filters, and understanding of which control is most likely to cause "empty dashboard" problems.

Reflection: In your operational role, how will you coach junior analysts who report "the dashboard shows nothing"?

Lab 2.3: Choose Graph Types and Rebuild a Widget

Objective: Practice selecting appropriate graph types for different data shapes and understand how a badly chosen graph can make data invisible.

Ability to add or edit widgets on your Dashboard; your Dashboard has or you can add a widget showing multiple data series (e.g., threats by engine, health by OS, or similar)

Steps:

- On your Dashboard, locate a widget that displays data across five or more categories (e.g., threats detected by Static AI, Behavioral AI, Cloud Reputation, Ransomware, Suspicious).

- Note the current graph type. Is it a pie chart, bar chart, line, donut, or word cloud?
- If it is a pie chart with more than four categories, reorder it to show a horizontal or vertical bar chart instead. Observe how the data becomes easier to read.
- If the widget shows a trend over time (e.g., 7-day window), ensure the graph type is a line or vertical bar chart, not a pie. Pie charts cannot show time trends.
- Create a new widget (or duplicate this one) and set it to a different graph type. Compare readability. Document which graph type makes the data easiest to understand.
- Export the widget configuration or take a screenshot showing the before and after.

Expected Outcome: Firsthand experience that graph type matters, and confidence in choosing the right visualization for your data.

Reflection: If a widget has the right data but looks like it has no data, what should you suspect?

What's Next

Chapter 3 covers Ranger, SentinelOne's network-asset-discovery engine. You'll deploy Ranger, interpret its four device classifications, use its discovery methods to find rogues and unmanaged endpoints, and build a weekly device-review workflow so you actually know what is on your network before an attacker does. The Dashboard told you the shape of your endpoint security. Ranger tells you the shape of your network.

Mastering SentinelOne

Expanded Chapter 3, Draft for Review

by Kendrick Washington, Technology Interpreters, Inc.

Chapter 3

Ranger

Learning Objectives

- Understand what Ranger is and why network visibility is fundamental to endpoint security.
- Identify the four device classifications that Ranger produces: Secured, Unsecured, Unsupported, and Unknown.
- Recognize how Ranger discovers devices using passive network traffic analysis and active scanning protocols.
- Use Ranger filters to find rogue devices, unmanaged endpoints, and inventory gaps in your environment.
- Configure active scan methods (ICMP, SNMP, multicast DNS, SMB, DNS, TCP/UDP port scans) and understand which are safe to run in production.
- Apply device review workflows and compliance tagging to reduce alert fatigue and accelerate incident response.

Chapter Opener

You have endpoints running SentinelOne agents. You believe they are your primary line of defense. But if you have never seen a complete inventory of devices actually plugged into your network, you are living in a dangerous blind spot. A security engineer at a 500-person financial services firm once told me they thought they had 350 managed endpoints. Ranger showed them 680 devices on the network, printers, IoT devices, guest laptops, rogue access points, and dozens of unmanaged workstations. Within a week of running Ranger, they found three business-critical servers running no endpoint protection at all. They had been invisible until Ranger looked.

This is what Ranger does. It listens to the network chatter your managed endpoints already have access to, builds a fingerprint of every device talking on the wire, with or without an agent, and answers the question that keeps chief information security officers awake: what is on my network that I do not know about? This chapter walks you through deploying Ranger, interpreting its output, hunting for rogues and gaps, and turning its findings into a remediation workflow that actually works.

3.1 What Ranger Is

Ranger is SentinelOne's network-asset-discovery engine. It is not a separate product you install. It is a capability your existing agents provide, every endpoint running the SentinelOne agent can participate in Ranger scanning at no extra cost. Think of each agent as a listener on your network. It passively monitors the traffic flowing past its network interface, reads the packets, extracts device identifiers (MAC addresses, IP addresses, hostnames, operating systems), and reports back to the management console what it sees.

The real intelligence happens at scale. One agent might see 50 devices on a subnet. Another might see a different 40. When you have dozens or hundreds of agents distributed across multiple locations and network segments, their collective view creates a comprehensive map of everything connected to your infrastructure. Ranger correlates all that data and presents it in a single dashboard where you can filter, search, tag, and remediate.

The key insight: Ranger does not require agents on the target devices. Your managed endpoints do the listening. They see broadcasts, DNS queries, DHCP handshakes, and protocol exchanges happening around them, and extract enough information to identify what is on the network even if the device itself is unmanaged. This is why Ranger is so powerful in discovering rogue devices, guest endpoints, and IoT gadgets that your IT team may not have inventoried.

3.2 The Four Device Classifications

When you open the Ranger interface, the first thing you see is the device summary. Every device Ranger finds is placed into one of four categories based on whether it has an agent and whether SentinelOne supports it.

Secured

These devices have a SentinelOne agent installed and are fully managed. They are running the Ranger listener themselves, which means they are actively contributing to the network discovery process. Secured devices are your primary enforcement boundary, these are the systems where

SentinelOne can detect, block, quarantine, and remediate. If your endpoint count in Ranger is lower than your agent deployment count, you have a decommissioning problem or a scope issue (a device has logged out and not registered back in).

Unsecured

These devices have no SentinelOne agent and SentinelOne can install one on them. They represent enforcement gaps in your infrastructure. In a well-run environment, the Unsecured count should be as close to zero as possible. Unsecured devices are your primary hunting ground. Some are workstations new to the network pending deployment, others are servers in non-standard deployment zones, and a handful are genuinely forgotten endpoints. Your job is to review the Unsecured list regularly and either deploy an agent or document a waiver explaining why the device does not need one.

Unsupported

These devices have no agent and cannot accept one. Unsupported devices are typically Linux IoT gadgets, network appliances, printers, and smart home devices that lack the operating system or architecture SentinelOne targets (Windows, macOS, Linux on standard hardware, Kubernetes, select cloud workloads). You cannot change this status, and you should not treat Unsupported as a failure. But you should log it. Knowing which Unsupported devices are on your network and where they are is crucial for incident response, if an adversary compromises a printer or a network appliance, you need to know it was there.

Unknown

These are devices Ranger observed on the network but could not classify. Ranger tried fingerprinting them using MAC address, IP behavior, DNS resolution, and protocol patterns, but did not have enough signal to place them in a category. Unknown devices require investigation. Sometimes they are asymmetric, your agent can see them sending packets, but cannot determine what they are. Sometimes they are on the network so briefly or so quietly that they do not reveal enough telemetry. Pull these devices manually. Cross-reference against your DHCP server logs, your network access control list, or your router's connected-device list. Unknown devices are where rogues hide.

3.3 How Ranger Discovers Devices

Ranger uses a combination of passive and active techniques to identify devices. Understanding how discovery works helps you evaluate the data Ranger reports and tells you when a device might not be fully classified.

Passive Discovery

Your agents are always listening. When a device joins the network or talks to other devices, it broadcasts information, MAC addresses, hostnames, IP addresses, operating system hints, at Layer 2 (the data link layer). Your agents capture these broadcasts without sending any packets. This is the quietest, fastest form of discovery. A new device plugged into the network will be visible in Ranger within seconds of sending its first broadcast, often before it has finished booting. Passive discovery is how Ranger scales to networks with thousands of devices without generating significant network overhead.

Active Scanning Protocols

When passive observation is not enough, Ranger uses active methods. These send packets to suspected devices and listen for responses. The four most common active methods are:

- ICMP (Ping): The simplest check. "Are you there?" Most devices respond, and the response helps Ranger confirm the device is alive and potentially classify its operating system.
- SNMP (Simple Network Management Protocol): Queries network equipment like switches and routers. Most network gear ships with default SNMP credentials unchanged. If SNMP is open and readable, Ranger learns the manufacturer, model, and sometimes inventory of connected devices. Many organizations do not realize how much network topology information leaks through unprotected SNMP.
- Multicast DNS (mDNS): Used by printers, smart home devices, and Bonjour-enabled endpoints to advertise themselves locally. Ranger listens for mDNS announcements and uses them to classify device types.
- SMB (Server Message Block): Queries Windows-like systems for share information. SMB shares reveal which devices are likely workstations or servers and sometimes leak information about installed software.

- DNS Traffic Observation: Ranger watches DNS queries and responses. A device requesting DNS resolution for a Philips Hue server is likely a smart home hub. A device resolving to a domain controller is likely a Windows endpoint.
- TCP and UDP Port Scans: Ranger probes common ports (SSH, RDP, HTTP, HTTPS, Kerberos, etc.) to infer device type and purpose. A device listening on port 3389 (RDP) is likely a Windows server. A device listening on port 22 (SSH) is likely Linux.

Active scanning generates network traffic. In a lab or test environment, this is fine. In production, you must be careful. Scanning your entire network continuously can create notification fatigue for your network team and may trigger security alerts on tightly monitored segments. This is why Ranger lets you exclude certain networks and configure scan frequency.

One common pitfall: PLC networks and industrial control systems. Programmable Logic Controllers are sensitive automation equipment used in manufacturing and utility control. A port scan against a PLC can sometimes cause it to crash or malfunction. Before enabling Ranger, check with your operations team. If you have PLCs, configure the exclusion list in Ranger settings to prevent scanning those IP ranges.

3.4 Reading the Ranger Dashboard

The Ranger dashboard shows you four lists and a powerful filter interface. Learning to work through this interface quickly is the difference between spending ten minutes finding a rogue and spending an hour.

At the top, you see the four-category summary: how many Secured, Unsecured, Unsupported, and Unknown devices your environment contains. Glance at these numbers every week. A sudden jump in Unknown devices might indicate a new office or network segment. A climb in Unsecured devices might mean a deployment lag. These metrics are your environmental health indicators.

Below that is the device list, which defaults to showing all devices but respects several filters. The most important filters are:

- Device Review Status: Allowed, Not Reviewed, or Under Analysis. When you first set up Ranger, most devices are Not Reviewed. As you classify them, you mark them Allowed (it belongs here) or keep them Under Analysis (uncertain).

- Device Type: Workstation, Server, Printer, Router, IoT, etc. Use this to quickly find all printers or all servers.
- Operating System: Windows, Linux, macOS, iOS, Android. Use this to find devices by operating system.
- Discovery Method: Port Scan, Ping, SNMP, DNS, mDNS, SMB, or Passive. This tells you which Ranger technique identified the device. If a device was found only via Port Scan and nowhere else, it might be barely on your network.
- Manufacturer: Automatically extracted from MAC address prefixes and protocol responses. Use this to find all Cisco devices, all Hewlett Packard printers, etc.
- Site: Which Site in your account the device was discovered on. In a multi-tenant environment, this keeps customer devices segregated.
- Network: Which logical network the device is on (if you have configured Ranger to identify them).

Click into any device and you get more detail: IP address, MAC address, last seen timestamp, all discovery methods that detected it, and the fields Ranger extracted. For Unknown devices, this is where you do the detective work. Look for hostname hints, MAC address patterns, and which other devices it talked to. Cross-reference against your router logs or DHCP server.

One thing to remember: Ranger does not identify everything on a single pass. A device that first appeared as Unknown might be re-classified to Unsupported after Ranger gathers more telemetry. It might later be identified as an unsecured Linux server. The classifications are not final until you have reviewed the device.

3.5 Finding Rogues and Gaps with Filtering

The real operational power of Ranger is hunting. You know your network should have exactly 320 managed endpoints. Ranger shows you 320 Secured devices, 12 Unsecured, and 8 Unknown. That Unknown count should not exist. Here is how to find them.

The Rogue Hunt

Filter by Device Review Status = Not Reviewed. This shows every device your organization has not yet classified. Start with the Unsecured devices in this list. These are the potential enforcement gaps. Read the details for each.

Are they servers in your data center? Workstations at a satellite office? Unknown contractors' laptops? For each one, either deploy an agent immediately, or document in the device record why the endpoint does not need one (it is isolated, it is temporary, it is undergoing decommissioning, etc.). Once you have reviewed all Unsecured devices, move to Unknown. This is where rogues hide. If the device has an unexpected manufacturer, unexpected OS type, or is talking to unexpected internal servers, you have found something that should not be on your network.

The Coverage Gap Hunt

Compare the number of endpoints you think you have with the Secured count in Ranger. If you deployed agents to 320 workstations but Ranger shows only 310 Secured devices, you are missing ten agents. Filter by Operating System = Windows (or whatever your managed OS is) and Device Review Status = Not Reviewed. This shows unmanaged devices that look manageable. These are candidates for agent deployment. Missing agents often hide in remote offices, servers added outside the standard deployment process, or machines handed to contractors who kept them offline during onboarding.

The IoT Audit

Filter by Device Type = IoT or Operating System = Linux and Device Type != Server. This isolates all your smart home devices, printers, and IoT gadgets in one view. For each one, note the manufacturer and IP range. You may have no control over these devices, but knowing where they are and what they do is critical. If an attacker compromises a printer to pivot into your network, you need to know that printer was there to track the attacker's movements in incident response.

Ranger Intelligence: The Unknown Device Workflow

When you find an Unknown device, start with the MAC address prefix. The first half of the MAC identifies the manufacturer.

Cross-reference the IP address against your DHCP server logs or your router's connected-devices list.

Check whether the device is talking to specific internal servers (via Ranger network connections, if available).

For persistent Unknown devices, manually connect to the network segment and use your own tools (nmap, arp, etc.) to identify them.

Once identified, change the Device Review Status to Allowed (if it belongs) or block the IP (if it does not).

3.6 Tagging and Review Workflows

Raw discovery data is useless without a review process. Ranger gives you three mechanisms to scale from "I have no idea what this device is" to "I understand and accept this device on my network."

Device Review Status

Every device in Ranger has a status: Not Reviewed, Under Analysis, or Allowed. Not Reviewed is the default for all newly discovered devices. As you classify them, move them to Under Analysis if you are still investigating, or Allowed if you have confirmed they belong on your network. The Allowed status tells Ranger and your team, "I have seen this device, I understand what it is, and it is supposed to be here." Allowed devices no longer generate alerts or appear in your daily hunting list.

Notes and Tags

You can attach notes to any device. Use this. Write "Printer in Building C, Accounting department, do not patch" or "Contractor laptop, temporary access until 2026-05-15, see contract in ticket #4521." These notes are searchable and will help the next analyst understand why the device is on the network and whether it still should be.

Bulk Workflows

If you discover 50 printers in a single scan, you do not need to click each one individually. Use the filter to show Device Type = Printer and Manufacturer = Xerox, then select all and bulk-apply the Allowed status and add a tag "Xerox Printers - Accounting." This scales your review process. A junior analyst can spend two hours filtering and tagging known good devices, and reduce the daily "Not Reviewed" list from 200 devices to 20, leaving only the truly uncertain ones for manual investigation.

3.7 Configuring Ranger for Your Environment

Ranger has several configuration options. Get these right and your discovery process will run quietly. Get them wrong and you will generate network noise and miss devices.

Enable Ranger

Ranger is disabled by default. You must enable it at the Account or Site level in Settings. This is not a deployment step on individual endpoints, Ranger capability exists in the agent already. You are just flipping the switch to tell the console to start collecting and displaying the network discovery data. Many operators miss this and wonder why Ranger shows zero devices. Check the toggle.

Scan Scope and Subnet Limits

By default, Ranger scans only the local subnets where your agents reside. If you have agents on 192.168.1.0/24 and 192.168.10.0/24, Ranger scans those two subnets. If you want Ranger to probe deeper (for example, to discover devices on adjacent subnets your firewall permits), you can enable cross-subnet scanning. Be cautious here. Aggressive scanning of unfamiliar networks can trigger alerts or cause problems. Test in a lab first. The "Scan only on subnets with agents" setting keeps Ranger conservative and safe for production.

Scan Frequency and Snapshots

Ranger can scan between every 5 minutes and every 20 minutes. More frequent scans catch device changes faster but generate more network traffic and consume more back-end processing. In most environments, every 15 minutes is a reasonable middle ground. You also set a timeline for how long to keep network snapshots. Networks change constantly. When a device disappears from your network, when does Ranger remove it from the list? The default is 7 days: if a device has not been seen for a week, it is automatically removed. You can adjust this if you have high churn (add a lot of guest devices and remove them frequently) or if you want a longer historical record.

Minimum Agent Requirement

You can configure Ranger to skip scanning a subnet if it has fewer than a minimum number of agents. For example, if you set "minimum 3 agents per subnet," Ranger will not scan any subnet with only 1 or 2 agents. This is a cost control and accuracy measure. Scanning with too few agents on a subnet yields incomplete data. If you want visibility into a subnet, first deploy enough agents to that subnet, then Ranger will engage.

Active Scan Methods

In the Active Scan Configuration section, you can enable or disable individual discovery methods. Check which ones make sense for your environment. ICMP and DNS are safe and low-noise. SNMP can be noisy if your network equipment is misconfigured. SMB can trigger alerts on tightly monitored systems. Port scans generate the most noise. If your network team complains about port scan alerts, toggle it off and rely on passive discovery and ICMP.

Global Restrictions and Exclusions

If you have sensitive networks that should never be scanned, PLC networks, medical devices, legacy systems, add them to the Global Restrictions list. Enter the IP range or CIDR block, and Ranger will skip it entirely. This is a hard guardrail. Use it to prevent Ranger from probing systems that could malfunction if probed.

Credential Groups for SMB Enumeration

If you want Ranger to enumerate SMB shares, you can store domain credentials in Ranger settings. This allows Ranger to connect to Windows systems with authenticated SMB queries and learn more about them. This is optional and requires careful credential management. If you go this route, use a service account with minimal permissions, store it only in Ranger, and rotate it regularly.

Operational Best Practice: Ranger in Production

Enable Ranger in test or staging first. Monitor network traffic and alert logs for a week.

Configure scan frequency to 15 minutes and start with local subnet scanning only.

Disable active methods that trigger false positives (usually SMB and port scans in highly monitored environments).

Run your first rogue hunt manually, outside of your normal incident response flow.

Tag and classify at least 80% of devices before you rely on Ranger alerts for operational decisions.

Review your Not Reviewed list at least weekly to catch drift.

3.8 Common Pitfalls and How to Avoid Them

Ranger is powerful, but it is also easy to misconfigure. Here are the problems I have seen most often.

Turning Ranger On and Never Looking at It

The biggest mistake: enable Ranger, assume it works, and only open it when you suspect a rogue. This leaves you reactive instead of proactive. Spend 20 minutes per week on your Ranger list. Filter for Not Reviewed devices, bulk-tag the known ones, investigate the outliers. This habit catches problems before they become incidents.

Confusing Unsupported with Rogue

An Unsupported device is not a threat. It is a device that SentinelOne simply cannot run on. Printers, smart home hubs, network switches, and IoT appliances are all expected to be Unsupported. Your job is to catalog them and keep them on your inventory, not to remove them. Rogues are Unsecured devices you do not expect to see, or Unknown devices that do not match your environment. Do not confuse the categories.

Network Noise Breaking Your Workflow

If Ranger scanning is generating so much network traffic that your network team is complaining, you have enabled too many active scanning methods for your environment. Pull back. Disable port scans and SMB enumeration. Rely on passive discovery and ICMP only. Passive discovery is fast and quiet, it will catch the devices that matter.

Scanning Sensitive Networks

If you have never run Ranger and you have a PLC network or medical device network in your environment, check with operations before enabling Ranger. A port scan or SNMP probe can destabilize critical infrastructure. Add the network to Global Restrictions first. Then enable Ranger. Then verify nothing broke.

Assuming Ranger Sees Everything

Ranger is powerful, but it is not omniscient. Devices on isolated VLANs, devices that rarely communicate, and devices that spoof MAC addresses might evade Ranger discovery. VPN-only devices might not be seen. Air-gapped networks will show nothing. Ranger is your primary visibility tool, not your only one. Use it alongside DHCP server logs, your access point client lists, and your network administrator's knowledge. The combination of those sources will give you more confidence than Ranger alone.

Chapter Summary

Ranger is network asset discovery baked into your existing SentinelOne agents. It listens to network traffic, fingerprints devices, and classifies them into four categories: Secured (has an agent), Unsecured (can have an agent), Unsupported (cannot have an agent), and Unknown (unclassified). The real value is in the hunt: running filters to find rogue devices, documenting inventory gaps, and preventing surprise compromises. Ranger uses passive observation (listening to broadcasts) as its primary discovery method and active methods (ICMP, SNMP, SMB, DNS, port scans) when more information is needed. Configure Ranger carefully in your production environment, enable only the scanning methods that make sense for you, protect sensitive networks with exclusions, and establish a weekly workflow for reviewing unclassified devices. The network visibility Ranger provides is not a luxury, it is a requirement for knowing whether you are actually secure.

Three takeaways to carry forward: First, Ranger closes the gap between what you think is on your network and what is actually there. Second, rogue device detection and enforcement gaps are prevention opportunities, find them before an attacker does. Third, your job as an operator is not to deploy Ranger and walk away, but to read it, classify what you find, and use those findings to harden your footprint every week.

Key Takeaways

- Ranger discovers all devices on your network using existing endpoints as listeners. No separate deployment required.
- The four device classifications, Secured, Unsecured, Unsupported, Unknown, tell you what needs your attention and what you can leave alone.
- Passive discovery is Ranger's quiet foundation; active scanning methods (ICMP, SNMP, SMB, port scans) should be tuned to your environment to avoid generating unnecessary network noise.
- Filter and hunt weekly: find Unsecured devices to deploy agents, find Unknown devices to classify, find IoT devices to catalog.
- Tag and review everything. The device you do not understand today becomes the rogue endpoint that compromised you in three months.
- Exclude sensitive networks (PLCs, medical devices, legacy systems) before you enable active scanning to prevent outages.
- Ranger is visibility, not perfection. Cross-reference Ranger output with DHCP logs, access point lists, and network operator knowledge for a complete picture.

Hands-On Exercise

Before moving to the next chapter, do the following:

- Enable Ranger at your Account or Site level (Settings > Network > Ranger). Set scan frequency to 15 minutes, keep local-subnet scanning on, and disable active methods that might generate noise in your environment.

- Let Ranger run for 24 hours. Then open the Ranger dashboard and count the devices in each category (Secured, Unsecured, Unsupported, Unknown). Does the Secured count match your expected agent deployment count? If not, you have a deployment gap or a device that has gone offline.
- Filter to show Device Review Status = Not Reviewed. Pick 20 devices at random. Classify each one using the device details (manufacturer, OS, discovery method). For the ones you cannot identify, cross-reference against your DHCP logs or router. Write a one-sentence note for each explaining why you allowed or rejected it.
- Filter to show Device Type = Printer or IoT. Count how many you have. Document the manufacturer and approximate location of three of them. This is your inventory baseline.

Review Questions

- 1. What are the four device classifications Ranger produces, and what does each one tell you about remediation urgency?
- 2. You enable Ranger and within 24 hours it shows 320 Secured devices, 18 Unsecured, 7 Unsupported, and 3 Unknown. Your endpoint inventory is supposed to be exactly 320 endpoints. Is this normal? What does the Unknown count mean?
- 3. Ranger uses both passive and active discovery methods. Name three active discovery methods and explain which one generates the most network noise.
- 4. True or False: If Ranger classifies a device as "Unsupported," you should immediately block it from the network. Explain.
- 5. When would you use the "Device Review Status" field, and what are the three values it can take?

Answer Key: Review Questions

1. (1) Secured: has an agent, managed fully, lowest remediation urgency. (2) Unsecured: can have an agent installed, medium urgency, deploy an agent or document a waiver. (3) Unsupported: cannot have an agent, lowest remediation urgency, just catalog it. (4) Unknown: unclassified, highest urgency, investigate manually.

2. Normal. You have 320 managed endpoints (Secured). The 18 Unsecured are deployment gaps or devices pending agent installation. The 7 Unsupported are IoT or network appliances. The 3 Unknown require investigation, they might be rogues, might be asymmetric network devices, or might reveal themselves with more telemetry.

3. ICMP (ping), SNMP, multicast DNS (mDNS), SMB, DNS observation, TCP/UDP port scans. Port scans generate the most noise; ICMP and DNS are quietest.

4. False. Unsupported devices are often expected (printers, network switches, IoT). You should catalog them, not block them. Rogues are Unknown or Unsecured devices you do not recognize.

5. To track whether you have reviewed and classified each device. Values: Not Reviewed (new device, not yet classified), Under Analysis (investigating, uncertain), Allowed (confirmed it belongs, stop alerting on it).

Discussion Questions

- 1. You discover a Ranger Unknown device with a MAC prefix belonging to Cisco and an IP that talks to your file servers. Describe your investigation workflow. What would you check, and how would you determine whether this is a rogue or a legitimate network appliance?
- 2. Your network ops team complains that Ranger port scans are triggering alerts on their monitoring platform. How would you approach reducing network noise while maintaining visibility into rogue devices?
- 3. In an MSSP environment managing 30 customer Sites, how would you scale Ranger review and device classification across your team without creating review bottlenecks?

Hands-On Lab Exercises

Lab 3.1: Enable Ranger and Baseline Your Network

Objective: Enable Ranger, observe initial discovery, and create a baseline of your network device inventory.

Access to Settings at Site level; no active Ranger deployment

Steps:

- Work through to Settings > Ranger (or equivalent) and enable Ranger for your current Site.

- Set the scan frequency to 15 minutes. Enable passive discovery and ICMP only; disable SNMP, SMB, and port scans for now.
- Let Ranger run for 24 hours to collect baseline data.
- Return to the Ranger dashboard. Count devices in each category (Secured, Unsecured, Unsupported, Unknown). Record these numbers and the time.
- Compare Secured count to your expected endpoint inventory. Document any discrepancies.
- Create a one-line note summarizing: "Baseline: X Secured, X Unsecured, X Unsupported, X Unknown. Expected agents: Y. Status: [Gap/Aligned]."

Expected Outcome: A baseline inventory count for comparison in future labs.

Reflection: If Secured count is lower than expected agents deployed, where might those agents be?

Lab 3.2: Hunt for Unknown Devices and Cross-Reference

Objective: Identify Unknown devices and manually investigate them using DHCP logs or router data.

Ranger running for at least 24 hours; access to your DHCP server logs or router's connected-devices list

Steps:

- In the Ranger dashboard, filter to Device Review Status = "Not Reviewed" and Device Classification = "Unknown."
- Pick any Unknown device. Record its MAC address, IP address, manufacturer (if detected), and last-seen timestamp.
- Open your DHCP server logs or router. Search for the IP or MAC address. Note the hostname assigned.
- Cross-reference the hostname or manufacturer against your network inventory or asset list. Determine if it is a rogue or a legitimate device.
- In Ranger, update the device with a note explaining what it is. Set the status to "Allowed" if legitimate or mark for escalation if suspicious.
- Repeat for three Unknown devices.

Expected Outcome: Three Unknown devices investigated and classified, demonstrating your ability to manually identify devices.

Reflection: If an Unknown device has no DHCP entry and no obvious owner, what is your next step?

Lab 3.3: Tag and Bulk-Classify Known Device Types

Objective: Use filters to identify device types (printers, servers, etc.) and bulk-apply tags and status changes.

Ranger dashboard with many devices, ability to filter and bulk-select

Steps:

- In Ranger, filter to Device Type = "Printer" (or another type if printers are not discovered).
- Note the count. If more than 5, select all and bulk-apply: Status = "Allowed," and add a tag like "Printer - Infrastructure" or "IoT - Monitored."
- Repeat for any other device type that appears frequently (servers, IoT, wireless access points).
- Document which device types you have and how many of each.
- Review the Not Reviewed count. Did bulk operations reduce it? By how much?

Expected Outcome: Reduced Not Reviewed count via bulk classification, and tags applied to device types.

Reflection: How could you automate this workflow if you discovered 500 printers from a new office?

Lab 3.4: Configure Active Scan Methods and Monitor Network Impact

Objective: Understand the trade-off between discovery completeness and network noise.

Ranger enabled with passive discovery running; ability to adjust scan methods and monitor network logs

Steps:

- In Ranger settings, currently enable ICMP scans only. Let this run for 2 hours and count the Unknown devices.
- Then enable SNMP in addition to ICMP. Run for another 2 hours. Count Unknown devices again. Did SNMP reveal new devices?
- Optionally, enable SMB (if you have Windows systems). Run for 2 hours. Compare Unknown count.

- Check with your network ops team: did they see any alert spikes during your SNMP or SMB runs?
- Based on your findings, document a recommendation: "For our environment, we should enable [methods] and disable [methods] because [reason]."

Expected Outcome: Understanding of how each discovery method contributes to visibility and network impact.

Reflection: Which discovery method would you recommend disabling in an environment with strict change controls?

What's Next

Chapter 4 shifts to the Sentinels interface, where you deploy agents, manage groups, and push policies. You now understand what is on your network (Ranger). Next you will learn how to put SentinelOne on every device that matters (Sentinels) and how to configure the detection engines that keep them safe.

Mastering SentinelOne
Sample Expanded Chapter 4, Draft for Review
by Kendrick Washington, Technology Interpreters, Inc.

Chapter 4

Sentinels: Endpoint Fleet Management

Learning Objectives

- Work through the Sentinels endpoint list and understand what each column reports about device state and connectivity.
- Filter and search the endpoint list by device name, group membership, health status, and agent version.
- Assign tags and customer identifiers to endpoints for organizational and automation workflows.
- Read device detail pages: status fields, agent health indicators, last activity timestamps, and what they tell you about remediation readiness.
- Execute bulk actions across multiple endpoints: agent upgrades, group reassignments, and mass-remediation operations.
- Interpret endpoint status: online vs. offline, last activity windows, and how to distinguish active endpoints from stale ones.

Chapter Opener

The Sentinels section of the SentinelOne console is where fleet management lives. This is not just a list of computers, it is the operational nerve center where every endpoint reports its state, where you push policies and actions, where you tag and organize your deployed agents, and where you make first contact with an infected or misbehaving machine. When something goes wrong in your environment, you start here. When you need to roll out a new policy or remediate at scale, you work from here. This chapter walks the endpoint list, the device detail page, filtering, tagging, bulk operations, and the field-team workflows that depend on Sentinels working efficiently.

The key to mastering Sentinels is learning to read the interface the way it was designed: fast, categorical, and built for decision-making. A single glance at the endpoint list should tell you how many machines are healthy, how many are offline, how many are waiting for your action. The detail page of any endpoint should show you everything you need to decide: is this machine active right now, when was it last seen, what version of the agent is running, and what remediation options are available. This chapter teaches you to move through Sentinels with confidence.

4.1 The Endpoint List: What You Are Looking At

When you click Sentinels in the left navigation, you land on a table. This table is your master list of endpoints. Every computer running a SentinelOne agent in your Site shows up here. In a small deployment you might see a handful; in an MSSP environment managing a thousand customers, you will be looking at millions of rows across all Sites.

The list uses columns to surface the most critical information at a glance. The first column is usually the device name, the hostname of the machine. Next to it, you typically see the group the endpoint belongs to, its current status (online, offline, disconnected), and timestamps showing when it last checked in with the console. Some columns are customizable, and we will cover that in a moment. But the pattern is consistent: every column answers one of these questions: What is this machine? Where does it belong? Is it healthy? What did it do recently?

The reason this matters is that in the field, you do not have time to click into every machine. When you are the one responding to an incident at 2 a.m. or troubleshooting a deployment issue, you need to absorb the state of your environment in seconds. The endpoint list is designed for exactly that: categorical decisions made fast. A good operator learns to scan the list, spot the machines that need attention, and drill into detail only when necessary.

4.2 Reading the Columns: Status, Health, and Activity

The most critical columns to understand are Status, Health, Infected, Last Activity, and Agent Version. Status tells you whether the endpoint is online or offline. Online means the agent has checked in within the last few minutes, when I train this with my team, we use the rule of thumb that "last four minutes" essentially means it is active, since the console pulls agent telemetry every five minutes. Offline means you have not heard from the agent in longer than your policy-defined timeout window, usually hours or days. Disconnected is a special state you create manually when you isolate a machine due to malware and want it to talk only to the console for remediation, we cover that in Chapter 5.

Health tells you whether the agent itself is functioning properly. A healthy endpoint is one where SentinelOne is running, the detection engines are loaded, and the agent can phone home to the console. An unhealthy agent might mean the service crashed, it lost its connection to the console, or it is running into permission issues on the endpoint. When you see a warning or error in the Health column, that is your signal that you need to look deeper.

Infected is self-explanatory but critical: it tells you at a glance whether any threat has been detected on that endpoint. If the column shows a red flag or a threat count, you drill into Incidents to understand what was found and what remediation steps are available.

Last Activity is perhaps the most underappreciated column. Knowing that a machine is online is good; knowing what it did and when tells you whether it is actually in use. An endpoint online but inactive for six months is probably decommissioned or in a closet somewhere. That timestamp helps you identify machines that should probably be offboarded.

Agent Version tells you what release of the SentinelOne agent is running. Keeping agents current is a fundamental hygiene task in an EDR deployment. You will frequently run queries like "show me all endpoints running agent version 7.6 or older" so you can push an upgrade. We cover that in the bulk actions section.

4.3 Filtering: Finding What You Need

The endpoint list can grow very large very fast. In an MSSP environment managing thousands of customers, a single Site can easily have ten thousand endpoints. Browsing is not an option. You need to filter.

SentinelOne Sentinels supports filtering on several key dimensions: device name, group membership, online status, agent version, tag values, and threat status. The fastest path is the search box at the top of the list. Type in a hostname and you immediately narrow to machines matching that pattern. If you are looking for all endpoints in a specific group, use the group filter dropdown. If you want to surface only machines that have detected threats, toggle the threat filter. If you are looking for agents running a specific version older than your current standard, use the version filter.

In practice, here are the filters you will use most often. First, filter by online status to separate active machines from stale ones; this is your starting point for any operational task. Second, filter by group; this is how you scope an action to the right set of endpoints. Third, filter by agent version; this is how you identify what needs upgrading. Fourth, filter by tags; if you have tagged critical servers or a pilot group for testing new policies, you access them this way. Fifth, filter by threat status to surface only infected machines when you are conducting incident response.

These filters can be combined. You can ask for "all endpoints in Group Alpha that are online and running agent version 7.5 or older." That single query becomes the scope for a bulk upgrade operation. Building proficiency with filters is one of the biggest time savers in the Sentinels workflow.

4.4 Tags and Customer Identifiers: Organizing Your Fleet

Tags and customer identifiers are your tools for organizing endpoints beyond the built-in hierarchy of Groups. A tag is a key-value pair. You define the key, maybe "Environment" or "Department" or "BusinessCriticality",and then you assign values to each endpoint: Production, Development, or Pilot; Sales, Finance, Engineering; Tier1, Tier2, Tier3. Customer identifiers are simpler: a single custom text field per endpoint that you can populate with whatever identifier makes sense for your workflow, a username, a serial number, a location code.

Tags are powerful because they become the basis for filtering and scoping. Once you have tagged all your endpoints, you can write a filter that says "show me all endpoints tagged Production=True AND Department=Finance." You can also use tags in policies and automation: a policy can apply differently to Tier1 machines than to Tier3 machines, and a remediation script can be scoped to run only on Development endpoints, protecting your Production fleet.

The key-value structure sounds simple but confuses teams at first. The key is the category. The value is the specific assignment. Think of it like metadata: every endpoint gets a label, and that label has structure. Some endpoints might have ten tags; others might have three. The point is that tags let you overlay arbitrary organizational logic on top of the built-in Groups.

Customer identifiers are used primarily in MSSP and multi-tenant environments where you want to associate an endpoint with a business identifier. Maybe you tag an endpoint with the customer's ticket system ID or an internal asset tag. That way, when you need to log an incident or request a change, you have the context baked into the agent record.

We will see tags and customer identifiers used in the bulk actions section, because once they are assigned, they become the basis for targeting large remediation campaigns without having to click through every affected machine.

Operator's Checklist: Tag Governance

Before you deploy tags across your fleet, write down the keys you will use and what values each key can take. Tags without a governing schema become messy fast.

Enforce the schema through policy in your Automation scripts: do not let ad-hoc tagging proliferate without review.

Tag new endpoints at installation time using scripts or group policies in Active Directory, not manually after the fact.

Audit your tags monthly; remove endpoints that have been decommissioned, and verify that critical tags (like "Tier1" or "Production") are still accurate.

4.5 The Device Detail Page: Everything About One Machine

When you click into an endpoint from the list, you land on the device detail page. This page is your window into every piece of telemetry and metadata about that single machine. It is dense, and navigating it efficiently separates seasoned operators from novices.

The detail page typically opens to a summary tab showing the most critical information: the device name, UUID (the unique identifier SentinelOne assigns to the agent), last activity timestamp, online status, and agent version. Below that you see hardware details: CPU, RAM, installed operating system, and network adapters with both the external IP address you see from the console and the internal MAC and IP addresses.

One field that frequently comes up in operations is the console IP address. This is the public IP (or the VPN IP if you are using a VPN, which most people should be) that the agent uses to reach back to the SentinelOne servers. If you are trying to troubleshoot connectivity, this tells you what address the agent thinks it is using.

The UUID field is important because it is what you use to uniquely identify an endpoint in queries and APIs. If you ever need to write an automation script or run a query against a specific machine, you grab the UUID from this page.

Below the summary you typically see tabs for Agent Actions, Response, Policies, and more. The Agent Actions tab is where you can do administrative tasks: manage tags, change the customer identifier, move the endpoint to a different site, generate an uninstall passphrase, initiate full disk scans, upgrade the agent, or disable and re-enable the agent itself. The Response tab is where you conduct remediation when a threat has been detected, we will cover that in detail in Chapter 5. The Policies tab shows you which policies are in effect for this endpoint and allows you to troubleshoot policy inheritance.

When I work with my team on a troubled endpoint, we always spend a moment reading this page carefully. A machine that looks infected might not be if you understand what you are reading. A machine that looks offline might actually be fine if the last activity timestamp shows it checked in three minutes ago, the display might just be slow to refresh. The detail page is the source of truth.

4.6 Remote Shell, File Fetch, and Remote Actions

Buried in the detail page and the Agent Actions tab are several capabilities that represent the real power of EDR. We will not do a deep dive here, this is Part 4a, and Part 4b covers policies and detection, but you need to know they exist.

Remote Shell is the marquee feature. It opens an interactive session to the endpoint (as PowerShell on Windows, shell on Mac/Linux) where you can run commands directly on the machine. You authenticate with a temporary token that changes every few minutes, and once authenticated, you have a full command prompt. You can use remote shell to query running processes, manipulate the file system, disable a malicious service, or test whether an application is actually vulnerable. It looks like a reverse shell, and it feels like you are SSHing into the machine, except you are doing it through SentinelOne's encrypted tunnel to the agent, not directly to the network. This is the foundation of remediation for sophisticated incidents.

File Fetch lets you download a file directly from the endpoint to the console. If you suspect a machine was infected and you want to grab the malware sample for analysis, or you want to pull Windows event logs to understand what happened during an incident, File Fetch is how you do it.

Disconnect from Network is a critical response action. When you have a machine that you believe is actively spreading malware or exfiltrating data, you can isolate it from the corporate network, but not from the console. The agent will disconnect from everything except SentinelOne's servers, meaning you can still remote shell into it, grab files, run remediation scripts, all while it is quarantined from your network.

These three, Remote Shell, File Fetch, and Network Disconnect, are why you buy an EDR product instead of just running an antivirus. With these tools, you can forensically investigate what happened, grab the evidence, remediate the malware, and bring the machine back online, all without physically touching it. Understanding how to use them will be critical in Chapter 5.

4.7 Bulk Actions: Working at Scale

One endpoint at a time is impractical when you have thousands to manage. SentinelOne Sentinels allows you to select multiple endpoints and perform actions on all of them simultaneously.

The most common bulk action is agent upgrade. When a new version of the SentinelOne agent is released, you do not manually upgrade each machine. You select all machines running the old version (using the filter we discussed earlier), then execute a bulk upgrade action. You choose the target version, you might upgrade to the very latest, or you might upgrade to a stable version from a few weeks ago if you are being conservative. Within minutes, all selected endpoints begin pulling and installing the new agent.

Another frequent bulk action is group reassignment. If you have migrated customers from one managed account to another, or if you are restructuring your deployment, you might need to move a hundred endpoints from one group to another. The bulk action handles that in a single operation.

Tag assignment at scale is also possible. If you have onboarded a batch of endpoints for a new customer and want to tag them all with that customer's identifier, you select them all and tag them in one operation.

Full disk scans can also be triggered in bulk. If you have encountered a malware strain that might exist on multiple machines, you can initiate scans across your entire fleet to look for indicators of compromise.

The principle behind bulk actions is the same: filter to the right set of endpoints, verify that the set is correct (because getting this wrong can have consequences), then execute. The SentinelOne interface typically asks you to confirm before bulk operations execute, which is a safeguard you should always take seriously.

4.8 Status Interpretation: What "Online" Really Means

The endpoint list shows status as a simple categorical field, but status is deceptively subtle. Understanding the difference between online, offline, disconnected, and stale is fundamental to not chasing ghosts.

Online means the agent has checked in with the SentinelOne infrastructure within the last few minutes. Practically speaking, if the status shows online, you can remote shell into it, fetch files from it, and push actions to it. If I see an endpoint online at 2 a.m., I know someone is using that machine right now.

Offline means the agent has not checked in within the timeout window defined in your policy, usually twelve to twenty-four hours. An offline endpoint might be turned off. It might be disconnected from the network. It might be a laptop that someone took home and has not connected to WiFi. Or it might be a decommissioned machine that you have not removed from the list yet. You cannot assume offline is bad; you just need to investigate.

Disconnected is a status you create by hand. When you perform the "Disconnect from Network" action on an infected machine, it moves to disconnected status. The agent is still talking to SentinelOne, but it cannot reach anything on your network. This is the remediation state.

Stale is the most important distinction that many new operators miss. An endpoint that has never checked in, or has not checked in for weeks or months, is stale. This is different from offline. An offline machine might come back online. A stale machine is probably gone for good. You periodically need to audit your endpoint list and remove stale machines; otherwise, you end up maintaining records for thousands of decommissioned computers, and your dashboards and reports become noisy.

The rule I teach: online machines are active and you should monitor them closely. Offline machines might be dormant or sleeping; check in once a week to see if they have come back. Stale machines should be decommissioned within thirty days of their last check-in. Disconnected machines are in remediation; monitor them until they are clean, then reconnect them.

4.9 Field-Team Workflows: Getting Work Done

In the real world, the Sentinels section becomes the operational hub for field teams. Here are the workflows you will see most often.

The Onboarding Workflow: A new customer is signed up, and you need to install the SentinelOne agent on fifty machines. You generate the installation package from Sentinels (more on that in Chapter 5), distribute it via Group Policy or manual installation, and watch as the endpoints appear in your list. As they come online, you verify they are reporting healthy, assign them to the appropriate group, and tag them with the customer identifier. Once all fifty are online and tagged, you move to policy configuration.

The Remediation Workflow: You have received an alert that a machine has detected malware. You open the Sentinels list, find the affected machine (using the filter for its hostname or customer ID), click into the detail page, and review the threat. You might open Remote Shell to understand what is running on the system, use File Fetch to grab a sample for your lab, and then execute a kill command through the Response tab. Once you believe the machine is clean, you trigger a full disk scan to verify, then document what you did in your ticketing system.

The Bulk Upgrade Workflow: Every quarter, SentinelOne releases a new agent version. You evaluate whether your environment should update, and if so, you filter the Sentinels list to show all endpoints running the version you want to replace. You verify the count matches what you expect. You initiate the bulk upgrade action with a schedule that staggers the updates so you do not overwhelm your network. You monitor the dashboard to watch the agent version distribution shift over the next few hours.

The Customer Migration Workflow: A customer has left your MSSP and is moving to a competitor, or you are consolidating multiple customer accounts. You filter Sentinels to show all machines belonging to that customer (using their tag), select them all, and use the bulk site-move action to transfer their endpoints to the new account, or you execute the uninstall action to remove the agents entirely if they are leaving. You verify the migration in the Activity log.

The Capacity Planning Workflow: You are managing several thousand endpoints and need to understand which customers are consuming the most resources. You can group the Sentinels list by customer tag and look at endpoint counts. You can pivot to the Applications tab (which we cover in Chapter 7) to see what software is running. This data informs your conversations with customers about licensing and support.

These workflows all start with Sentinels, with the list, with filtering, with understanding what you are looking at. The operators who master Sentinels early move through these workflows without friction. The ones who do not end up clicking randomly through the console and accidentally pushing the wrong policy to the wrong group.

Chapter Summary

The Sentinels section is your endpoint management control center. The endpoint list surfaces the most critical information at a glance: device name, status, health, last activity, agent version, and threat status. Every column answers one of the core operational questions: What is this machine? Is it healthy? Is it active right now? What version of the agent is running?

Filtering is how you scale operations beyond manual browsing. Filter by online status, group, agent version, tags, and threat status. Use filters to build the scope for bulk actions. Tags and customer identifiers let you organize endpoints beyond the built-in Groups hierarchy; they are essential in MSSP and multi-tenant environments. The device detail page shows everything about one machine: UUID, hardware, agent health, and access to powerful remote actions like Remote Shell and File Fetch. Bulk actions, upgrades, group moves, tag assignments, and scans, are how you work at scale. Status interpretation matters: online machines are active, offline machines are dormant, disconnected machines are in remediation, and stale machines should be decommissioned. The real-world field-team workflows, onboarding, remediation, bulk upgrades, customer migrations, and capacity planning, all run through Sentinels. Master this section and you have the foundation for everything that follows.

Key Takeaways

- The endpoint list is your interface to fleet state. Read it for categorical information: status, health, last activity, and threat presence.
- Filters are your friends. Learn to filter by status, group, version, tag, and threat to build scopes for bulk operations without browsing.
- Tags and customer identifiers provide a second organizational dimension beyond Groups. Use them for tagging at scale.

- The device detail page is your source of truth for any single endpoint. Check the UUID, status, last activity timestamp, and policy inheritance before making changes.
- Remote Shell is the power move: it lets you execute commands directly on endpoints through an encrypted SentinelOne tunnel, which is foundational for incident response.
- Bulk operations save hours. Filter correctly, verify the scope, then execute upgrades, moves, or scans across hundreds of endpoints at once.
- Status is subtle. Online is active. Offline is dormant. Disconnected is remediation. Stale is decommissioned.

Hands-On Exercise

Before you continue to Chapter 4 Part B, do the following in your SentinelOne tenant.

- Open Sentinels and examine the endpoint list. Identify the status, health, and agent version of at least five endpoints. Take note of which are online and which are offline. Then filter the list to show only online endpoints. How does the count change?
- Click into one endpoint detail page. Work through the tabs: read the UUID, locate the console IP, and note the last activity timestamp. If the endpoint has an associated tag, record what it is.
- Use the filter to find all endpoints running an agent version older than your current standard. Select a few and perform a test agent upgrade to the latest version. Watch the version number update in the list within the next five minutes.
- If you have multiple groups in your Site, filter by group and count how many endpoints are in each. Consider whether that distribution aligns with your network segmentation strategy.

Review Questions

- 1. In the Sentinels endpoint list, you see an endpoint with Status = "Online" and Last Activity = "6 months ago." What does this discrepancy mean, and what action would you take?

- 2. You filter the endpoint list to show all endpoints in Group "Production" running agent version 7.5. Why would you create this filter?
- 3. True or False: Tags and customer identifiers serve the same purpose. Explain the difference.
- 4. What is a UUID, and why is it more reliable than a hostname for identifying an endpoint in APIs or queries?
- 5. When you issue a bulk agent upgrade command, what parameter prevents all endpoints from upgrading simultaneously, and why does this matter?

Answer Key: Review Questions

1. The endpoint is online (checking in within the last few minutes) but has been inactive for six months. It is probably powered on in a closet or storage and not being used. Plan to investigate, confirm it is not needed, and decommission it within 30 days.

2. To identify endpoints that need agent upgrades. You can then select all of them and push a bulk upgrade to version 7.6 or later.

3. False. Tags are key-value pairs (e.g., Environment=Production, Department=Finance); you can apply many tags per endpoint. Customer identifiers are single text fields. Tags are more flexible; customer IDs are simpler.

4. A UUID is the unique identifier SentinelOne assigns to an agent instance. It is more reliable than a hostname because hostnames can change, be duplicated across environments, or be unset on some devices. UUIDs are immutable and globally unique.

5. The concurrent-deployment limit parameter (e.g., "upgrade 50 endpoints at a time"). This prevents network saturation and distributes the load across your infrastructure.

Discussion Questions

- 1. A customer's IT director claims that 50 new laptops were deployed last week, but Ranger shows only 40 Secured endpoints for that customer. Sentinels shows the same 40. Where did the 10 laptops go, and how would you investigate?
- 2. You manage an MSSP with 30 customers spread across 30 Sites. You want to create a tag governance policy so that all endpoints are tagged consistently (e.g., Site name, customer tier, department). Describe your tagging schema and how you would enforce it.

- 3. Your team is considering automatic agent decommissioning after 21 days of no check-in. What are the risks of this policy, and how would you mitigate them?

Hands-On Lab Exercises

Lab 4.1: Work through the Endpoint List and Interpret Columns

Objective: Learn to read the endpoint list at a glance and extract operational insights.

Access to Sentinels with at least 10 endpoints visible

Steps:

- Open Sentinels. Review the columns displayed: Device Name, Group, Status, Health, Infected, Last Activity, Agent Version, and any custom columns.
- Identify three endpoints with Status = "Online." For each, note the Last Activity timestamp. Is it within the last 5 minutes? If not, what might that mean?
- Identify one endpoint with Status = "Offline." Click into it and check whether it is legitimately offline (maintenance window) or stale. Document your finding.
- Filter the list to show only endpoints running an agent version older than the current standard (e.g., older than 7.6). Count them. These are candidates for a bulk upgrade.
- Create a one-sentence summary for each finding: "Three online endpoints checked in within 5 minutes (active). One offline endpoint last seen [date] (candidate for decommissioning). [X] endpoints running outdated agent (need upgrade)."

Expected Outcome: Comfort reading the endpoint list and extracting meaning from each column.

Reflection: In your operational role, what would you check first when an endpoint goes offline unexpectedly?

Lab 4.2: Use Filters to Build a Bulk-Action Scope

Objective: Develop proficiency filtering the endpoint list to target specific remediation campaigns.

Access to Sentinels with diverse endpoints (multiple Groups, versions, tags if available)

Steps:

- Create Filter 1: "Group = 'Pilot', Status = 'Online', Agent Version <= 7.5." Count matching endpoints.
- Create Filter 2: "Group = 'Production', Threat Status = 'Infected'." Count matching endpoints. (These are candidates for isolation/remediation.)
- Create Filter 3: "Tag = 'CriticalServer', Status = 'Offline'." Count matching endpoints. (These warrant investigation.)
- For each filter, verify the count makes sense operationally. If Pilot group has 0 endpoints, either the filter is wrong or Pilot is empty.
- Document each filter's purpose and action: "Filter 1 targets [number] endpoints for agent upgrade because [reason]."

Expected Outcome: Confidence building filters that match your operational scenarios.

Reflection: Why is filtering before a bulk action safer than selecting all endpoints and hoping for the best?

Lab 4.3: Examine a Device Detail Page and Plan Remediation

Objective: Read a device detail page and extract information necessary for response or remediation.

Access to at least one endpoint in Sentinels (preferably one with detected threats or suspicious status)

Steps:

- Click into an endpoint. Review the Summary tab: note Device Name, UUID, Last Activity, Status, Online IP, and MAC address.
- Click the Policies tab. Verify which policy is applied. Is it the Group default, or is an override in place? Document what you find.
- Look for the Agent Actions tab (or equivalent). Scroll to see available actions: manage tags, move to group, upgrade agent, disconnect, remote shell, file fetch, scan.
- If the endpoint has detected threats, click the Response tab (if available). Note what mitigation options are presented.
- Create a one-sentence remediation plan: "If this endpoint were infected, I would [action 1], then [action 2], then [action 3]."

Expected Outcome: Ability to work through a device page and understand what actions are available.

Reflection: Before taking a remediation action, what information would you gather to inform your decision?

Lab 4.4: Execute a Bulk Agent Upgrade (Test)

Objective: Gain hands-on experience with bulk operations, including filtering, confirmation, and monitoring.

Access to Sentinels; permission to initiate agent upgrades; at least 3 endpoints eligible for upgrade

Steps:

- Filter endpoints to show Status = "Online" AND Agent Version = "[known old version]." Record the count.
- Select all matching endpoints. Verify the selection count is as expected.
- Initiate an agent upgrade to the next stable version (not necessarily the latest, check what your team standards recommend).
- Set concurrent-deployment limit to 2 or 3 (to avoid network saturation). Set a maintenance window if your infrastructure requires it.
- Review the confirmation dialog carefully. Verify scope, target version, and concurrent limit. Then confirm.
- Over the next 5-10 minutes, watch the endpoint list. Observe agent versions changing from old to new. Document the upgrade progress.
- Once complete, filter again to verify all selected endpoints are now on the new version.

Expected Outcome: Successfully upgraded multiple endpoints and gained confidence in bulk operations.

Reflection: What would you do if after upgrade, an endpoint became unresponsive or reported "agent unhealthy"?

What's Next

Chapter 4 Part B (the second half of the Sentinels workflow) dives into policy configuration, detection engine tuning, and how the policies you build at the Site level inherit and override at the Group level. We will explore what separates Detect-Only mode from Full Enforcement mode, how to configure the behavioral AI engines, and how to write policy exceptions without blinding your platform to real attacks.

Mastering SentinelOne

Chapter 5, Draft for Review

by Kendrick Washington, Technology Interpreters, Inc.

Chapter 5

Sentinels: Remediation and Lifecycle

Learning Objectives

- Distinguish between disconnect, isolate, and quarantine actions and understand when each is the right choice.
- Execute a full isolate-and-remediate workflow: respond to a detection, disconnect the endpoint, run remediation scripts, and reconnect.
- Understand the four core remediation actions, kill, quarantine, remediate, and rollback, and what each does on disk.
- Configure automatic decommissioning to keep your fleet inventory clean and reduce console noise.
- Design a re-enrollment and agent-upgrade strategy that keeps endpoints current without disrupting the network.
- Interpret what happens to telemetry and forensics when an endpoint goes offline, and how to preserve evidence.

Chapter Opener

Chapter 4 taught you how to organize, group, and manage your fleet at scale. This chapter is where you act on what you find. A detection fires. An endpoint is infected. A user has installed something that does not belong. What do you do now? SentinelOne gives you six major action categories: disconnect the endpoint from the network, isolate it while keeping the management connection open, kill malicious processes, quarantine suspicious files, remediate by rolling changes back to a snapshot, and finally decommission or uninstall the agent altogether. Each action is surgical, designed to solve a specific problem without collateral damage, but each has different implications for forensics, downtime, and evidence preservation.

This chapter walks you through every action from first detection to endpoint recovery, and introduces the lifecycle operations that keep your console clean and your endpoints current. You will learn which action to reach for first, how to chain them together for complex incidents, and what to do when remediation fails and you need to roll back. You will also learn why some companies never clean their console, and why that choice is quietly expensive.

5.1 The Four Core Remediation Actions

Before we talk about the actions you take on infected endpoints, you need to understand the four remediation primitives that SentinelOne uses to neutralize threats. These four actions, kill, quarantine, remediate, and rollback, work together and form the foundation of everything that follows.

Kill means to terminate a running process. When SentinelOne detects malicious activity in a process that is currently executing, the fastest way to stop it is to terminate the process immediately. This does not remove the process from disk; it only stops the currently running instance. If the malware has a persistence mechanism (a scheduled task, a registry auto-start entry, or a service), killing the process alone will not solve the problem permanently. But it does stop active damage in real time.

Quarantine means to isolate a file on disk by moving it to a protected vault that the agent maintains. When SentinelOne detects a malicious file during write or execution, it does not delete the file, deletion can be destructive if the detection is wrong, it quarantines it. The file is moved to an encrypted vault on disk where it cannot be accessed, executed, or modified. This preserves the file for forensics while preventing it from executing again. If you later decide the detection was a false positive, you can restore the file from quarantine back to its original location.

Remediate means to repair the endpoint by removing or disabling the changes malware made. Malware often modifies registry keys, creates scheduled tasks, installs services, or injects code into legitimate system files. Remediation actions reverse those changes. SentinelOne can kill a malicious process, then remove the registry entry that was auto-starting it, then delete the malware binary, all as a coordinated remediation action. The scope of remediation depends on what SentinelOne detected and how aggressive the policy is configured.

Rollback is the most powerful but also the most disruptive action. SentinelOne takes periodic snapshots of the endpoint, volume shadow copies on Windows, similar mechanisms on macOS and Linux, and stores them in a protected partition. When an endpoint is severely compromised and remediation is uncertain, you can roll the endpoint back to a pre-infection snapshot. Everything the malware did, registry modifications, file creation, process injection, scheduled tasks, is undone in a single operation. The endpoint restarts and comes up clean. This is expensive in terms of downtime and user disruption, but it is your nuclear option when you have high confidence that containment and incremental remediation will not work.

5.2 Disconnect vs. Isolate: The Key Distinction

Many practitioners use the terms "disconnect" and "isolate" interchangeably, but in SentinelOne they are different actions with different outcomes. Understanding this distinction is critical to responding effectively.

Disconnect means to physically or logically remove the endpoint from the network. When you disconnect an endpoint, it loses all network connectivity, it cannot reach other machines, cannot reach the Internet, cannot reach the management console. A disconnected endpoint becomes, from a security perspective, inert. It cannot spread malware, exfiltrate data, or participate in a worm. But a disconnected endpoint also cannot be remediated, because you have no way to send commands to it or execute scripts on it.

Isolate is a finer-grained action that SentinelOne implements at the agent level. When you isolate an endpoint, the agent blocks all outbound network connections except for the connection back to the SentinelOne management console. The endpoint cannot reach other machines, cannot reach the Internet, but the management console can still reach it. This is the magic: isolation stops the threat from spreading while leaving you a remediation channel.

The practical difference shows up immediately. Disconnect is useful in two scenarios: when the infection is so severe that you do not trust any remediation plan, or when the endpoint will be wiped and reimaged anyway. Isolate is your primary response action. Isolate the endpoint, then use remote shell to run diagnostics and remediation scripts. Once you have confirmed that the endpoint is clean, reconnect it and move on. If something goes wrong during remediation, rollback restores the endpoint to its pre-infection state.

One final subtlety: when you issue an isolate command in SentinelOne, you are telling the agent to enforce network isolation. The agent blocks egress at the OS level using Windows Firewall rules (Windows), network filters (macOS), or iptables rules (Linux). This happens at the endpoint itself. If an attacker has root or system-level access and can disable those rules, isolation can be bypassed. But against most commodity malware and standard lateral-movement techniques, isolation is extremely effective.

5.3 The Isolate Workflow End-to-End

Here is the sequence of actions you perform when you receive a critical detection on a production endpoint.

- Detection fires. A SentinelOne detection engine produces a threat alert. You see it in Incidents. The threat shows a process name, a file hash, a detection category (malware, suspicious, exploit, etc.), and the endpoint it was detected on. This is your entry point.
- Triage the threat. Open the threat details. Look at when it was detected, what user was logged in, what process triggered it, and what file is on disk. Ask: Is this a known legitimate application that is in a group without an exclusion? Is this a user who commonly downloads suspicious files? Is this a real threat or likely a false positive? If you are confident it is malicious, proceed to isolate. If you think it is a false positive, create an exclusion instead and do not proceed.
- Isolate the endpoint. Go to the Sentinels screen, find the endpoint, and click Response Actions. Select "Isolate this endpoint." The agent will immediately enforce network isolation. The endpoint will lose access to the Internet and other machines but will maintain the connection to SentinelOne. The user may see a network error ("No Internet") but the endpoint is fully responsive to remediation commands.
- Wait for the agent to confirm isolation. After you issue the isolate command, wait 30 seconds to 1 minute for the agent to acknowledge. You will see the endpoint status change to "Isolated" in the console. Do not proceed to the next step until the status has changed.
- Run diagnostics. Open Remote Shell. Execute commands to understand what the malware did. Common first steps: tasklist /v (Windows) or ps aux (macOS/Linux) to see running processes; Get-ScheduledTask (Windows) to check for new scheduled tasks; reg query HKLM\Software\Microsoft\Windows\CurrentVersion\Run (Windows) to check auto-start entries. Look for artifacts that match the threat details you saw in the alert.

- Execute remediation. Based on what you found, execute remediation commands. Kill the malicious process, delete the malware file, remove the persistence mechanism (scheduled task, registry entry, service). SentinelOne policy may have already killed or quarantined the malware, but use remote shell to confirm and clean up any remnants. If the malware is persistent and complex, consider a rollback instead of manual remediation.
- Validate the cleanup. Run the diagnostic commands again. Confirm that the process is gone, the persistence mechanism is removed, and no new suspicious files are present. Reboot the endpoint and run diagnostics once more after boot to confirm nothing re-executes.
- Reconnect the endpoint. Once you are confident the endpoint is clean, go back to Response Actions and select "Reconnect this endpoint." Network isolation will be lifted and the endpoint will regain normal network access. Monitor the endpoint closely for the next 24 hours for any re-infections.
- Close the incident. Mark the threat as resolved in Incidents. Document in your ticket system what was found, what was done, and the outcome. If the threat class was something you had not seen before, create an exclusion or policy update to prevent similar false positives in the future.

5.4 Decommissioning Endpoints: Keeping the Console Clean

One of the operational headaches that every MSSP and large enterprise faces is console bloat. Endpoints are deployed. Users leave the company or are issued new machines. Hardware fails. Devices get shelved in closets. And without active lifecycle management, those endpoints sit in your SentinelOne console forever, consuming licenses and cluttering your dashboards.

SentinelOne addresses this with automatic decommissioning. When you enable the decommissioning policy, any endpoint that has not checked in for 21 days is automatically hidden from the main Sentinels view. It does not get deleted; it is not uninstalled from the machine. It is simply marked as decommissioned and moved out of the active inventory.

Why 21 days? Because 21 days is long enough to capture endpoints that are legitimately offline for a few weeks, machines being repaired, sent in for imaging, or stored in warehouses, but short enough to prevent years of stale entries building up. If a decommissioned endpoint powers back on, it will immediately check back in to the console and will automatically re-commission itself.

The operational pattern is this: Enable automatic decommissioning at the Site level. Let SentinelOne hide offline machines. Once per quarter, review the decommissioned inventory to identify machines that are truly dead (drives failed, hardware replaced, devices sold) versus machines that are just in storage. For truly dead machines, you can contact the customer and discuss uninstalling the agent. For machines in storage, leave them; when they are reimaged and re-used, they will re-commission.

Without automatic decommissioning, you end up with console inventory that grows unbounded. We have seen MSSP consoles with 50,000 stale endpoints mixed into 10,000 active ones. The result: dashboards are useless, searches are slow, and analysts cannot tell what they are actually securing. Decommissioning solves this with minimal effort.

Operator's Insight: Decommissioning Is Not Uninstall

Many teams confuse decommissioning with uninstallation. Decommissioning hides the endpoint from the console view. It does NOT uninstall the agent from the machine.

If you want to actually remove the agent, you must manually request uninstall (which the user can approve or deny) or use remote shell to forcibly remove it.

Decommissioning is automatic housekeeping. Uninstall is a customer-initiated action. Know the difference.

5.5 Agent Uninstall, Passphrase, and Re-Enrollment

Uninstalling a SentinelOne agent is straightforward in theory but has enough operational nuance that you need to understand it fully.

When you want to remove the agent from an endpoint, you have three options. First: request uninstall via the console. You initiate an uninstall request, and if the endpoint is online, a notification appears on the user's desktop asking for approval. The user approves, the agent uninstalls, and the endpoint drops out of inventory. This is the safest option because it gives the user visibility and control. It also takes the most time because it depends on user action.

Second: force uninstall via remote shell. If you have remote shell access and administrator rights, you can execute an uninstall command directly without user involvement. On Windows, this is typically msiexec /x

{GUID} /quiet. The agent will uninstall and the endpoint will drop from inventory immediately. Use this only when time is critical or the user cannot be reached.

Third: manual agent removal. If the agent is broken and cannot be uninstalled via console or remote shell, you can manually delete the agent directory and registry entries. This is messy and should be a last resort, but it works when everything else fails.

Now, passphrases. When you install a SentinelOne agent, the installer generates a random passphrase that is stored in the agent configuration. If you later want to uninstall the agent, the agent can demand that you provide this passphrase before proceeding. This is a tamper-protection measure: it prevents malware from quietly uninstalling your security software.

As an operator, you can see the passphrase in the console under the endpoint details. If you initiate an uninstall, you can provide the passphrase and the uninstall proceeds silently. If you do not provide it, the agent will refuse to uninstall. If you have lost the passphrase and the endpoint is inert, you will have to do a manual agent removal or reimage the machine.

Re-enrollment means to install the agent on an endpoint again after it has been uninstalled. When you uninstall an agent, the endpoint drops from inventory. When you run the installer again on that same machine, the agent will check in as a new endpoint (possibly with a new UUID) depending on how the installation was parameterized. If you used a site key in the installer, the agent will register to the correct Site. If you used a group ID, it will register to that specific Group. Plan your re-enrollment strategy in advance: decide whether new installs go to a pilot group first or straight to production.

5.6 Agent Upgrade and Maintenance Windows

SentinelOne agents do not auto-upgrade. By default, upgrades require explicit action from you. This is intentional: upgrading thousands of endpoints simultaneously can disrupt network bandwidth and endpoint performance. You need control.

The agent upgrade workflow has three parts: version selection, concurrent-deployment limits, and maintenance windows.

Version selection: SentinelOne releases new agent versions on a regular schedule. When a new version is available, you can view it in the Sentinels console and decide whether to upgrade. A version released three days ago might not be tested in your environment yet. You can choose to wait a few weeks before upgrading, or you can run a phased pilot: upgrade a test group first, observe for any issues, then roll to production. The console allows you to select which version to deploy, so you are not forced to the absolute latest.

Concurrent-deployment limits: When you issue an upgrade command, you can specify how many endpoints should upgrade simultaneously. The default might be "unlimited," which means all endpoints upgrade at once. In a large deployment, this can overwhelm the network. Instead, set a limit like 25 or 100 concurrent upgrades. SentinelOne will queue the rest and upgrade them in batches. This keeps network bandwidth smooth and prevents a traffic spike that could alert users to unusual activity.

Maintenance windows: You can configure a maintenance window policy that restricts agent upgrades to a specific time window. For example, "upgrades only between 2 AM and 6 AM on weekends." When you issue an upgrade command, the agent will not actually upgrade until it is within the maintenance window. This prevents upgrades during business hours and gives users a predictable time when their endpoint might restart.

The typical pattern: Push an upgrade to all endpoints with a concurrent limit of 50 and a maintenance window of 2 AM to 5 AM on Saturday. The console will queue the upgrade and deploy it in batches throughout the night. By Monday morning, 95% of the fleet is updated. The remaining 5% that were offline during the window will upgrade the next time they are online during the window.

5.7 Telemetry and Forensics When an Endpoint Goes Offline

One of the most common questions after an incident is: "What happened on that endpoint during the two hours it was isolated?" The answer depends on whether the endpoint was offline or just network-isolated.

When you isolate an endpoint (agent-enforced isolation), all SentinelOne telemetry continues to flow to the management console. The agent is still running, deep visibility is still collecting process activity, and you can still run remote shell commands. If you need to investigate what happened during the isolation, you have a complete telemetry record because isolation does not stop the agent, it only stops the endpoint from reaching the network.

When an endpoint is truly offline, powered down, disconnected from power, or physically removed from the network, the agent stops reporting. Any activity that happened while the endpoint was offline is lost unless the agent logs it locally. For this reason, SentinelOne agents write activity logs to local disk. When the endpoint comes back online, those local logs are uploaded to the console and become part of the forensic record. By default, local logging is enabled, but it consumes disk space. You can disable it in the policy if disk space is critical, but you accept the loss of forensic data from offline periods.

Volume shadow copies (Windows snapshots) are also important for forensics. If you roll back an endpoint to a pre-infection snapshot, you are replacing the entire disk state at that moment in time. Any changes the malware made between the last snapshot and the rollback are lost. For this reason, SentinelOne takes multiple snapshots throughout the day, not just one. You can choose to roll back to a specific snapshot (say, from 2 hours ago) rather than the most recent one, if you want to preserve evidence from a particular time window.

If an endpoint becomes inert and you cannot recover it through isolation and remediation, you have two options: rollback (if you trust the snapshots and are willing to lose the last few hours of data) or offline forensics (power off the endpoint, remove the drive, and image it to a forensic workstation for detailed analysis). The local SentinelOne logs will still be on disk and can be examined in detail.

5.8 Case Studies: When to Use Which Action

Case 1: Ransomware on a File Server. A SentinelOne detection flags a suspicious process that is rapidly creating encrypted files in SMB shares. This is classic ransomware behavior. Your response: Isolate immediately. Do not delay. The isolation will prevent the endpoint from encrypting files on other machines. While isolated, use remote shell to confirm the process is running, kill the process, and check for persistence. If you find persistence, use remote shell to remove it. Quarantine the malware binary if it is still present. Once confident the process is stopped and will not restart, reconnect. If ransomware has already encrypted files, you will need to restore them from backup after the endpoint is clean. Isolation buys you time to stop the encryption without losing the evidence.

Case 2: Potentially Unwanted Application on a User Laptop. A detection fires on a PUA (potentially unwanted application),maybe a bundled toolbar or adware that came with something the user legitimately downloaded. Your response: Do not isolate. The user may be actively working. Instead, create an exclusion for the application hash. If it continues to trigger, collect the hash, move the endpoint to a test group with stricter policies, and observe. If the PUA is confirmed malicious and the user has unintentionally installed it, use remote shell to remove it. If it is legitimate software that looks suspicious, an exclusion is the right call.

Case 3: Server That Was Just Imaged and Came Online as a Duplicate UUID. You detect that two endpoints have the same UUID, usually because a server was cloned. Your response: Do not isolate. The UUID conflict is a registration issue, not a security issue. Go to the endpoint details for one of the clones and click "Change UUID." Generate a new random UUID for that endpoint. The two endpoints will now register separately and you will be able to manage their policies independently.

Case 4: Critical Production System with Uncertain Malware. A detection fires on a production system that you depend on. You have confirmed it is malware, but you are not certain whether a rollback will lose critical data. Your response: Isolate and escalate. Use remote shell to collect forensic data (process dumps, registry exports, file metadata). Document exactly what was detected and what you found. Get buy-in from the system owner that rolling back is acceptable. If they approve, roll back. If they do not, perform incremental remediation and monitor very carefully. This is where you need escalation and stakeholder consensus.

Case 5: Endpoint That Has Not Checked in for 60 Days. An endpoint has been offline for two months. It is probably a user who left the company, or a machine that was decommissioned. Your response: If automatic decommissioning is enabled, the endpoint was already hidden 21 days ago. If it is still in your active inventory, review the endpoint owner. If the user has left, contact the IT team and request the endpoint be uninstalled or wiped. If it is a test machine or spare hardware, ask whether it should be re-commissioned or remain in storage. Document the decision.

Case 6: Macro-Based Malware in an Office Document That You Cannot Remediate. A user received a malicious Word document. SentinelOne detected the macro when it tried to execute. The document is quarantined, but the user insists it is legitimate. Your response: Do not restore the file from quarantine without verification. Ask the user for the source and context. If they cannot verify it, delete the quarantined file. If they can verify it is from a trusted source, coordinate with that source to provide a version without the malicious macro, or confirm with them that the macro should not be there and request a clean version.

Chapter Summary

Remediation in SentinelOne is built on four primitives: kill (stop a running process), quarantine (vault a suspicious file), remediate (reverse malware changes), and rollback (restore to a pre-infection snapshot). Each action solves a different problem and can be chained together for complex incidents.

Isolate and disconnect are different actions with different outcomes. Isolate tells the agent to block all network traffic except to the management console; you retain a remediation channel. Disconnect breaks all connectivity; the endpoint becomes inert. Use isolate for active incidents where you need to remediate while contained. Use disconnect only when isolation is insufficient or the endpoint will be wiped.

The isolate-remediate-reconnect workflow is the bread and butter of incident response. Isolate, run diagnostics and remediation via remote shell, validate the cleanup, then reconnect. Monitor the endpoint closely afterward for re-infection.

Decommissioning keeps your console clean. Enable automatic decommissioning at the Site level to hide offline endpoints after 21 days. Decommissioned endpoints do not consume active licenses and do not clutter your dashboards. If they come back online, they re-commission automatically.

Agent upgrades are not automatic. Use version selection to stage upgrades cautiously, concurrent-deployment limits to prevent network spikes, and maintenance windows to schedule upgrades during off-hours. Uninstall is manual and can require a passphrase; re-enrollment must go through the installer again with the correct Site Key or Group ID.

Telemetry during an offline period is only as good as your local logging. When an endpoint is truly offline, SentinelOne cannot send data to the console. Local logs preserve the forensic record. When an endpoint is isolated, telemetry flows normally because the agent is still connected to the management console.

Isolation, remediation, and rollback all have different implications for evidence and downtime. Choose the lightest-touch action that solves the problem. Reserve rollback for severe infections where incremental remediation is likely to fail or take too long.

Key Takeaways

- Kill, quarantine, remediate, and rollback are the four core remediation primitives. They work together and can be chained.
- Isolate is your primary containment action when you need to remediate. Disconnect is your last-resort action when isolation is not enough.
- The isolate-remediate-reconnect workflow is the standard incident-response cadence: isolate, diagnose with remote shell, execute remediation, validate cleanup, reconnect.
- Automatic decommissioning hides offline endpoints after 21 days, keeping your console clean and your license count accurate. It does NOT uninstall the agent.
- Agent upgrades are not automatic and should be deployed in batches with maintenance windows to avoid network spikes.
- When an endpoint is isolated, telemetry continues to flow. When truly offline, local logs preserve the forensic record. Understand the difference.
- Rollback is powerful but disruptive. Use it when incremental remediation is unlikely to work, and only after escalating to stakeholders.

Hands-On Exercise

If you have access to a SentinelOne console with a test environment, perform the following exercises.

- Create a test endpoint group (do not use production) and generate a fake threat detection if possible (some consoles have a synthetic threat tool). Practice the isolate-remediate-reconnect workflow from start to finish without actually executing remediation on a real system.
- In your Site settings, enable automatic decommissioning if it is not already enabled. Review your current endpoint inventory and count how many are inactive or have not checked in recently. Document the number.

- Locate the Agent Upgrade policy for one of your groups. Review the concurrent-deployment limit and maintenance window settings. If you do not have limits in place, consider configuring them (in a test group first).
- Go to Activity and search for any decommission events from the past 30 days. Understand what triggered them and whether they were expected.
- If you have a quarantine that contains a file, review its properties, check the detection reason, and decide whether to delete it or restore it. Document your decision logic.

Review Questions

- 1. Explain the operational difference between "Kill," "Quarantine," and "Remediate" as remediation actions.
- 2. True or False: "Disconnect from Network" and "Isolate" are the same thing. Explain the difference.
- 3. You suspect an endpoint is infected. You isolate it, connect via Remote Shell, and confirm malware is present. What is your next action, and why?
- 4. After 21 days without a check-in, an endpoint is automatically decommissioned. Does this uninstall the agent? Explain what decommissioning does.
- 5. When you push an agent upgrade with a maintenance window of "2 AM to 5 AM on Saturdays," when will an endpoint that was offline during that window actually upgrade?

Answer Key: Review Questions

1. Kill terminates a running process (reversible; file remains on disk). Quarantine moves a malicious file to a vault (file preserved for forensics; cannot run). Remediate deletes malicious files and reverses system changes (more complete; less reversible).

2. False. Disconnect is physical/network removal (no connection to anything). Isolate is agent-enforced network blocking (agent still connected to SentinelOne for remediation commands).

3. Use Remote Shell to run diagnostics and remediation commands. Kill the malware, remove persistence (scheduled tasks, registry entries), delete the payload. Then run a full disk scan to verify. Do not reconnect until confident.

4. No. Decommissioning hides the endpoint from the console view (it no longer clutters the list). The agent remains on the machine. To actually uninstall, you must explicitly request uninstall.

5. The endpoint will upgrade the next time it is online during a maintenance window. If it remains offline for weeks, the upgrade will not happen until it comes back online within the window.

Discussion Questions

- 1. An incident response reveals that five endpoints were infected with ransomware. Three can be cleaned and brought back online within hours. Two have been too corrupted to remediate safely. Describe your end-to-end response workflow for each group.
- 2. Describe the challenges of managing agent upgrades across an MSSP with 500+ customers. How would you design an upgrade strategy that balances risk, testing, and deployment speed?
- 3. A customer's SOC wants to enable automatic remediation (kill, quarantine, remediate) globally across all endpoints. What are the risks, and what safeguards would you recommend before enabling auto-remediation?

Hands-On Lab Exercises

Lab 5.1: Understand the Four Remediation Actions

Objective: Read policy settings and understand what each remediation verb does.

Access to Sentinels policies; at least one policy visible

Steps:

- Work through to Sentinels. Open a policy (any group's policy).

- In the policy settings, find the Threat Response or Remediation section. You should see toggles or settings for: Kill, Quarantine, Remediate, Rollback.
- For each, note whether it is enabled or disabled. Read any description or tooltip.
- If you have access to Incidents, look at any past threat. Check which remediation action was taken. Correlate it to the policy setting.
- Document: "In the [Policy Name] policy, Kill/Quarantine/Remediate/Rollback are [enabled/disabled]. When a threat fires on an endpoint in this policy, the expected behavior is [action]."

Expected Outcome: Understanding of how policy settings determine what actions SentinelOne takes automatically.

Reflection: Under what circumstances would you disable Quarantine but leave Kill enabled?

Lab 5.2: Trace an Isolate-and-Remediate Workflow (Simulated)

Objective: Map out a complete incident response using isolation and remote actions.

Understanding of Isolate, Remote Shell, and remediation concepts; access to documentation or a simulation

Steps:

- Write down the steps you would take if an endpoint detected a suspicious process:
- - Step 1: Verify threat details in Incidents.
- - Step 2: Move to isolated state.
- - Step 3: Gather diagnostics via Remote Shell.
- - Step 4: Execute remediation commands.
- - Step 5: Validate cleanup.
- - Step 6: Reconnect and monitor.
- For each step, document: what command/action you would use, what outcome you expect, and how you would confirm success.
- Identify potential failure points: What if Remote Shell times out? What if remediation leaves remnants? What if reconnecting triggers re-infection?

Expected Outcome: A documented isolation and remediation workflow for your environment.

Reflection: At which step would you escalate to a senior analyst or customer for approval?

Lab 5.3: Plan an Agent Upgrade with Maintenance Windows

Objective: Design an upgrade strategy that respects maintenance windows and minimizes disruption.

Understanding of maintenance windows and concurrent-deployment limits

Steps:

- Assume your customer has 200 endpoints spread across three locations: East (100), West (75), Central (25).
- You want to upgrade all endpoints from agent version 7.5 to 7.7.
- Plan your upgrade: Which location would you upgrade first? Why? What concurrent limit would you use? What maintenance window?
- Document: "Phase 1: Upgrade West (75 endpoints, 25 concurrent, Saturday 2-5 AM) because [reason]. Phase 2: Upgrade East... Phase 3: Upgrade Central..."
- For each phase, identify a rollback plan: if agents become unhealthy or slow, what version would you roll back to?

Expected Outcome: A phased upgrade plan that balances risk and throughput.

Reflection: If Phase 1 encounters "agent unhealthy" on 10 endpoints, how would you respond before proceeding to Phase 2?

What's Next

Chapter 6 moves from operational response to investigative threat hunting. You have isolated the endpoint, killed the malware, and confirmed it is clean. Now you want to understand how the malware got there in the first place. Deep Visibility is where you run queries against your endpoint telemetry to follow attack chains backward: which process spawned the malware? Which URL did the user visit that delivered it? What network reconnaissance did the attacker perform? Chapter 6 walks you through building and executing Deep Visibility queries to answer these questions.

Mastering SentinelOne

Sample Expanded Chapter 6, Draft for Review
by Kendrick Washington, Technology Interpreters, Inc.

Chapter 6

Incidents: Triage, Investigation, and Response

Learning Objectives

- Open an incident in the SentinelOne Incidents queue and distinguish threats from alerts.
- Read the Storyline view to understand the sequence of process execution and file activity that triggered a detection.
- Interpret the Thread Details panel, including threat indicators, MITRE ATT&CK classifications, and publisher signatures.
- Use manual mitigation actions, kill, quarantine, remediate, and rollback, to contain threats in real time.
- Mark incidents with the correct analysis verdict (true positive, false positive, suspicious, or undefined) and status workflow (New, In-Progress, Resolved, Unresolved).
- Correlate threats across the fleet using threat IDs, storyline IDs, and the filtering surface to identify fleet-wide campaigns.

Chapter Opener

It is 8 a.m. on Monday morning. You open the SentinelOne console and work through to the Incidents tab. Your inbox is full. Three customers have threats. One endpoint has four detections in the same attack chain. Another has a suspicious process that may be a false positive. A third has a ransomware detection you need to roll back immediately. You have no notes in the system yet. You do not know the priority order. Your job, as the SOC analyst, is to triage this queue: open the right incidents, read the telemetry, make a judgment call on each one, take the action that fits, and close the ticket with enough documentation that when the next analyst or the auditor asks what happened, you have the answer ready.

This chapter is about that workflow. It walks you through every tool in the SentinelOne Incidents surface: how to work through the threat queue, read the Storyline view, correlate events across time, understand what each mitigation action actually does, mark incidents with the right status and verdict, and close with confidence. By the end of this chapter you will know how to move from "alert fired" to "incident resolved" with the precision that real operations demand.

6.1 The Incidents Queue and Filtering

When you open the Incidents tab, you are looking at a table of threats and alerts. Each row is either a threat detected by SentinelOne's AI engines or an alert you have configured through a query rule. At the top of the queue you will see summary counts: the total number of New incidents, how many are In-Progress, how many are Resolved but unreviewed, and critical metrics like the number of unique endpoints affected.

The queue is not chronological by default; it is organized by threat classification and recency within that classification. You will see malware at the top, followed by ransomware, suspicious behavior, potentially unwanted applications, and other categories. This ordering is by design: the most dangerous categories rise to the top so your eye goes where the risk is greatest.

To the left of each threat is a shield icon with a number. That number tells you how many detections are in the same attack chain, the same Storyline. If a threat shows a 4, that means four related events fired in sequence. If you click one and move through it with the arrow navigation at the top, you will work through through all four. This is critical: many analysts make the mistake of clicking the next arrow expecting to go to the next detection in a different chain, when in fact they are cycling through all four detections in the current chain. Pay attention to the counter,"1 of 4",to know where you are.

The filtering surface at the top of the queue is your second-most-important tool. By default you see all threats across all Sites and Groups, which can be overwhelming. Click View More Filters to expose the full filtering vocabulary. Here you can narrow by threat status (Mitigated, Not Mitigated, Benign), analysis verdict (True Positive, False Positive, Suspicious, Undefined), incident status (New, In-Progress, Resolved, Unresolved), endpoint state (Online, Offline), reboot requirement, OS version, detection engine, classification, and several others. The professional analyst uses these filters as a first-pass triage tool. Filter to Online endpoints only, there is no point trying to remediate a machine that is not connected. Filter to Not Mitigated, you want to see what is still active. Then sort by classification and work the queue systematically.

6.2 The Storyline View

When you open a threat, the first thing you will see is the Storyline. This is SentinelOne's visual representation of the process tree and file activity that led to the detection. It is a timeline drawn left to right, with process launches as boxes and file operations as labels, all connected by arrows showing causality.

Read the Storyline from left to right. The leftmost box is the originating process, the entry point. As you move right, you see what that process launched, what files it created or modified, and what child processes spawned from there. At the end of the chain, you see the red highlight indicating where the detection fired. This visualization is worth its weight in gold when you are trying to understand whether something is actually malicious or a false positive.

The Storyline is interactive. Hover over any element to see a timestamp showing when that event occurred relative to the attack chain's start. This helps you answer the question: "Did all of this happen in two seconds (which might be a legitimate installer), or did it happen over fifteen minutes (which might be reconnaissance)?" You can also zoom in and out to focus on different parts of the chain. In the top right, you can export the Storyline as a PNG or SVG for inclusion in your report or your incident ticket.

Below the Storyline is an Advanced view option. Click it to see the same information in tabular form: process ID, event type, timestamp, and details. The table form is searchable and is sometimes easier to work with when the Storyline gets large or complex. The process ID is especially important if you are doing forensic follow-up or if you need to correlate this event with logs from another system.

One more critical element: the Timeline tab beneath the Storyline view. This is not the process tree; this is the operational timeline. It shows actions you or other analysts have taken on this incident, moving it to a Site, initiating a scan, applying mitigations, so that when you come back to the incident later, you can see the history of what happened and by whom. The timeline is searchable and is your primary forensic record.

6.3 Thread Details and Threat Indicators

To the right of the Storyline, you will see the Thread Details panel. This is where SentinelOne packages everything it knows about the detected file: its hash, its file size, whether it is signed, what the publisher signature says, the detection engines that flagged it, and a summary of threat indicators.

The first thing to look for is the Signed field. If a binary is signed with a legitimate publisher certificate, you will see names like "Epic Games" or "Fortnight Launcher" or "Microsoft Corporation",that is a strong signal of legitimacy. Signatures are difficult to forge. If an executable is unsigned, that is not proof of malware, but it is a yellow flag. If a signed executable is labeled as something but the signature says something different, that is a red flag. A file claiming to be Windows Update but signed by someone else is immediately suspicious.

Below the signature is the classification: Malware, Ransomware, Potentially Unwanted Application, Suspicious, or other categories. This is SentinelOne's assessment of the threat's severity. Malware and Ransomware are high-confidence detections. PUA is lower confidence but still worth acting on in a corporate environment where users should not be installing gaming software or cryptocurrency miners. Suspicious is the catch-all for things that look malicious but have not been definitively classified.

The engines section shows you which detection engines flagged this file. You might see Behavioral AI, Static AI, Cloud Reputation, or several others. Behavioral AI means the file did something malicious, injected into a process, created a persistence mechanism, modified system files. Static AI means the file's code or structure matched a known malware signature. Cloud Reputation means the file has been seen in the wild and flagged by SentinelOne's global sensor network as malicious. If multiple engines agree, your confidence in the detection goes up.

Lower in the Thread Details panel, you will see Threat Indicators. These are mapped to the MITRE ATT&CK framework, which is a comprehensive catalog of adversary tactics and techniques. You might see indicators like "Privilege Escalation," "Lateral Movement," "Defense Evasion," or others. These are not proof of malice, many legitimate tools exhibit these behaviors, but they tell you what the file was trying to do. Understanding MITRE ATT&CK mapping is essential for translating SentinelOne detections into actionable intelligence.

Pay attention to the Threat ID and Storyline ID at the top of the Details panel. These are unique identifiers you can use to search across the console to see if this same threat or pattern appears elsewhere in your environment. If you find the same Threat ID on ten endpoints, you have a fleet-wide campaign. If you find the same Storyline pattern on five endpoints even with different Threat IDs, you have a coordinated attack.

6.4 Manual Mitigation Actions

When you have read the Storyline and the Thread Details and you are confident you need to act, the Actions tab is where you make it happen. SentinelOne offers four primary mitigation verbs, and understanding what each one does is non-negotiable.

Kill stops the process immediately. If Explorer.exe launched a malicious DLL that is currently running, you can kill that DLL's process. This is fast and reversible. However, kill does not remove the file from disk. If the malicious process restarts, the threat returns. Use kill as an immediate containment action while you investigate further.

Quarantine moves the malicious file to a secure location on the endpoint or makes it non-executable. The file is still there, you can restore it later if it was a false positive, but it cannot run. This is the standard mitigation for most detections. Quarantine is safer than delete because you have recovery options, but it is permanent enough that the threat cannot restart unless the file is explicitly restored.

Remediate is stronger. It deletes all files and system changes that the malware created. This is appropriate for malware that has made multiple modifications, registry keys, scheduled tasks, additional files. Remediate cleans up the attack completely, not just the initial payload. Use this when you are certain of a true positive and want the system returned to a clean state.

Rollback is the most powerful and most dangerous mitigation. It uses Windows Volume Shadow Copy to revert the endpoint to a previous point-in-time snapshot captured before the malware executed. If the malware executed at 3 p.m. and you roll back to 2 p.m., all of its file and registry changes vanish. However, rollback also reverts any legitimate work the user did between 2 p.m. and 3 p.m., so it is a decision that needs coordination with the endpoint owner. Rollback often requires a reboot to complete.

These actions can be applied preemptively, SentinelOne does them automatically as part of your policy, or manually, after you have opened the incident and inspected it. When you apply an action manually, you have the opportunity to add notes before clicking the action button. Always add notes. Document what you saw, why you took this action, and what you expect the outcome to be. Your notes are your forensic record and your protection if anyone questions the decision later.

6.5 Analysis Verdict and Incident Status

Two parallel workflows run on every incident: the analysis verdict and the incident status.

The analysis verdict is your judgment of whether the detection is actually malicious. You have four options. True Positive means you are confident this is a real threat and the detection is correct. False Positive means this is legitimate software and SentinelOne was wrong to flag it. Suspicious means you are not sure, there is something odd about it, but it does not cleanly fit into either category. Undefined means you have not yet made a judgment.

Set the verdict after you have read the Storyline and the Details, after you have taken (or decided not to take) mitigation action, and after you have added your notes. The verdict is what the next analyst reads to understand your thinking. Always set it to something other than Undefined. Analysts who open incidents and leave them Undefined are creating work for everyone downstream.

The incident status is separate and describes the progress of your investigation. An incident is New when you first open it. You mark it In-Progress when you start working on it, this is critical in a team environment because it tells other analysts that this is not available for them to pick up. Once you have taken your action and documented your reasoning, you mark it Resolved. An incident marked Unresolved stays in the queue for follow-up; this is typically used when you have run out of time or need more information before you can close it.

The mistake many analysts make is leaving incidents in New status while actively investigating them, then being surprised when a teammate opens the same ticket and starts duplicate work. Make it a habit: the moment you click into an incident, mark it In-Progress. The moment you finish, mark it Resolved. This simple discipline scales your team's throughput and eliminates duplicate investigation.

6.6 Notes and Collaboration

Do not underestimate the Notes field. This is where you document what you found, what you did, and why you did it. The notes are indexed and searchable, and they become part of the permanent record of the incident. They are also what saves your job if someone later claims you mishandled something.

Professional incident notes follow a simple pattern. First, state what you observed in the Storyline or the Thread Details. "Process explorer.exe launched rundll32.exe with command-line argument -silent." Second, state what you did. "Applied Quarantine action to the detected file." Third, state your reasoning. "The file is unsigned, flagged by multiple detection engines, and has an inline command-line argument suggesting evasion. Confidence: high."

If you are working in a multi-analyst environment, the notes become a conversation. One analyst investigates, adds notes, and marks the incident In-Progress. A second analyst comes in, reads the notes, and either agrees and marks Resolved, or disagrees and adds their own notes. This asynchronous collaboration is how you avoid rework and how you build institutional knowledge.

The notes also capture timestamps. Even though the event happened at 2 a.m., if you are entering the notes at 9 a.m., include that temporal information. The next person reading will want to know when you opened the incident and when you took action. Be explicit: "Opened incident at 2026-04-24 09:15 UTC. Threat timestamp 2026-04-24 02:00 UTC. Applied Quarantine and marked Resolved."

6.7 Threat Hunting and Sweep Across the Fleet

Once you have closed a single incident with confidence, the natural question is: "Is this threat anywhere else?" The answer lives in the Threat ID and Storyline ID fields at the top of the Thread Details panel.

Copy the Threat ID. Open the Incidents queue. Use the search bar at the top to search for that Threat ID. SentinelOne will return every endpoint in your entire fleet that has seen this same threat. If you get ten results, you have a fleet-wide detection event that requires different communication and remediation strategy than a single-endpoint incident.

Alternatively, copy the Storyline ID. This identifier represents the exact attack pattern, not just the file. A Storyline search will show you endpoints that have experienced the same sequence of process launches and file operations, even if the file hash is different (which might happen if the attacker modified the payload slightly). Storyline matching is a powerful way to detect coordinated campaigns.

Once you have identified the fleet-wide scope, apply bulk remediation. SentinelOne allows you to select multiple endpoints and apply the same mitigation action to all of them at once. This is where the platform's power becomes apparent: instead of manually clicking on fifty endpoints to kill a process, you can queue the action once and have it execute across the fleet. However, always filter first. Never apply bulk actions without scoping down to the exact set of affected endpoints. A careless bulk remediation can take down critical systems.

Keep a running list of threat and storyline IDs that have fired in your environment. These become the basis for your block list and your threat intelligence. When you see a repeat, you escalate it immediately because it means either the attacker is coming back or you have another compromised endpoint.

6.8 VirusTotal Integration and External Intelligence

Every threat you open has a VirusTotal link embedded in the Details panel. VirusTotal is a public repository where you can upload a file hash and see how many commercial antivirus and behavioral analysis vendors have flagged it.

Before you dismiss a detection or add it to your false positive list, check VirusTotal. If SentinelOne flags something as suspicious but VirusTotal shows zero detections, you have a strong signal it is a false positive. If SentinelOne flags it and VirusTotal shows fifteen vendors agreeing it is malicious, your confidence in the SentinelOne verdict goes up dramatically.

The Details tab in VirusTotal shows vendor detection names and any behavioral analysis available. The Community tab shows comments from other analysts who have seen the file. Read the comments, sometimes the context provided by experienced analysts saves you from a poor decision.

However, do not blindly trust VirusTotal or any external source. VirusTotal has false positives too. A single vendor flagging something does not mean it is malicious, and a file with high VirusTotal detections might still be legitimate in your specific environment. Use VirusTotal as a data point, not as truth.

6.9 Closing Procedures and Handoff

When you are ready to close an incident, verify that you have done the following. First, you have opened the incident and read the Storyline and Thread Details. Second, you have set the analysis verdict to one of True Positive, False Positive, or Suspicious. Third, you have taken the appropriate mitigation action or explicitly decided not to take one. Fourth, you have added notes explaining your reasoning. Fifth, you have searched for the same Threat ID or Storyline ID across the fleet and remediated other affected endpoints if applicable.

After all of that, mark the incident as Resolved. If the incident involved a multi-step remediation or requires follow-up from the customer, create an external ticket. SentinelOne has an integration field for this, you can link the incident directly to your ticketing system so that customer follow-up is tracked separately from the incident close.

Finally, add a disposition summary to the notes. This is a one-sentence statement of the outcome: "Marked true positive. Applied Quarantine. Confirmed no other endpoints affected. Closed 2026-04-24."

The entire incident record, Storyline, Thread Details, Actions, Notes, Verdict, Status, becomes part of your compliance record. In a breach investigation or an audit, every closed incident will be reviewed. Close incidents as if every one of them will be examined by a lawyer.

6.10 The Daily Analyst Workflow

A professional SOC analyst's daily rhythm follows a pattern. First, you arrive and open the Incidents queue. You immediately filter to Online endpoints and Not Mitigated threats. This removes the noise, offline machines cannot be helped anyway.

You scan the filtered list for anything with a threat count greater than 2. Multi-detection chains are usually more interesting than single detections; they suggest a coordinated attack. You open the threat with the highest count, read the Storyline, and spend no more than five minutes deciding whether it is credible.

If it is credible, you take the appropriate mitigation action immediately. Do not deliberate. Behavioral AI detections are highly accurate; trust the engine. If it is not credible, mark it false positive and move on.

Once you have handled the high-count threats, you work through the rest of the queue systematically, filtering by classification. Ransomware first, then Malware, then suspicious behaviors. You aim to move each incident to Resolved status within 5-10 minutes.

As you work, you record Threat IDs and Storyline IDs that appear to be the same. At the end of your shift, you review those duplicates for fleet-wide patterns. You escalate any pattern to your security team and update your block list.

Finally, you pull the Activity log and scan it for entries that do not look right. Unexpected policy changes, remote shell sessions, or admin logins at odd times are early warnings of a compromised account. This weekly habit, just a five-minute scan of Activity, will often catch the breach before the incident queue does.

Analyst's Guide: The Five-Minute Incident Decision

Spend no more than five minutes on an incident open-close cycle: Read the Storyline, check the Thread Details, verify with VirusTotal if necessary, take action or decide not to, add one-sentence notes, set verdict, mark Resolved.

If an incident needs more than five minutes of analysis, it is either not a real incident, or you are missing context. In the latter case, escalate to your security team. Do not sit on ambiguous incidents in New status.

Warning: Bulk Remediation Requires Care

Never apply bulk mitigation actions without filtering first. A careless bulk remediation can disable critical endpoints or production systems.

Always verify the scope before you click. Count the affected endpoints. If it is more than you expected, investigate why. If it is a critical system, reach out to the endpoint owner before applying Remediate or Rollback.

6.11 Worked Example: Triage of a Suspected False Positive

It is 9:14 a.m. on Tuesday. Your inbox shows a new SentinelOne incident with severity Medium. The threat name is "Suspicious PowerShell Execution Pattern." The endpoint is FIN-DESKTOP-04. Your morning coffee just got more interesting.

We open the Incidents queue and filter to FIN-DESKTOP-04. We see the threat listed as In-Progress (someone else has already opened it, but let us verify what they found). We click into the incident and read the Storyline.

First-Look Triage

The Storyline shows: explorer.exe launched powershell.exe. PowerShell then executed a remote session connect (connection to a named-pipe endpoint). The Thread Details show the alert was triggered by the Behavioral AI engine on a "suspicious command-line pattern." The file is signed by Microsoft. The classification is "Suspicious" (not Malware), and no other engines flagged it.

This is immediately interesting because multiple engines are not agreeing. If five engines all flagged this, we would move to remediation. But one engine with a "Suspicious" verdict suggests a false positive is possible. We make a note: "Initial assessment: low confidence. PowerShell is legitimate, signature is Microsoft. Behavioral flag alone warrants investigation before action."

Pivoting to Context

We look at the endpoint details. FIN-DESKTOP-04 is owned by a Finance department user. We check the ownership log and see this endpoint has been active for 18 months with no prior security incidents. We search the Activity log for this user and find no evidence of credential compromise or unusual login times. We then check the Incidents history on this endpoint over the past 90 days: zero other detections.

This user has a clean history. That is a significant data point. We next ask: who is this user, and what is their job function? We find they are a Senior Finance Analyst. Finance teams often run scripting workflows, reporting automation, and data pulls. PowerShell is a standard tool in that department.

We make a second note: "Endpoint and user context suggests legitimate business use. No prior incidents. No credential compromise indicators. Recommend communication with user before remediation."

The False-Positive Determination

We decide we need to talk to the user before making a judgment. We message the Finance Analyst: "Hi, we saw an alert on your machine at 9 a.m. related to PowerShell execution. Did you initiate a script or remote connection this morning?" Within five minutes, they respond: "Yes, I was running our monthly expense report automation. It connects to our data warehouse via PowerShell remoting to pull vendor spend data."

Bingo. This is a legitimate business script, not an intrusion. The script uses PowerShell remoting (which explains the named-pipe pattern the Behavioral AI caught). The analyst is the endpoint owner, so they are authorized to run it.

We then do a quick check: we ask the user for the script path and verify it is stored in the shared Finance folder on the network, not in a suspicious location. We also verify with IT that the data warehouse remote endpoint is an approved data source. All checks pass.

We make a final note: "User confirmed running legitimate expense report automation script. Script stored in approved network location. Data warehouse connection is authorized. No malicious indicators. Verdict: False Positive."

The Right Way to Close

Now we close this incident properly. We do the following:

1. Set the analysis verdict to "False Positive".

2. Set the incident status to "Resolved."

3. Add comprehensive notes documenting the investigation. Our full note reads: "Alert triggered by Behavioral AI on PowerShell remoting pattern. Endpoint is clean (18 months, zero prior incidents). User is Finance Analyst. Confirmed via direct communication that PowerShell script is part of monthly expense reporting automation. Script location verified as approved network path. Data warehouse connection is authorized. Conviction: High. This is legitimate business use. Created exclusion by process name (powershell.exe) and script path hash to prevent re-alerting on this specific automation."

4. Create an exclusion. Rather than just marking it False Positive, we create a precise exclusion: we exclude alerts on powershell.exe when the command line includes the specific parameters from the expense report script. This prevents the same alert from firing next month when the user runs the same automation. We do NOT create a blanket exclusion for all PowerShell activity, that would be too broad and defeat the purpose of detection.

5. Add a tag to the incident: "finance-automation" so we can trend these types of business-process false positives.

6. We send a note to the Finance Analyst: "Alert has been resolved. We have updated our detection rules to prevent this alert from appearing again for your monthly process. If you see similar alerts in the future, please reach out."

What NOT to Do

Many new analysts make predictable mistakes on false positives. Let us call them out:

Closing without documenting. Some analysts click "Mark Resolved" and move on. Six months later, an auditor asks: "Why was this false positive marked resolved?" and there are zero notes to explain the reasoning. This creates credibility risk.

Creating overly broad exclusions. A mistake-prone analyst might exclude "all PowerShell alerts" to stop this one alert from firing again. That is catastrophic. Now real PowerShell-based attacks slip through undetected.

Suppressing the rule entirely. Some analysts find the Behavioral AI rule in the policy and disable it entirely because "it is generating too many false positives." This throws out the baby with the bathwater. A better move is to tune the rule or create a targeted exclusion, not disable it.

Not updating the team. The analyst marks it Resolved but does not tell anyone else in the SOC. Next month, when the same alert fires on another Finance analyst's machine, a different analyst investigates from zero, wasting time and creating duplicate documentation.

Assuming "False Positive" means "never trust this rule again." Some analysts mark a few false positives on a rule and then mentally dismiss all future alerts from that rule. But false positives do not mean the rule is broken. It means the rule needs tuning or context. Treat each incident independently.

The Follow-Up

This kind of incident shapes future detection tuning. At the end of your shift, we make a note in our team channel: "Resolved false positive: Behavioral AI flagged legitimate Finance automation script using PowerShell remoting. Created exclusion. Recommend: (1) Review Behavioral AI alerting parameters to reduce noise on scripts with specific command-line patterns, (2) Coordinate with Finance to centralize script monitoring so similar automation elsewhere in the company is visible. (3)

Consider creating a Finance-specific policy with loosened Behavioral AI thresholds since scripting is part of their normal workflow." This kind of feedback becomes the basis for the next tuning cycle.

False-Positive Discipline

Always document why you concluded it is a false positive. One sentence is not enough. Write the reasoning: what you observed, what you checked, what confirmed it was legitimate.

Never create an exclusion broader than the specific scenario. Exclude the exact process, path, or hash, not the entire category. Broad exclusions blind your defenses.

Tag the incident for trend tracking. Use tags like "finance-automation," "vendor-tool," or "shadow-it" to group similar false positives. Trends reveal tuning problems.

Tell the team what you found. Post a note to your security channel or incident log. The next analyst facing a similar alert will find your documentation and close it faster.

Revisit recurring false positives. If you see five similar false positives in a month from the same process or script, that signals a tuning problem, not just analyst nuisance. Escalate to your detection engineering team to refine the rule.

Chapter Summary

The SentinelOne Incidents workflow is the core daily tool for every SOC analyst. You begin with the queue, filtered to the threats that matter most, those on online endpoints that have not yet been mitigated. You open a threat, read its Storyline to understand the attack chain, and examine the Thread Details to verify the verdict. You apply one of four mitigation actions, Kill, Quarantine, Remediate, or Rollback, based on your confidence in the detection. You set the analysis verdict (True Positive, False Positive, Suspicious, Undefined) and the incident status (New, In-Progress, Resolved, Unresolved), add detailed notes, and close the ticket. Throughout, you search for the same Threat ID or Storyline ID across the fleet to catch coordinated campaigns.

Speed and consistency are the metrics of a mature SOC. A well-trained analyst can open, investigate, act on, and close an incident in five to ten minutes. The key is knowing what to look for in the Storyline, trusting the detection engines when they agree, using external sources like VirusTotal to validate edge cases, and documenting every decision in notes. The incidents you close today become the threat intelligence and tuning feedback that makes tomorrow's detections more accurate. Close incidents as if they will be audited, because one day, they will be.

Key Takeaways

- The Incidents queue surfaces threats from AI engines and alerts from your custom detection rules. Filter to Online and Not Mitigated as your first triage step.
- The Storyline view shows the attack chain left to right. Read it to understand causality and timing.
- Thread Details contains signature, classification, detection engines, threat indicators, and MITRE ATT&CK mappings.
- Four mitigation actions: Kill (stop the process), Quarantine (isolate the file), Remediate (delete and roll back changes), Rollback (revert to a prior snapshot).
- Set the analysis verdict (True Positive, False Positive, Suspicious, Undefined) and the incident status (New, In-Progress, Resolved, Unresolved) before closing.
- Use Threat ID and Storyline ID to search for fleet-wide patterns. Always scope before bulk remediation.
- Document every decision in notes as if the incident will be audited.
- The professional analyst closes five to ten incidents per shift, filtering ruthlessly and trusting the engines.

Hands-On Exercise

Before you continue to Chapter 7, do the following in your SentinelOne tenant.

- Open the Incidents tab and filter to Online endpoints and Not Mitigated threats. Identify the threat with the highest detection count. Open it, read the Storyline, and examine the Thread Details. Write down three observations about the attack chain.
- For that same threat, search for the Threat ID across your entire fleet. Document whether it appears on other endpoints. If so, apply a bulk remediation action to all affected endpoints.
- Pick a threat you have marked as False Positive. Open VirusTotal and verify that the file has zero or near-zero detections from commercial vendors. Document your findings in the incident notes.

- Spend fifteen minutes moving threats from New to Resolved status. Mark each incident with the correct verdict and incident status. Aim to close at least five incidents with documented notes on each.

Review Questions

- 1. In the Incidents queue, a threat shows a shield icon with "2 of 4". What does this mean, and why is it important to pay attention to the counter?
- 2. Describe the difference between an analysis verdict and an incident status. Can an incident be marked "Resolved" if the verdict is still "Undefined"?
- 3. In the Storyline view, you see a process tree: explorer.exe → cmd.exe → powershell.exe → rundll32.exe. The detection fired on rundll32.exe. How would you interpret this chain, and what would you look for to confirm malice?
- 4. True or False: If VirusTotal shows zero detections for a file hash, the file is definitely benign. Explain.
- 5. When you mark an incident as "Resolved," what additional action should you take to ensure it does not become orphaned or forgotten?

Answer Key: Review Questions

1. The incident is part of a chain of 4 related detections (same Storyline). The counter shows you are looking at detection #2 of 4. Navigating through all 4 gives you the complete attack chain. This is important because related detections are stronger evidence of a coordinated attack.

2. Analysis verdict is your judgment (True Positive, False Positive, Suspicious, Undefined). Incident status is your progress (New, In-Progress, Resolved, Unresolved). Best practice: never mark Resolved if verdict is Undefined, set a verdict first. If you must leave it unresolved, mark it Unresolved, not Resolved.

3. This chain suggests: user opened a file → explorer.exe opened cmd.exe → cmd.exe launched PowerShell → PowerShell launched rundll32.exe. This is a suspicious chain because rundll32 is often used for code injection or loading DLLs directly. Look for the original file (e.g., email attachment, downloaded file), check what DLL is being loaded, and verify the command-line arguments.

4. False. VirusTotal can have false positives, and absence of detections does not guarantee benignity. A file might be new, custom, or targeted. Use VirusTotal as a data point, not as truth.

5. If it is a multi-step remediation or requires customer follow-up, create a ticket in your external ticketing system and link it to the incident. Then close the incident in SentinelOne. This prevents orphaned work.

Discussion Questions

- 1. You receive three detections: one marked "Malware" with 8 vendor detections on VirusTotal, one marked "Suspicious" with 0 VirusTotal detections, and one marked "PUA" with 3 VirusTotal detections. Rank them by priority and explain your reasoning.
- 2. A customer reports that SentinelOne is generating dozens of daily "Suspicious" alerts on software they claim is legitimate (a custom in-house application). What is the root cause, and how would you resolve it?
- 3. Describe a scenario where bulk threat remediation across a fleet would be faster and safer than individual endpoint remediation.

Hands-On Lab Exercises

Lab 6.1: Open an Incident and Read the Storyline

Objective: Practice opening incidents and interpreting the process-tree visualization.

Access to Incidents; at least one threat or alert available

Steps:

- Work through to Incidents. If no threats are available, skip to a recent resolved incident for this exercise.
- Click on any threat. Observe the Storyline visualization. Identify: the originating process (leftmost box), any child processes, and the detection point (usually highlighted in red).
- Read the timeline left to right. Does the attack chain make sense? Is it rapid (few seconds, might be installer) or slow (many minutes, might be lateral movement)?
- Hover over key elements to see timestamps. Calculate the duration from first event to detection.
- Below the Storyline, click Advanced view. Compare the tabular representation to the visual. Which is easier to understand?
- Document: "This incident shows a chain of [number] events over [duration]. The attack appears to be [type: installer/lateral movement/reconnaissance] because [evidence]."

Expected Outcome: Fluency reading Storyline visualizations.

Reflection: If you saw the same Storyline pattern on five other endpoints within an hour, what would that indicate?

Lab 6.2: Manually Analyze and Verdict an Incident

Objective: Practice the analysis workflow: read details, check VirusTotal, set a verdict, document reasoning.

Access to an incident; ability to open external links (VirusTotal)

Steps:

- Open an incident. Read the Thread Details panel: check the file hash, publisher signature, detected classifications, and threat engines that flagged it.
- Click the VirusTotal link (if available). In a new tab, review vendor detections, community comments, and behavioral analysis.
- Return to the incident. Based on Storyline + Thread Details + VirusTotal, decide: True Positive, False Positive, or Suspicious.
- Set the verdict. Add a note explaining your reasoning: "File is [classified] by SentinelOne, [X] vendors on VirusTotal agree, Storyline shows [pattern]. Verdict: [choice] because [reason]."

- If True Positive, select a remediation action (Kill, Quarantine, Remediate) and document why. If False Positive, create an exclusion and mark resolved.

Expected Outcome: One completely analyzed incident with verdict, notes, and remediation plan.

Reflection: If this same incident fires on another endpoint, what would you do differently?

Lab 6.3: Bulk-Remediate a Fleet-Wide Threat

Objective: Identify a threat across multiple endpoints and apply bulk remediation.

Access to Incidents and ability to filter by threat ID or storyline; at least 2 endpoints with the same or similar threat

Steps:

- Open an incident. Copy the Threat ID from the Thread Details panel.
- Go back to the Incidents queue. Search or filter for this Threat ID. How many endpoints show the same threat?
- If more than 5 endpoints are affected, you have a fleet-wide detection. Select all affected endpoints from the Incidents queue (if the interface supports it), or go to Sentinels, filter by threat status = "Infected with [Threat Name]," and select all.
- Initiate a bulk remediation action: Kill, Quarantine, or Remediate (whichever you decided was appropriate).
- Set a concurrent limit to avoid overwhelming the network (e.g., 50 endpoints at a time).
- Confirm the action. Over the next few minutes, observe the threat status change to "Mitigated" across the fleet.
- Document the campaign: "Threat [ID] affected [number] endpoints across [Sites]. Bulk [action] applied. Status: [X] mitigated, [Y] pending, [Z] failed."

Expected Outcome: Experience bulk threat remediation and understanding of fleet-wide coordination.

Reflection: If 80% of endpoints were successfully mitigated but 20% failed, what would be your next step?

Lab 6.4: Create and Test a Custom Alert (If Feature Available)

Objective: Design a custom alert (proactive detection) based on a pattern you want to watch for.

Access to Alerts or Custom Queries; familiarity with PowerQuery or your alert DSL

Steps:

- Identify a pattern you want to alert on (e.g., "all instances of rundll32.exe with command-line containing 'shell'," or "file writes to the System32 directory from non-system processes").
- In the Alerts section, create a new alert with a PowerQuery or equivalent query.
- Name it descriptively (e.g., "Suspicious rundll32 Activity").
- Set the alert to trigger on matches and assign it to a test Group or a single endpoint.
- If possible, simulate the pattern (e.g., manually run rundll32 with a suspicious command) and verify the alert fires.
- Review the alert in Incidents to confirm it appears as an Alert (not a Threat).
- Document the alert definition and its purpose.

Expected Outcome: Understanding of how custom alerts extend SentinelOne's detection beyond the AI engines.

Reflection: Would you recommend alerting on this pattern company-wide, or only in a test group?

What's Next

Chapter 7 goes deep on Applications: how to identify vulnerable software on your managed endpoints, how to export vulnerability lists to your remediation workflow, how to prioritize which vulnerabilities matter most in your environment, and how to measure remediation progress over time.

Mastering SentinelOne

Chapter 7, Draft for Review

by Kendrick Washington, Technology Interpreters, Inc.

Chapter 7

Applications: Software Inventory for Security Operations

Learning Objectives

- Work through the Applications inventory and understand what information each column surface.
- Use filters and sorting to isolate vulnerable applications, specific vendors, and version-mismatch patterns.
- Pivot from a vulnerable application to affected endpoints to remediation guidance via CVE cross-reference.
- Distinguish between critical, high, medium, and low CVSS severity scores and understand what each means for your response priority.
- Identify unapproved software and shadow IT through inventory review and scope-aware querying.
- Integrate vulnerability data from SentinelOne Applications with your broader vulnerability management and patch workflows.

Chapter Opener

Most security teams treat vulnerability management as a separate problem from endpoint detection and response. You have a vulnerability scanner over here, an EDR platform over there, and an ITSM system somewhere else. The Applications menu in SentinelOne exists to collapse that boundary: because the agent already knows what software is installed on every endpoint and what version it is, SentinelOne can cross-reference that against the National Vulnerability Database in real time and hand you a prioritized list of what needs to be patched, where it lives, and what the actual risk is. For small organizations, this can replace a dedicated vulnerability scanner altogether. For larger organizations that already have Tenable Nessus or Qualys in place, Applications serves as a fast, agile complement that fills in the gaps between scan windows.

This chapter is titled "favorite module" because it is. Not because it is flashy, it is not. But because it solves a real gap in endpoint security that too many teams leave unresolved: the gap between "we have vulnerability data somewhere" and "we know which vulnerabilities are on which endpoints and we are actively remediating them." The Applications inventory closes that gap. And once you learn to hunt with it, you will start spotting patterns you never saw before: deprecated versions of software still in use, applications that should not be there, license compliance issues hiding in plain sight. This is the kind of tool that pays for itself quietly.

7.1 Understanding the Applications Inventory

When you work through to Applications in the SentinelOne console, you land on a list of every application that has been detected across the scope you are viewing (Global, Account, Site, or Group, remember the hierarchy matters here). For each application, SentinelOne displays:

Application Name: the human-readable name (Safari, Python Launcher, etc.)

Vendor: the publisher (Apple, Microsoft, etc.)

Version: the specific version detected

CVSS Score: the severity ranking from the National Vulnerability Database (NVD)

Severity Label: Critical (9-10), High (7-8.9), Medium (4-6.9), Low (0.1-3.9), or False Positive

Affected Endpoints: the count of machines running this version

CVE ID(s): the specific vulnerability identifiers associated with this version

Days Since Detection: how long the agent has known about this application

The key insight here is scope. If you are viewing at the Account level in an MSSP environment, you might see 347 unique applications across all your customers. If you filter down to a single Site, that number drops dramatically, maybe 52 applications. This matters because it tells you how wide a patch campaign has to be and whether you need to coordinate across customers or just focus on one. Every filter you apply narrows the scope.

7.2 Reading the Vulnerability Data: CVSS Scores and Severity Bands

The CVSS score is the backbone of the Applications inventory. CVSS stands for Common Vulnerability Scoring System, and it is the standard that virtually every vulnerability researcher and scanning product uses to measure how bad a flaw really is. SentinelOne pulls these scores directly from the National Vulnerability Database (NVD) maintained by NIST.

The scoring bands are:

Critical: 9.0-10.0. A flaw that can be exploited remotely without user interaction, leads to complete compromise of the system, or affects hundreds of thousands of endpoints. If you have critical vulnerabilities, they should be in your queue today.

High: 7.0-8.9. A flaw that requires modest attacker skill to exploit, leads to significant loss of confidentiality or integrity, or affects your most sensitive systems. High vulnerabilities should reach your patch window within days.

Medium: 4.0-6.9. A flaw that requires moderate attacker skill, affects non-critical systems, or has limited real-world exploitability. Medium vulnerabilities are part of your regular patch cycle.

Low: 0.1-3.9. A flaw with limited impact, requires unusual configuration, or affects systems that are already at lower risk. Low vulnerabilities are still worth knowing about, but they do not drive your patch priority.

False Positive: SentinelOne has flagged an application version as having known vulnerabilities, but either the vulnerability does not apply to your configuration or the vendor has already patched it and the agent has not seen the update yet. These get easier to recognize the more you use the tool.

The CVSS score alone is not actionable. A critical score on a rarely-used utility matters less than a high score on your company's standard email client. But paired with endpoint count and your own risk model, whether the machine is internet-facing, what data it touches, whether it runs privileged code, the score becomes a powerful triage tool.

7.3 Filtering, Sorting, and Hunting

The Applications inventory comes with a filter bar that lets you narrow results by five dimensions simultaneously:

Vendor: filter to Microsoft, Apple, Adobe, Zoom, or any vendor in your environment. This is your first move when a vendor announces a major vulnerability. Microsoft Exchange zero-day? Click the Microsoft filter and see every affected product across your organization.

Application Name: search by exact name or substring. Good for finding a specific tool you know is in use.

Version: filter to specific version ranges. This is how you identify machines that have missed a patch or are running a deprecated build.

CVSS Score Range: filter by severity band (critical, high, medium, low). Most teams start by filtering to critical and high to clear the most dangerous items first.

Endpoint Name or UUID: find applications on a specific machine or by the machine's unique identifier.

You can combine these filters. "Show me all Microsoft products with a CVSS score of 8 or higher that are running on machines in the Finance department." The interface applies filters as you type, letting you narrow your result set in seconds.

Sorting is equally important. By default, the inventory sorts by highest CVSS score first, which is a sensible default. But you can also sort by affected endpoint count (find applications that are wide rather than deep), by vendor (useful when you are trying to coordinate a patch campaign with external teams), or by days since detection (find older machines that have been off the update cycle). The key is: sorting and filtering work together. Filter to a vendor, then sort by endpoint count to see which of their products affect the most machines.

7.4 From Vulnerability to Remediation: The CVE Cross-Reference Workflow

The real power of Applications emerges when you click into a specific vulnerable application and follow the remediation path. Here is the workflow:

1. Spot a vulnerability: you see Safari 16.3 with a CVSS score of 9.8 (critical).

2. Click the application name: SentinelOne takes you to a details page showing every endpoint running that version.

3. Review the affected endpoints: you see it is running on five Mac endpoints in the design department.

4. Click the CVE ID: SentinelOne opens the corresponding entry in the National Vulnerability Database (NVD) or MITRE CVE registry.

5. Read the remediation details: the NVD entry tells you: "Fixed in Safari 16.4 and later" or "Update to macOS Ventura 13.3." Now you have a specific patch version to deploy.

6. Integrate with your patch workflow: create a patch task in your ITSM system, send a request to the Mac team, or use SentinelOne's Automation surface to push the update yourself.

The entire workflow from "we have a critical vulnerability" to "here is the patch version and which endpoints need it" takes minutes instead of hours, because you are not toggling between five different systems. Everything is connected. This is why vulnerability management without good endpoint inventory is broken. You can know that Safari 16.3 is vulnerable, but without knowing where it lives, remediation becomes a guessing game.

7.5 Finding Unapproved Software and Shadow IT

One of the hidden benefits of the Applications inventory is that it reveals shadow IT: software running in your environment that you did not authorize and sometimes do not even know about. This can be benign (a developer installed a library they needed) or malicious (someone running unauthorized cryptocurrency mining software).

To hunt for shadow IT, change your approach. Instead of starting with vulnerability data, start with inventory data. Go to the Inventory tab within Applications and ask: "What applications are running on my endpoints that should not be here?"

Some hunting patterns:

Compare against your software approval list. If your company only approves Chrome, Firefox, and Safari as browsers, any installation of Brave, Opera, or Tor is a flag.

Look for deprecated versions of business software. Old versions of Slack, Teams, or Salesforce might indicate someone is running a copy they found lying around instead of using the corporate license.

Hunt by endpoint. Select a single machine and ask: what is installed that does not match the standard build? Often you will find personal productivity tools, game emulators, or development environments that were never formally requested.

Use vendor clustering. Group by vendor and sort by smallest installation count. Single-instance vendors often indicate one-off installations, which can be legitimate research tools or unauthorized security risk.

When you find something suspicious, drill down to the endpoint, talk to the user, and either add it to your approved list or request immediate removal. The Applications inventory is your first line of visibility into what is actually running, and that visibility is your first line of defense against shadow IT.

7.6 Scope Awareness: Scanning Across Sites and Accounts

A critical operational principle in the Applications menu: scope matters more here than almost anywhere else in the console. When you click the "Scan Now" button, you are triggering an application detection scan on every endpoint in your current scope.

If you are at the Account level in an MSSP environment and hit Scan Now, you just initiated a scan on every customer's endpoints. This is usually a low-impact, background-priority scan that does not interfere with normal operations. But it is a significant action, and you should be intentional about it. Most teams set a policy of scanning once weekly and let it run on schedule rather than manually triggering scans.

The same applies to filters and vulnerability counts. If you are viewing at the Account level and you see "347 total applications with critical vulnerabilities," that number represents critical vulnerabilities across all your customers. Drill down to the Site level to see which customer has the most critical issues. Drill down further to a Group to see which department or team is at risk. Every level of the hierarchy changes the context of the numbers.

Practical rule: when you are investigating a vulnerability or hunting for shadow IT, drill down from Account to Site to Group, the same way you would when investigating an incident. The headline-level numbers are useful for reporting, but the work happens at the scope where you can actually take action.

7.7 Integration with Vulnerability Management and Patch Workflows

The Applications menu is not a replacement for a dedicated vulnerability management platform unless you are a very small organization with a tight patch window. Most enterprises use both: a specialist like Tenable or Qualys for network-wide scanning, OS patching, and compliance reporting, and SentinelOne Applications as a real-time, agent-based complement that catches installed software that network scanners might miss (especially on laptops and remote endpoints).

The integration pattern:

Use SentinelOne Applications to inventory software and cross-reference against NVD in real time. This is fast and agent-native.

Use your vulnerability scanner to validate patch deployment and check for network-accessible services that should not be running.

Use the Automation surface (covered in Chapter 10) to push patches to groups of endpoints based on vulnerability findings from Applications.

Use Reports (Chapter 9) to generate monthly or quarterly vulnerability reports showing critical and high vulnerabilities by application, by Site, by group, and trending over time.

The policy tab in Applications also includes an option to enable "Extensive Vulnerability Scan," which improves the fidelity of the data at the cost of slightly more agent load. For compliance-heavy environments, enabling this gives you higher confidence in your vulnerability counts.

The practical benefit: if a vendor announces a zero-day or critical update on a Tuesday morning, you can be patching by Tuesday afternoon because you already have the inventory, the affected endpoints, and the patch guidance all in one place.

7.8 License Compliance as a Side Benefit

While your primary goal in the Applications menu is vulnerability management, the inventory data also gives you visibility into software licensing. Many organizations pay for a Site license (five hundred users) but discover through the Applications inventory that they have actually installed the software on seven hundred endpoints. Or they have a budget for fifty copies of an enterprise tool and find that a department has deployed one hundred.

The Applications inventory is not a replacement for a dedicated software asset management (SAM) tool, but it is a powerful sanity check. Pull a report of all installed instances of your top ten software expenses and compare it against your license count. The gap between license count and installation count is either evidence of under-licensing (and budget leakage) or evidence of unlicensed installations (and compliance risk).

When you audit the Applications inventory for licensing purposes, pay special attention to version numbers. A vendor might have provided a newer license model in version 5.0, but your inventory shows you still have two hundred machines on version 3.1. That is a licensing conversation waiting to happen.

Analyst's Workflow: The Saturday-Morning Vulnerability Check

Set a weekly reminder (Friday afternoon) to open Applications and filter for Critical and High vulnerabilities.

Drill down by Site. For each Site, export or screenshot the critical/high list and send it to the customer's IT team with the subject "Vulnerabilities requiring immediate attention."

For each critical vulnerability, click through to NVD, confirm the patch version, and note whether it requires a reboot. That information goes in your escalation email.

Check back Monday morning to see which vulnerabilities have been patched. Use the "Days Since Detection" column to identify machines that have not received the update, those are your follow-ups.

This twenty-minute ritual prevents critical vulnerabilities from aging in your queue and demonstrates a level of proactivity that customers notice.

7.9 Case Study: Coordinating a Cross-Endpoint Vulnerability Remediation

Wednesday morning, 8:47 a.m. You open the Applications inventory and filter to Critical vulnerabilities. The list is short (thank goodness), but one item catches your eye: Adobe Reader 22.001, CVSS 7.8 (High, not Critical, but significant). Affected Endpoints: 47.

The Discovery

You click into Adobe Reader to see the affected endpoints. The list populates: 47 machines across three Sites. The CVE is CVE-2024-45631, publicly disclosed and rated 7.8 (High severity). You click the CVE link and land in the National Vulnerability Database. The description reads:

"Arbitrary code execution vulnerability in Adobe Reader 22.x versions before 22.1.47. Requires user interaction (opening a crafted PDF) but leads to complete process compromise." Fixed in version 22.1.47 and later.

This is not critical, but it is not low-risk either. User interaction is required (someone has to open a PDF), but this organization handles a lot of PDFs. Insurance claims, contracts, vendor documents. The attack surface is real.

Risk Assessment: Mapping Exposure

You decide to drill down and map the 47 affected endpoints to risk tiers based on who uses them and what they do.

You scope to Site 1 (your largest customer with 200 endpoints) and filter by the affected list. You see 12 machines. You look at the Sentinels list and note the endpoint owners: eight are Finance and Accounting staff, four are Executive team (C-suite and senior management). These are high-exposure users. They handle external documents constantly, vendor contracts, financial statements, insurance forms. High risk.

You scope to Site 2 (120 endpoints). You find 25 affected machines. The user roles are mixed: Customer Service (15 machines), IT Help Desk (5 machines), General Admin (5 machines). Medium exposure. They handle external documents but with less frequency than Finance.

You scope to Site 3 (30 endpoints). You find 10 affected machines. The users are Data Center operators and Infrastructure team. Low exposure. They rarely open external documents; their work is mostly infrastructure management.

Your mental risk matrix: Tier 1 (High exposure): 12 machines, executives and finance staff. Tier 2 (Medium exposure): 25 machines, customer service and admin. Tier 3 (Low exposure): 10 machines, infrastructure team.

Prioritization Decision

You do not dump 47 patch tickets on IT all at once. Instead, you contact the IT teams and propose a phased approach: Tier 1 (12 machines, high exposure) within 24 hours. Tier 2 (25 machines, medium exposure) within 5 business days. Tier 3 (10 machines, low exposure) in the next maintenance window (up to 30 days).

This approach balances risk and operational impact. The executives are less likely to tolerate a reboot forced on them, so we make it a priority to get their systems patched first, before they hit a malicious PDF in their inbox. The customer service team can wait a few days; the infrastructure team can wait much longer.

You prepare a quick remediation request with details. Here is a sample message to IT:

Sample Communication to IT/Desktop Team:

Subject: Urgent: Adobe Reader Vulnerability (CVE-2024-45631), 47 Endpoints Priority: High We have identified 47 endpoints running Adobe Reader 22.001, which is vulnerable to CVE-2024-45631 (CVSS 7.8, arbitrary code execution). This affects our highest-exposure users (executives, finance, customer service). The fix is available in Reader 22.1.47 and later. Proposed Remediation Timeline: • Tier 1 (12 endpoints, executives/finance): patch by Thursday EOD • Tier 2 (25 endpoints, customer service/admin): patch by Friday next week • Tier 3 (10 endpoints, infrastructure): patch by end of month Affected endpoint list: [attached or linked] Benefits of this timeline: (1) Shields high-exposure users within 24 hours, (2) distributes the patch load across the week to avoid IT bottleneck, (3) allows testing before pushing to lower-priority groups. Please confirm receipt and provide an ETA for Tier 1 patching. Questions? Contact [your name].

Coordination with IT/Desktop Team

IT responds within a few hours. They confirm they can handle Tier 1 by Thursday. They need a few clarifications: Does the patch require a reboot? (Yes, it does, Reader is a user-level application, but a restart is safest). Can we test it on one machine first? (Absolutely, we send them one endpoint from Tier 1 for validation.) Are there any known compatibility issues? (No, this is a straightforward update with no backward compatibility breaks.)

IT pushes the patch to Tier 1 on Thursday morning. By Thursday afternoon, you check the Applications inventory again: 10 of the 12 machines now show Adobe Reader 22.1.47. Two machines still show 22.001. You check the Sentinels list and see that both endpoints are currently offline (one is a remote laptop, one is in a dock but powered down). You note in your remediation tracker: "Two endpoints offline as of Thursday 3 p.m. Retry patching when endpoints come online."

Verification After the Patch

Friday morning, you re-pull the Applications inventory and scope to the Tier 1 list. All 12 machines now show Adobe Reader 22.1.47. Two machines took an extra 18 hours to come online and receive the patch, but they are now current. You move to Tier 2.

For Tier 2, you check in with IT on Monday morning. They confirm they are planning to push the patch in the Wednesday-to-Friday window to avoid weekend emergency calls. You ask: "Can you exclude the Customer Service team on Monday and Tuesday? They support end-users, and we don't want a reboot disrupting their calls in the middle of the week." IT adjusts the plan to patch Tier 2 on Thursday-Friday only.

By the following Wednesday, you check Applications inventory again. You scope to the Tier 2 list: 24 of 25 machines now show 22.1.47. One machine is still 22.001. You check the endpoint details: it is a loaner laptop that has not been returned to the office yet (traveling employee). You tag it in your notes and follow up with the employee's manager: "We have identified a traveling employee whose laptop is missing a critical software patch. Can we schedule 15 minutes for them to dock the laptop and allow patching?"

Three days later, the loaner laptop comes in, gets patched, and the Tier 2 remediation is complete. You move to Tier 3, which IT schedules for the following month during their standard maintenance window. By the end of that month, all 47 endpoints are running Adobe Reader 22.1.47 or later.

The Closing Report

You prepare a short executive summary for your CISO and send it to the customer's leadership. Here is the report:

Vulnerability Remediation Report, April 2026

Vulnerability: Adobe Reader CVE-2024-45631 (CVSS 7.8, High severity) Discovery Date: 2026-04-24 Affected Endpoints: 47 (out of 350 total) Risk Level: High (affects finance, executive, and customer-facing teams) Action Taken: We identified 47 endpoints running vulnerable Adobe Reader 22.001 and coordinated patching in three priority tiers based on business risk and user roles. Tier 1 (executives/finance, 12 endpoints) patched by 2026-04-25. Tier 2 (customer service/admin, 25 endpoints) patched by 2026-05-02. Tier 3 (infrastructure, 10 endpoints) patched by 2026-05-30. Outcome: As of 2026-05-30, all 47 endpoints are running Adobe Reader 22.1.47 or later. Zero vulnerabilities remain. No incidents related to this CVE were observed during the remediation window. Key Learning: This remediation demonstrates the value of endpoint-based vulnerability detection. Using SentinelOne Applications inventory, we identified the vulnerable software, mapped it to business risk, and coordinated patching without disrupting operations. Integration with IT workflows ensures both security and operational continuity.

What This Case Study Teaches

The Applications module is a security tool because it lets analysts move from "we have stuff installed" to "we have a measurable, prioritized, coordinated remediation outcome." The journey looks like this:

1. Inventory step: Applications inventory shows us 47 machines with Adobe Reader 22.001.

2. Risk assessment step: We map those 47 endpoints to user roles and business context (executives, finance, customer service, infrastructure).

3. Prioritization step: We do not treat all 47 equally. We create three tiers based on risk and operational impact.

4. Coordination step: We communicate with IT in a structured way (timeline, affected list, impact assessment) so they can plan and execute.

5. Verification step: We re-scan Applications inventory after patching to confirm all machines are updated. We identify laggards (offline endpoints) and follow up.

6. Reporting step: We document the outcome for compliance and future reference.

Analysts who skip steps 2-3 (jumping straight from "we have 47 affected machines" to "patch all 47 now") create operational friction. IT rebels against aggressive patching that disrupts business. But analysts who invest 30 minutes in risk mapping and phased planning get IT buy-in and smoother execution.

The Applications inventory + analyst judgment + IT coordination = the complete remediation cycle. That cycle is where vulnerability management actually lives. Tools like Tenable or Qualys can flag vulnerabilities. But it is the analyst, working with IT and the business, who turns those flags into actual risk reduction. The Applications module is your lever for moving from detection to remediation.

From Inventory to Outcome: The Analyst's Remediation Checklist

Identify vulnerable applications in the Applications inventory. Filter by CVSS score and endpoint count.

Map affected endpoints to user roles, business units, and data sensitivity. Create risk tiers (high, medium, low).

Propose a phased remediation timeline to IT that balances risk and operational impact. Do not dump all tickets at once.

Communicate clearly. Include CVE details, patch version, affected endpoints, and timeline in writing. Let IT plan around it.

Verify remediation. Re-scan the Applications inventory after patching to confirm all endpoints are updated. Follow up on laggards.

Report the outcome. Document what was patched, when, and what the current status is. Use this for compliance audits and trend analysis.

Close the loop with the business. Let the customer or CISO know the remediation is complete and the risk is closed.

Chapter Summary

The Applications menu is SentinelOne's lightweight vulnerability management surface. It leverages the agent's knowledge of what software is installed on every endpoint and cross-references that against the National Vulnerability Database in real time. The result is a prioritized, endpoint-aware view of where your vulnerabilities are, how many machines are affected, and what the patch version should be. The CVSS scoring system (Critical 9-10, High 7-8.9, Medium 4-6.9, Low 0.1-3.9) provides a standard framework for triage, but real-world risk also depends on endpoint count and business context.

Beyond vulnerability management, the Applications inventory is a powerful tool for shadow IT discovery, license compliance auditing, and patch-campaign planning. The filters (vendor, version, CVSS range, endpoint) work together to let you narrow your focus from "all applications in my organization" to "all critical versions of Safari running in the Finance department" in seconds. The remediation workflow is fast: spot a vulnerability, click through to the affected endpoints, click through to the CVE for patch guidance, then integrate into your patch system. Scope awareness is critical, filtering at the Account level shows you everything; drilling down to a Site or Group shows you what you can actually act on.

Key Takeaways

- The Applications inventory gives you real-time visibility into installed software across your endpoints and vulnerability data cross-referenced to the National Vulnerability Database.
- CVSS scores are the standard for vulnerability severity, but must be interpreted alongside endpoint count and business context. A critical score on a rarely-used utility matters less than a high score on your standard email client.
- Filtering and sorting are your primary tools for triage. Start by filtering to Critical and High, then sort by endpoint count to find the vulnerabilities that affect the most machines.
- The remediation workflow is fast: click the application → see affected endpoints → click the CVE ID → read the patch guidance → integrate into your ITSM or patch system.
- Shadow IT hunting uses the Applications inventory in reverse: instead of starting with vulnerability data, start with application inventory and ask what should not be there.
- Scope matters. A scan at the Account level triggers across all customers; drilling down to a Site or Group shows you what you can act on.
- Applications is a complement to, not a replacement for, dedicated vulnerability management tools in large enterprises, but can replace them entirely in small organizations.
- The license compliance side benefit should not be ignored: use the inventory to audit software installation counts against your license purchase.

Hands-On Exercise

Before you continue to Chapter 8, do the following in your SentinelOne tenant.

- Work through to Applications and filter to Critical and High severity vulnerabilities. Export or screenshot the list. For the top three vulnerabilities by endpoint count, click through to each CVE entry and note the patch version and any required reboot information.

- Go to the Inventory tab within Applications. Sort by application name and look for any products you do not recognize. Pick one and click through to see which endpoints have it installed. Research whether it is approved software or a shadow IT candidate.
- Select a single endpoint (a specific Group) and view the Applications list scoped to just that machine. Compare the application count to your standard build. Identify any unexpected installations.
- Go to the Policy tab and note whether "Extensive Vulnerability Scan" is enabled in your policy. If not, enable it and allow 24 hours for the data to become more granular.
- Create a simple report: count the number of applications with a CVSS score of 9.0 or higher across your Account. Then drill down to each Site and record the Site-level count. This comparison shows you where the most critical vulnerabilities are concentrated.

Review Questions

- 1. What does a CVSS score of 9.2 tell you, and what is your expected response time for remediation?
- 2. In the Applications inventory, you see "Microsoft Windows 10 Build 19042" with a CVSS score of 7.8 and "Affected Endpoints: 47." What does the 47 refer to?
- 3. True or False: The Applications menu can replace a dedicated vulnerability scanner like Tenable Nessus. Explain when Applications is sufficient and when you still need Tenable.
- 4. You filter Applications to show all products from a single vendor with CVSS >= 8.0. You plan to present this to your CISO as part of a quarterly remediation report. What additional data would you include to make the report actionable?
- 5. Why is "Days Since Detection" in the Applications inventory a useful metric, and what does a high number mean operationally?

Answer Key: Review Questions

1. CVSS 9.2 is Critical (range 9.0-10.0). Critical vulnerabilities can be exploited remotely, lead to complete system compromise, or affect wide populations. Expected response time: patch within 24-72 hours, or document a risk acceptance.

2. The 47 refers to the number of endpoints running that specific Windows build. If all 47 need a security patch, you have a bulk remediation campaign.

3. False, with nuance. Applications is sufficient for small organizations with tight patch windows and no compliance requirements. For enterprises, Applications is a complement: use it for real-time agent-based inventory and SentinelOne-managed endpoints; use Tenable for network-wide scanning, out-of-band systems, and compliance reporting.

4. (1) The affected endpoints by Site or Group (to identify customer-specific risk). (2) Patch version availability (to know what to deploy). (3) Trends (is the critical count decreasing month-over-month?). (4) Waivers or exceptions (which vulnerabilities have accepted risk).

5. Days Since Detection tells you how long that software version has existed in your environment. A high number (e.g., 180+ days) suggests the application is stale and the endpoint may not be receiving updates. This flags potential patch-cycle failures or inactive endpoints.

Discussion Questions

- 1. A shadow IT discovery using Applications reveals that 12 developers have installed different versions of Python, Node.js, and Java on their laptops. How would you approach this situation, and what is the balance between security and developer autonomy?
- 2. Your CISO wants to automate patching using SentinelOne Automation (scripts) to push updates for critical vulnerabilities. What are the risks of fully automated patching, and how would you stage the rollout?
- 3. Describe how you would use Applications inventory data to audit software license compliance alongside security patching.

Hands-On Lab Exercises

Lab 7.1: Inventory and Filter Applications

Objective: Work through the Applications menu and practice filtering to isolate vulnerable software.

Access to Applications inventory with data; at least 10 applications present

Steps:

- Work through to Applications. At the top level, note the total count of applications and affected endpoints.
- Filter to CVSS Score >= 8.0. How many applications are Critical or High? Record the count.
- Filter to Vendor = "Microsoft" (or another major vendor). Count applications. Sort by CVSS (highest first). Which Microsoft product has the highest vulnerability score?
- Clear filters and filter to Affected Endpoints >= 50. These are wide applications. Note the top five by endpoint count. Are any of these also high-CVSS?
- Create a two-column table: Application Name | Affected Endpoints | CVSS | Patch Version Available?. Fill in at least five applications.

Expected Outcome: Fluency navigating the Applications inventory and extracting vulnerability metrics.

Reflection: If you had to patch only three applications this month due to resource constraints, which three would you choose from your list, and why?

Lab 7.2: Pivot from Vulnerability to Remediation

Objective: Trace a vulnerable application to affected endpoints to patch guidance.

Applications inventory with at least one vulnerable application

Steps:

- Identify a vulnerable application with CVSS >= 7.0. Click on the application name.
- You should see a list of affected endpoints. Note the count and a few endpoint names/groups.
- Click the CVE ID link (if available). This takes you to the National Vulnerability Database or MITRE CVE registry. Read the remediation details. What is the patched version?
- Return to SentinelOne Applications. Look for a "Remediation Guidance" section or link. Document the recommended patch version and any caveats.

- Create a remediation ticket template: "Vulnerability: [CVE], Application: [Name], Affected Endpoints: [X], Patched Version: [Y], Deployment Risk: [Low/Medium/High], Estimated Downtime: [0/minimal/requires restart]."

Expected Outcome: Understanding the end-to-end workflow from vulnerability to remediation.

Reflection: Before patching, what would you check to understand the deployment risk?

Lab 7.3: Identify Shadow IT Using Applications

Objective: Use Applications to discover unapproved software and raise security awareness.

Applications Inventory tab; list of approved applications for your organization

Steps:

- Create a list of approved applications for your organization (e.g., approved browsers, office software, dev tools).
- In Applications, use the Inventory tab (not Vulnerabilities). Manually scroll or filter to find applications that are NOT on your approved list.
- Focus on developer tools, browsers, messaging apps, or gaming software. Document the unapproved applications and which endpoints have them.
- For one unapproved application (e.g., Brave browser or VS Code), click into it. See how many endpoints have it. Note any version fragmentation.
- Create an action: Will you add this to the approved list, request its removal, or block it via policy?
- Document your findings: "Unapproved application: [Name]. Found on [X] endpoints in [Groups]. Recommendation: [Allow/Block/Investigate]."

Expected Outcome: Demonstration of how Applications helps you see what is actually installed vs. what should be.

Reflection: How would you automate ongoing shadow IT detection?

What's Next

Chapter 8 covers the Activity log, SentinelOne's forensic record of every action taken in the console and on every endpoint. You will learn how to audit policy changes, investigate who accessed what, and build a timeline of actions that led up to an incident.

Mastering SentinelOne
Chapter 8, Draft for Review
by Kendrick Washington, Technology Interpreters, Inc.

Chapter 8

Activity Logs: Audit Trails and Operator Accountability

Learning Objectives

- Interpret every category in the Activity log and understand what user actions it tracks.
- Filter Activity logs by user, action type, date range, and severity to isolate specific events.
- Use Activity logs to answer forensic questions: "Who changed this policy?" "When was the agent decommissioned?" "What API tokens were created?"
- Export Activity logs for compliance audits and post-incident reviews.
- Recognize which actions do and do not appear in the Activity log, and why that matters for detecting insider misuse.
- Integrate Activity logs with SIEM and log aggregation platforms for centralized audit trails.

Chapter Opener

The Activity log is the forensic record of every meaningful action that happens inside the SentinelOne console. When a policy changes, when an agent is decommissioned, when someone logs in, when a manual scan runs, when a remote shell session opens, all of it is written to Activity. For change management and incident post-mortems, the Activity log is not optional. It is the answer to the question that keeps security teams up at night: who did what, when, and from where.

In this chapter you will learn to read the Activity log like an operator, not a user. You will understand which events matter, how to filter them down to actionable insights, and how to integrate Activity logs into your compliance workflow. You will also learn a critical lesson: there are actions that do not appear in the Activity log, and understanding that blind spot is key to detecting when a compromised admin account is being used to cover its tracks.

8.1 What the Activity Log Is and Why It Matters

The Activity log is the audit trail of the SentinelOne console. Every time a user performs an action in the UI, logging in, changing a policy, creating a group, decommissioning an agent, enabling a detection engine, deleting an exclusion, pushing a firmware update, or running a remote shell command, SentinelOne writes an entry to Activity with a timestamp, the actor, the action, the target, and the scope.

Activity is not optional for three reasons. First, compliance. If you are SOC 2 audited, ISO 27001 audited, or subject to regulatory requirements like HIPAA or PCI-DSS, your auditor will ask to see your admin audit log. The Activity log is what you hand them. Second, incident post-mortems. After a breach, the first question is: were there unauthorized changes to policies or detection engines that blindsided the platform? The Activity log answers that. Third, insider detection. If an admin account is compromised and an attacker uses it to cover their tracks, the Activity log will show policy changes, exclusions created, agents decommissioned, and other defensive actions that do not match the legitimate admin's typical behavior. Anomalous Activity entries are sometimes the earliest indicator of a compromised account.

Reading the Activity log well is a skill that separates operational security teams from reactive ones. You should develop the habit of reviewing Activity entries weekly, not just during incidents. That weekly scan can catch policy drift, unauthorized admin access, or suspicious patterns before they cause real damage.

8.2 The Activity Log Interface

The Activity section of the SentinelOne console presents a table of events. Each row is a single action, with columns for timestamp, user, action, category, affected resource, and status. By default, Activity is sorted newest-first, and the display shows the last seven days. You can immediately see the volume and type of activity in your console without filtering.

At the top of the Activity table are several controls. You can filter by user (dropdown showing all admin accounts that have logged in), by action type (dozens of categories covered below), by date and time range (with separate start and end time pickers), and by free-form search. In practice, you will almost always narrow by at least one dimension. If a customer calls asking about a policy change on Thursday, you filter to Thursday and search for the customer's Site name. If you want to know who created API tokens last month, you filter by action type "Enable API token generation" and set the date range. The filtering model is simple but powerful.

At the bottom right is an export button. Click it and SentinelOne generates a CSV file of all visible Activity entries (respecting whatever filters you have applied). This CSV is what you hand to auditors, include in incident reports, or ingest into your SIEM for long-term retention.

8.3 Understanding Activity Categories: Administration, Operations, Malware, and More

The Activity log is organized into top-level categories, each grouping related actions. Understanding these categories is key to knowing where to look for specific events.

Administration covers changes to users, roles, access control, API tokens, and account-level settings. Key events include:

2FA Configured (two-factor authentication turned on or off), Recovery Email Added (security recovery path set), Change Password (an admin changed their password), Forgot My Password (an admin used the password-reset flow), Enable API Token Generation (someone created an API key; this matters because API access does not log in via the UI), User Onboarding (an onboarding email was sent to a new admin), User Modified (an admin's permissions or role changed), and User Login (every console login is logged). Do not skip User Login entries; a login at 3 a.m. from a datacenter IP address when the admin is on vacation is a red flag.

Operations covers policy, group, tag, and detection-engine actions. Key events include:

Agent Decommission (an agent was hidden from the console), Agent Recommission (a decommissioned agent came back online), Agent Subscribed (an agent registered into the console), Policy Create and Policy Modify (policies were created or edited), Group Create and Group Rename (groups were created or renamed), Tag Create and Tag Removed (tags were added or removed from endpoints), and Detection Rules Created (if you are using custom detection rules). This category is where you track changes to detection engines and policies.

Threat Management covers threat verdict changes and notes. You can see when a threat was marked as a threat, marked as suspicious, marked as resolved, or when an analyst added notes. This is useful for post-incident review: you can see exactly when a threat was identified and by whom.

Exclusion covers all exclusion-related actions: New Browser Exclusion, New File Type Exclusion, New Exclusion (generic file or hash exclusion), Modified Exclusion, and Deleted Exclusion. This category is critical to understand. If you see an exclusion created for a malicious file hash, and that exclusion appears hours before the hash appeared in Incidents, you have a red flag. An inside actor creating exclusions to let malware run cleanly is exactly what the Activity log will catch.

Malware events show threat lifecycle: Cloud Marked as Threat, Mitigated, Not Mitigated, Preemptively Mitigated, and New Custom Rule Alert. These tell you the status of threats as the platform acts on them.

Block List covers hash-block and browser-block events: New Hash Block List, New Modified Browser Exclusion, Edit Browser Exclusion. These are similar to exclusions but represent intentional blocks rather than carve-outs.

8.4 Finding the Answer: Filtering by User, Action, and Date

In practice, you use the Activity log to answer operational questions. Here are the most common ones and how to find the answer.

Question: Who changed the monitoring policy on the Production group last Thursday?

- Filter to last Thursday (date and time pickers), filter by action "Policy Modify," then scan the results for "Production." The action column will show the policy name, the user column will show who made the change, and the timestamp will show when. Takes 30 seconds.

Question: What exclusions have been created in the last month?

- Filter by action "New Exclusion," set the date range to the last 30 days. You will see every exclusion added and by whom. Red flag: an exclusion created for a file hash that matches something currently in malware quarantine. Even more of a red flag: an exclusion created hours before that file showed up in Incidents.

Question: Has anyone created API tokens recently?

- Filter by action "Enable API Token Generation." API tokens are the way an attacker with compromised credentials can access your environment without using the web UI. Every token creation should be accounted for and correlated against your actual administrative needs.

Question: When was this agent decommissioned?

- Search for the agent's IP address or hostname in the free-form search box, filter by action "Agent Decommission." The result shows timestamp and actor. If an agent was decommissioned seconds before an incident alert fired, and the decommissioning came from an off-hours admin account, you have found your insider.

Question: What changes happened to Site X between 8 a.m. and 10 a.m. on March 15?

- Set the date range to exactly March 15, 8 a.m. to 10 a.m. Search for Site X in the free-form box. Apply any additional action filters if you are looking for policy changes, group changes, exclusions, etc. The results show every action that touched Site X during that window.

8.5 Exporting Activity for Compliance and Incident Review

At the bottom right of the Activity table is an Export button. Click it and SentinelOne generates a CSV containing all visible rows (respecting whatever filters you have applied).

The CSV includes: timestamp, user, action, category, description (the affected resource and what happened), source IP, and status. The CSV is plain text and can be opened in Excel, imported into your SIEM, or handed to an auditor.

Compliance use case: Your SOC 2 auditor asks for proof of admin activity for the past year. You export Activity with a date range filter covering the full year. You bundle the CSV with a cover letter explaining what the columns mean, which roles appear, and which actions are most significant. That is your auditor response.

Incident use case: After a breach, you export Activity for the 72 hours before the breach was detected. You look for policy changes, exclusions created, agents decommissioned, or API tokens generated. Any of those would indicate an attacker (or compromised admin) was laying the groundwork for the breach. The CSV is your forensic record.

Best practice: do not just export and leave. When you export, make a note of which time period you exported, which Site or Group scope the export covers, and why. If auditors ask questions six months later, you need to be able to say: "Here is what Activity looked like during the incident window," not "I exported something but I do not remember what was in it."

8.6 Activity Log Retention and Long-Term Integration

By default, SentinelOne retains Activity logs for a period that depends on your license tier. Enterprise licenses often get 90 days or more; smaller licenses may get 30 days. Check your SLA with your SentinelOne account team to know exactly what you have.

Ninety days is often not long enough for incident response, compliance audits, or regulatory retention requirements. The solution is to export Activity regularly and store the CSV files in a centralized location, or better yet, integrate SentinelOne with your SIEM.

SIEM integration: SentinelOne supports Syslog forwarding (covered in Chapter 11 under Notifications). You can configure SentinelOne to send all Activity entries to your Syslog endpoint in real time. Your SIEM (Splunk, Elastic, etc.) then ingests those logs, stores them indefinitely, and makes them searchable. This is the enterprise standard. With SIEM integration, you have a permanent forensic record of every administrative action.

If you do not have a SIEM, export Activity weekly to a file share or cloud storage with immutable backups. A weekly export that you retain for three to five years gives you the long-term record a compliance auditor will eventually ask for. Label each export with the date range and Site scope so you can find it quickly later.

8.7 Reading Activity Anomalies: The Insider Detection Pattern

The Activity log is your tool for detecting insider misuse. Legitimate admins have patterns. They log in at business hours from the same IP address range. They make policy changes that align with documented change requests. They do not create exclusions for random file hashes.

Suspicious patterns in Activity include:

Off-hours login: an admin logging in at 2 a.m. from an IP address outside your corporate range.

Exclusion before incident: an exclusion created for a file hash that appears in Incidents hours or minutes later.

Rapid policy changes: an admin making five major policy changes in three minutes when they normally make one change per week.

Agent decommission wave: an admin decommissioning ten agents in five minutes when nothing indicates a hardware refresh.

API token creation: an admin who has never created an API token suddenly creating one at midnight from a suspicious IP.

Password reset during incident: an admin account used in suspicious activity suddenly initiates a password reset, erasing the password history.

The Activity log does not tell you everything. See the next section for what is missing.

Best practice: set up an automated weekly Activity report. Export the last seven days of Activity, send it to your SOC lead or CISO, and have them scan for anomalies. Most weeks will be routine. But when an anomaly appears, you catch it while the account is fresh.

8.8 What the Activity Log Does Not Track: The Blind Spots

The Activity log is comprehensive but not complete. There are actions that do not leave Activity entries, and understanding that gap is critical.

The activity log captures administrative actions in the console: logins, policy changes, group modifications, agent decommissioning, and script execution. It does not capture agent-side activity. When an agent quarantines a file, kills a process, rolls back a change, or detects a threat, that action is logged in Incidents, not Activity. Activity is about who did what in the console, not what the platform did on endpoints.

Similarly, Activity captures when someone runs a Remote Shell command in the console, but it does not capture the commands that person types inside the shell session. If an attacker logs in to a remote shell and downloads tools, installs backdoors, or exfiltrates files, none of that appears in Activity. You have to look elsewhere (Deep Visibility, Incidents, or forensics on the endpoint itself) to see what happened inside the shell session.

API calls do not leave detailed Activity entries. You can see that an API token was created, but you do not see which API calls were made using that token. If an attacker creates an API token and uses it to query your environment, pull telemetry, or disable agents, those API calls are not logged in Activity. This is a significant gap and why API token creation is a red flag that warrants immediate investigation.

Finally, Activity does not capture when someone accesses a resource without modifying it. If an admin views a policy, reads a threat, or opens a report, that view is not logged. Activity only logs changes, not reads. An attacker with read-only access is invisible to Activity.

Implication: Activity is your audit log for administrative changes, but it is not a complete forensic record. For complete incident investigation, you need Activity plus Deep Visibility plus Incidents plus endpoint forensics. Activity is the first place to look; if it is clean, you go deeper.

Operator's Checklist: Post-Incident Activity Review

Within one hour of detecting an incident, export Activity logs covering the 72 hours before detection.

Filter for policy changes, exclusion creation, agent decommissioning, and API token generation.

Look for off-hours administrative activity or activity from IP addresses outside your corporate range.

Cross-reference Activity timestamps with Incidents timestamps: exclusions created just before threats appeared are a red flag.

If you find suspicious Activity entries, isolate the admin account immediately and begin a full account compromise investigation.

If Activity is suspiciously clean during a time window when you detected active compromise, suspect API access or attacker use of agent-side tools that bypass the console audit log.

8.9 Common Audit Questions the Activity Log Answers

Auditors and compliance teams repeatedly ask the same questions. Here is how Activity answers them.

"Show me every administrative change made to security policies in the past 90 days."

- Filter by action "Policy Create" and "Policy Modify," date range 90 days, and export. Done.

"Who has administrative access to our SentinelOne environment?"

- Go to Settings > Users and RBAC (Chapter 11). But you can also answer this in Activity: filter by action "User Login" and look at the unique set of users over the past 30 days. Anyone who logged in is an active admin.

"Have any exclusions been created that could have allowed malware to run?"

- Filter by action "New Exclusion," "New Hash Block List," "New Browser Exclusion." Export, then compare those hashes and file paths against your malware quarantine for the same period. Any matches require investigation.

"Were any agents decommissioned without authorization?"

- Filter by action "Agent Decommission," check the user and timestamp, and compare against your IT asset management system. If an agent was decommissioned but the asset was not decommissioned in your system, that is a gap.

"How do we know only authorized users access the console?"

- Activity logs every login. You export logins for the past 90 days, cross-reference the user list against your HR directory, and verify every login was from someone who should have had access. Missing a user from HR? Unauthorized access detected.

8.10 Integrating Activity with SIEM and Log Aggregation

Activity logs are most powerful when integrated into your centralized log platform. SentinelOne supports Syslog forwarding, which sends all Activity entries to a Syslog-compatible endpoint in real time. Your SIEM or log aggregator (Splunk, Elastic, Datadog, etc.) then ingests those logs, stores them long-term, and makes them searchable alongside other security logs.

To integrate Activity with SIEM, go to Settings > Notifications (Chapter 11) and configure a Syslog notification rule. You specify the Syslog endpoint (hostname and port), the message format, and which events to forward. Typically, you forward all Activity entries. SentinelOne then streams those logs to your SIEM in near-real-time.

Once Activity logs are in your SIEM, you gain search capability across all your logs at once. A query in Splunk might ask: "Show me all logins from user admin@company.com that happened outside business hours." Or: "Show me exclusion creation events that occurred within one hour before a malware incident." Or: "Find all API token creation events correlated with a spike in API calls to /api/threats." These queries are trivial in a SIEM and nearly impossible in the Activity UI alone.

SIEM integration also solves the retention problem. SentinelOne might only retain 90 days of Activity, but your SIEM retains three to five years. You have a permanent audit trail.

Best practice: if you have a SIEM, integrate it now. If you do not have a SIEM yet, export Activity weekly and store the CSV files in immutable cloud storage. When you eventually deploy a SIEM, you will be grateful to have the historical record.

Practical Example: Detecting Insider Misuse via Activity

Scenario: Friday afternoon, your SOC detects a lateral-movement incident affecting servers in the Production Site. You suspect insider involvement.

Step 1: Export Activity for the past 72 hours, filtering for the Production Site.

Step 2: Look for any exclusions or policy changes that would have hindered detection: exclusion created for a known malware family, detection engine disabled, quarantine disabled.

Step 3: Cross-reference Activity timestamps with Incidents: did any exclusion precede the alert?

Step 4: Check admin logins: did any admin log in outside business hours before the incident?

Step 5: Check for API token creation: did someone create an API token that could have been used to set up agent communication to a C2 server?

If you find policy changes, exclusions, off-hours logins, or token creation correlated with the incident timeline, you have a forensic record proving insider involvement.

Chapter Summary

The Activity log is the forensic record of every meaningful administrative action in the SentinelOne console. It shows who logged in, who changed policies, who created exclusions, who decommissioned agents, and who created API tokens. For change management, incident post-mortems, and compliance audits, the Activity log is not optional; it is your source of truth on administrative actions.

Activity is organized into categories: Administration (logins, users, API tokens), Operations (policies, groups, tags), Threat Management (threat verdicts and notes), Exclusion, Malware, and Block List. Each category groups related events. You work through Activity by filtering on user, action type, date range, and free-form search. Export function generates a CSV for auditors, incident reports, or SIEM ingestion. The Activity log captures console administrative actions but does not capture agent-side activity, detailed API call history, or view-only access. Audit trails are retained for a license-dependent period (often 90 days), so long-term retention requires SIEM integration or regular exports to cold storage. Suspicious Activity patterns like off-hours logins, exclusions preceding incidents, or API token creation are early indicators of insider misuse. Regular review of Activity logs, particularly weekly scans for anomalies, is one of the highest-value defensive practices in any SentinelOne deployment.

Key Takeaways

- The Activity log is your administrative audit trail. Every login, policy change, exclusion creation, and agent action is logged with timestamp, actor, and description.
- Filter Activity by user, action type, date range, and free-form search to answer operational questions: "Who changed this policy?" "When was that agent decommissioned?" "What exclusions were created this month?"
- Export Activity as CSV for compliance audits, incident reviews, and SIEM ingestion.
- Suspicious Activity patterns include off-hours logins, exclusions created just before malware alerts, rapid policy changes, and API token creation from unexpected users.
- Activity captures console actions but not agent-side activity, detailed API call logs, or read-only access. For complete incident investigation, combine Activity with Deep Visibility, Incidents, and endpoint forensics.
- Integrate Activity with your SIEM (via Syslog forwarding) or export weekly to ensure long-term retention beyond SentinelOne's native retention window.
- Make Activity log review a weekly habit, not just an incident-response tool. Early detection of anomalous admin activity often prevents insider misuse from escalating.

Hands-On Exercise

Before you continue to Chapter 9, do the following in your SentinelOne tenant.

- Open Activity and apply a date filter to the past 30 days. Without any additional filters, scan the raw activity stream and write down three entries whose action type you do not yet understand. Research those action types in this chapter and note what they indicate.
- Filter Activity by your own user account and look at your login history. Note the IP addresses and times. Do any entries look anomalous? What would a compromised account look like?

- Filter Activity by action type "Policy Modify" for the past 90 days. Identify at least one policy change, note the user and timestamp, and verify that change is documented in your change management system.
- If your organization has a SIEM, work with your SIEM administrator to configure Syslog forwarding of Activity logs. If not, export a 30-day Activity log and store it in a secure location with a label indicating date range and scope.
- Simulate a post-incident review: create a hypothetical breach scenario (e.g., "malware detected on Production servers at 3 p.m. Friday"), export Activity for the 72 hours prior, and identify which Activity entries would raise red flags.

Review Questions

- 1. You need to answer: "Who changed the Monitoring group policy on March 15?" Using Activity logs, what filter would you apply and what would you record?
- 2. True or False: All administrative actions in the SentinelOne console are captured in Activity logs. If False, name an action that might NOT be logged.
- 3. An exclusion for file hash "abc123xyz" appears in Activity, created on March 1 at 2 AM. Two hours later, the same hash appears in Incidents as a Threat. What should you suspect?
- 4. You are preparing for a SOC 2 audit and must provide admin activity logs for the past 12 months. SentinelOne only retains 90 days in the console. What should you have been doing all along to meet audit requirements?
- 5. A junior analyst asks: "How do I know if this Activity entry is suspicious?" What patterns or anomalies would you teach them to look for?

Answer Key: Review Questions

1. Filter by Action = "Policy Modify" and Date = "March 15". In the results, search for the Monitoring group name. The User column shows who made the change, and the Timestamp shows when.

2. False. Deep Visibility queries and some automated background actions might not be logged. More importantly: attempted login failures may or may not be logged depending on configuration, and some API calls might not show up if logging was disabled.

3. An insider may have created the exclusion to allow malware to run. This is a major red flag: an exclusion created hours before the hash appeared in Incidents suggests someone knew the attack was coming. Escalate immediately.

4. You should have exported Activity weekly and stored the CSV files in a secure, immutable location (S3 with versioning, network drive with long-term retention, or sent to your SIEM for permanent storage). Without this, you cannot meet audit requirements beyond 90 days.

5. Teach them to look for: off-hours logins from unusual IPs, rapid policy changes (5+ in 5 minutes), exclusions created for file hashes that later appear as threats, agent decommissioning waves, and API token creation without corresponding documentation.

Discussion Questions

- 1. An incident response reveals that a compromised admin account was used to create exclusions and disable detection engines before a ransomware attack. How would you use Activity logs to reconstruct the attack timeline, and what would you recommend to prevent similar attacks?
- 2. Design a process for your team to review Activity logs weekly without adding administrative burden. What would you look for, and how would you escalate suspicious patterns?
- 3. If you archive Activity logs to a SIEM, how would you ensure the data is secure, immutable, and available for audit review years later?

Hands-On Lab Exercises

Lab 8.1: Filter and Answer Operational Questions Using Activity Logs

Objective: Use Activity filtering to answer common operational questions.

Access to Activity logs with at least 7 days of history

Steps:

- Question 1: "What policies were modified in the last 7 days, and by whom?" Filter Activity by Action = "Policy Modify" and Date Range = "Last 7 days." Record the policy name, actor, and timestamp for each result.
- Question 2: "Have any agents been decommissioned recently?" Filter by Action = "Agent Decommission" and Date Range = "Last 30 days." If results exist, record which endpoints and by whom.
- Question 3: "Were any exclusions created?" Filter by Action = "New Exclusion." If results exist, record what was excluded and by whom. (Red flag if an exclusion was created for a hash that later appeared as a threat.)
- Question 4: "Who logged in during off-hours (e.g., after 10 PM or before 6 AM)?" Filter by Action = "User Login." Manually scan timestamps for off-hours entries. Record any anomalies.
- Document each finding in a table: Timestamp | Action | Actor | Target | Note.

Expected Outcome: Ability to frame operational questions and extract answers from Activity logs.

Reflection: If you found 10 policy changes but no documented change requests, what would you do?

Lab 8.2: Investigate a Suspicious Activity Pattern

Objective: Detect and investigate anomalous Activity entries that might indicate insider misuse or compromise.

Access to Activity logs; understanding of normal vs. suspicious patterns

Steps:

- In Activity, create a filter for a specific user (any admin account). Scan their activity over the last 30 days. Identify: their typical login times, typical actions, and typical number of changes per week.
- Now, hypothetically imagine that same user made five policy changes in 2 minutes, logged in at 3 AM from an unfamiliar IP, and created three exclusions. How would you know this is anomalous? (Compare to step 1.)
- Document: "This account's normal pattern is [description]. An anomaly would be [pattern]. If detected, I would [escalation action]."

- Optional: If you find a real anomaly in your Activity logs, escalate it to your manager with documented evidence.

Expected Outcome: Ability to spot behavior that deviates from norms and escalate appropriately.

Reflection: What additional data (IP logs, VPN logs, etc.) would help you confirm a compromised account?

Lab 8.3: Export and Retain Activity Logs

Objective: Practice exporting Activity logs and planning long-term retention.

Access to Activity logs; export functionality

Steps:

- In Activity, filter to a specific date range (e.g., last 30 days).
- Click the Export button. Download the CSV file.
- Open the CSV in Excel or a text editor. Verify the columns: Timestamp, User, Action, Category, Description, Source IP, Status.
- Create a folder structure for archiving: /Archives/Activity-Logs/2026/Q1/ and save the CSV there with a descriptive name: "Activity-Q1-2026-01-01-to-03-31.csv".
- Create a metadata file in the same folder listing: Date Range, Sites Covered, Number of Entries, Export Date, Exported By.
- If your environment has a SIEM, document the export path and retention policy. (E.g., "All Activity logs are exported monthly to [SIEM name] and retained for 7 years.")

Expected Outcome: A repeatable export and retention process for audit compliance.

Reflection: How would you ensure these archived logs remain readable and searchable 5 years from now?

What’s Next

Chapter 9 covers Reports: how to build scheduled reports that aggregate metrics, apply filters, and deliver to stakeholders on cadence. Activity logs are raw forensic data; Reports are curated summaries of that data designed for executives, customers, and auditors.

Mastering SentinelOne

Sample Expanded Chapter 9, Draft for Review
by Kendrick Washington, Technology Interpreters, Inc.

Chapter 9

Reports: Communicating Security Posture Upward

Learning Objectives

- Work through the five report types available in SentinelOne: Executive Insights, Executive Insights by Group, Mitigation and Response Insights, Application Insights, and Threat Insights.
- Schedule reports on appropriate cadence, daily, weekly, or monthly, and understand when reporting frequency becomes noise instead of signal.
- Customize reports for different audiences: board-level executives, the CISO, the SOC team, and external auditors.
- Build a metrics narrative that tells a story about your security posture rather than simply aggregating raw numbers.
- Recognize vanity metrics that look good in a presentation but hide real risk, and learn to avoid them.
- Develop strategies for communicating "bad news" reports upward when detections spike or adversaries evade your controls.

Chapter Opener

Reports are where security work becomes politics. You can identify a critical vulnerability, you can contain an active threat, you can reduce your attack surface by 40 percent, but if the report that documents it never makes it to the right person at the right time in the right format, none of that work matters. Reports are not just data visualization. They are stakeholder management, narrative control, and risk communication all rolled into one.

The challenge is that your audience is not homogeneous. The board wants to know whether security is a material risk to the business. The CISO wants to know whether the program is trending in the right direction. The SOC team wants to know what happened yesterday so they can plan their hunt for today. The external auditor wants documentation that controls are in place and operating. SentinelOne's reporting module is built to accommodate all of these audiences at once, but only if you understand what goes into each report, when to use it, and how to read the metrics so they tell the truth instead of the story you wish were true.

This chapter walks the five core report types, the scheduling strategies that keep stakeholders informed without spamming them, and the political nuance of reporting bad news when your organization finds out it is less secure than it thought.

9.1 The Five Core Report Types

SentinelOne ships with five main report templates. Each serves a different purpose, surfaces different metrics, and appeals to a different audience. Understanding the distinction is critical because a report that works for your executive sponsor will bore or confuse your SOC team, and a report built for an auditor will tell your board nothing about whether they should feel comfortable.

Executive Insights is the first. This report is designed for the C-suite and the board. It surfaces three categories of information: threats mitigated in the reporting period, the users and devices most at risk, and basic deployment statistics, how many agents you have, how many are new, how many were removed, and what the trend looks like. The idea is that a non-technical executive can glance at this report and understand at a high level whether the environment is getting healthier or sicker. Mitigated threats show action. New deployments show growth. At-risk users show where the work needs to focus. Executive Insights deliberately hides technical depth. There are no detection engine configurations. There are no incident statuses or verdict classifications. Those belong in other reports.

Executive Insights by Group is the second variant. It is the same report filtered to a single customer, business unit, or organizational group. If you are an MSSP with twenty customers, you generate Executive Insights for each one and deliver it to their security contacts or CISOs. If you are an enterprise security team managing departments separately, you generate one for Sales, one for Engineering, one for Finance, and deliver each to the respective business leaders. The report structure is identical to the top-level Executive Insights, but scoped down. If a group has no threats detected, the report will still be clean and professional, it simply shows green metrics instead of activity.

Mitigation and Response Insights is the third. This report is for the SOC or the incident response team. It breaks down actions taken in the reporting period: automatic mitigations (where the agent's policy was set to kill, quarantine, remediate, or roll back automatically), manual mitigations (where an analyst clicked a button in the console to take action), and threats that were detected but not mitigated (either because the policy was set to monitor-only, or because the analyst decided it was a false positive and marked it as benign). It also shows you periodic trends, are you trending up or down in automatic vs. manual actions? Are success rates improving or degrading? This is the report that tells you whether your policies are actually working and whether your team's remediation speed is keeping pace.

Application Insights is the fourth. This report turns the SentinelOne agent into a lightweight asset and vulnerability scanner. It counts total unique applications across your environment, breaks them down by operating system, identifies newly installed software, and flags applications that lack digital signatures from publishers. If you pair this with periodic application-base scans, Application Insights gives you a surprisingly complete picture of what is actually running in your environment without deploying a separate vulnerability scanner. It is particularly useful for organizations trying to understand software compliance or catch rogue applications that snuck in without approval.

Threat Insights is the fifth. This is the most technical report and the one that appeals most to security teams doing forensics or hunting. It surfaces individual threats detected in the reporting period, breaks them down by verdict (malicious, suspicious, undefined, false positive), incident status (resolved, unresolved, in progress), and the detection engines or policies that initiated them. It also shows the indicators of compromise associated with each threat and the timeline of activity. For a security team that needs to do retroactive analysis or explain to an external auditor what you detected and when, Threat Insights is the report you live in.

A sixth report type, Vigilance Verdict, exists if your organization has purchased SentinelOne's managed detection and response (MDR) service. Vigilance is a 24/7/365 SOC run by SentinelOne staff who monitor your environment in parallel with your internal team. The Vigilance Verdict report shows what the MDR team detected, what actions they took, their response times against published SLAs, and their recommendations. If you have Vigilance, this report is how you measure the value of that contract.

9.2 Scheduling Cadence: Daily, Weekly, Monthly

Once you have chosen a report type, the next decision is frequency. When should it run? How often should your stakeholders see it?

The temptation is to schedule everything daily. You think, 'More data is better. If we have new information every day, we can respond faster.' This is wrong. Daily reporting at scale becomes spam. Your inbox fills up. Your executives stop reading them. Your auditors miss the signal in the noise. The operational rule is simple: report only frequently enough that your audience will act on it.

Daily reports make sense only in two scenarios. First, if you are actively investigating an incident and you have created a custom report to track remediation progress hour by hour. Second, if your organization has such high volume that daily summary aggregation is genuinely useful, essentially a SOC daily standup report. For most organizations, neither applies.

Weekly reporting is the sweet spot for most teams. A weekly Executive Insights report gives your leadership team visibility into the week's activity without creating email fatigue. It arrives every Monday morning, your CISO has read it by 10am, and it informs the week's priorities. A weekly Mitigation and Response Insights report gives your SOC team a retroactive view of what the automated policies handled versus what required manual intervention. You can adjust policies on Friday based on Wednesday's data. Weekly is frequent enough to catch deterioration before it becomes critical, but infrequent enough that each report has signal.

Monthly reporting works for auditor-facing reports and for situations where you are managing many customers and generating a report for each one. A monthly Threat Insights report sent to your external auditors is professional, shows comprehensive data over a meaningful period, and gives them everything they need to verify that controls are operating. A monthly Application Insights report shows significant change over the period, new software deployments, vulnerabilities patched, compliance improvements. Monthly is also the right cadence if you are in a low-threat environment where weekly noise outweighs useful information.

The political rule underneath all of this: never let frequency outrun insight. If your stakeholder is deleting reports without reading them, you are reporting too often. If your stakeholder is asking 'did we miss something last week,' you are not reporting often enough. Hit the middle ground and then let the conversation with your stakeholder guide adjustments.

9.3 Audience-Appropriate Customization

A security program that serves only one customer or one department is rare. Most security teams answer to multiple stakeholders who all need to see different things. The SentinelOne reporting module is built with this in mind: you create a single report template, then generate variants filtered by Site or Group, and deliver each to its intended recipient.

An MSSP with twenty customers generates twenty variants of the same Executive Insights report. Each one is scoped to a single customer's Site. Each one includes only that customer's metrics. Each one is delivered to that customer's CISO or security contact. From the template you created once, you generate twenty different reports automatically. This is also how you manage internal business units. If you run security for a global company with Engineering in one region and Finance in another, you generate Executive Insights for each Site or Group, and each department head gets visibility into their own security posture without seeing anyone else's.

The key is the audience-appropriate filter. Ask yourself: 'Who is reading this? What decisions do they need to make? What information helps them make those decisions?' Your CFO does not care how many potentially unwanted applications were found. She cares whether security incidents put revenue at risk. Your VP of Engineering cares about the developer-targeted threats on that one team's machines. Your board wants trend arrows, is the environment trending toward less security or more security?

When you set up the Group-based variant, you also have the option to customize what metrics appear. You can toggle individual threat categories on or off, adjust date ranges, include or exclude specific policies or detection engines. The default template might show everything; your variant for the board might show only the three metrics that matter to them. This is not lying. This is good communication design. Your CFO's report should not have twenty tables if five tell the story.

9.4 Executive Reports vs. Analyst Reports

The Executive Insights report is intentionally shallow. It shows trends and aggregate numbers. It does not show verdict classifications or incident statuses. It shows 'threats mitigated' as a single green number.

The Threat Insights report is intentionally deep. It shows every detection, the verdict of each one (true positive, false positive, suspicious, undefined), the incident status (resolved, unresolved, in progress), and the detection engine or policy that initiated it. It shows you the raw evidence.

The operational mistake teams make is sending an Executive Insights report to the SOC and then wondering why analysts feel they are not trusted with information. Or sending a Threat Insights report to the board and watching them glaze over because the first page is seventy lines of malware verdicts. Wrong report for the wrong audience wastes everyone's time.

The political version of this mistake is sending a shallow report to leadership knowing it omits bad news. If your threat count spiked but you report only the mitigated count without context, leadership will eventually realize you were hiding information. That damages trust faster than just reporting the spike honestly.

The rule is straightforward: pair report type to audience. Executive Insights goes to non-technical stakeholders and leadership. Threat Insights goes to your SOC team, your incident response team, and your forensics team. Mitigation and Response Insights goes to the team running the security program because they need to understand whether the program is working. A report is not better because it has more data. It is better because it has the right data for the person reading it.

9.5 Building a Metrics Narrative

Raw numbers are not a story. A metrics narrative is. Consider two versions of a security report. Version one says: 'Mitigated threats: 127. New agents: 4. At-risk users: 3.' Version two says: 'We identified and contained 127 threats this month, bringing our cumulative mitigation rate to 99.2 percent over the past three months. We expanded deployment by four agents to cover two previously unmonitored subnets. Three users required security awareness training after we detected patterns consistent with phishing susceptibility.'

The difference is narrative. The second version puts each metric into a context that explains why it matters and what your organization should do about it. Mitigated threats is not impressive on its own, you need to show that the number is growing or that the rate is improving. New agents matter only if you explain why they matter: you are closing coverage gaps, or you are responding to growth, or you are replacing deprecated infrastructure. At-risk users is only actionable if you connect it to a remediation step: training, re-imaging, policy change.

This is where the political part enters. Every metric can be told two ways. You had three new threats from ransomware in the reporting period. You can tell it as: 'Ransomware attempts increased.' Or you can tell it as: 'We detected three ransomware attempts, investigated all of them, and found that only one succeeded in reaching a user. Policy was adjusted to block the delivery vector.' Both are true. One makes it sound like things are getting worse. One makes it sound like your defenses are working. The ethical obligation is to pick the second telling because it is the fuller truth.

Build your narrative around three elements. First, detection capability: 'Our engines are seeing X percent more activity than last quarter because we added rules and turned up detection sensitivity.' Second, remediation success: 'Of the threats we detected, Y percent were automatically contained without analyst intervention.' Third, trend: 'This is good because we are moving toward more proactive detection with less manual work. This is concerning because it means we are chasing our tails.' Always include the 'so what' for each metric. Do not report a number without explaining why it matters.

The most important rule: never lead with raw incident volume. If you had 10,000 detections last month and you say 'We had 10,000 detections,' your board thinks things are terrible. If you say 'We had 10,000 detections, of which 9,987 were automatically contained by policy and 13 required analyst review,' the board understands that volume is not the problem, it is being handled. Context is everything.

9.6 Avoiding Vanity Metrics

A vanity metric is a number that looks good in a presentation but does not tell you anything true about whether your security posture is actually better. The graveyard of security programs is full of organizations that congratulated themselves on metrics that looked impressive but did nothing to reduce risk.

Total agent count is a vanity metric if you are not paired it with coverage. You can have 10,000 agents installed and still have an unmanaged Linux server running in production because Linux was not part of your deployment plan. Reporting 'we have 10,000 agents' means nothing. Reporting 'we have agent coverage on 98 percent of devices, with known gaps on development servers that are isolated from production' is true security communication.

Threat count is a vanity metric if you do not distinguish between signal and noise. If you enable every detection engine at maximum sensitivity, you will detect thousands of potentially unwanted applications that users intentionally installed. The user installed Slack. Slack does something that matches your 'suspicious behavior' rule. Now you have a detection you cannot act on without annoying your users. You can report a huge detection count, but it is vanity. Report the mitigated-threat count instead, the ones you actually did something about.

Mean-time-to-respond (MTTR) is a vanity metric if your baseline is artificially low. If you measure MTTR as 'average time from detection to analyst acknowledgment,' that is meaningful. If you measure it as 'time from threat creation to any event in the incident timeline,' you can make MTTR look like 3 minutes because the system auto-replied to the detection in 3 minutes. Measure the metric that reflects actual work.

Percent threats mitigated can be a vanity metric if you cherry-pick the denominator. If you count only threats that your policies were configured to handle automatically, of course your success rate is 99 percent. If you count all threats including the ones your policy was set to monitor-only, the percentage drops because you never tried to mitigate them. Be precise about what you are measuring. Say: 'Of threats that our policies were configured to remediate, 98 percent were successfully contained.' Not: '98 percent of all threats were mitigated' if that is not true.

The test for vanity is simple: if a metric makes you look good but does not help you make a decision about security posture, it is vanity. Do not include it. A report that is honest and boring will serve you better over time than a report that is impressive but misleading.

9.7 Handling Bad News Reports

Every organization eventually has a month when threat counts spike. An adversary finds a new way in. A malware variant spreads faster than expected. A policy misconfiguration inadvertently disabled detection on a critical asset. Now you have to report bad news upward. This is where tone and context matter more than the numbers themselves.

The first rule of bad news reporting is: report it early and report it yourself. Do not let bad news reach leadership from someone else first. The moment you detect a significant spike or a major evasion event, you notify your leadership immediately, not in a monthly report, not in next week's standup, but in a separate communication that day. You own the narrative. You provide context. You present next steps.

The bad-news report should follow a specific structure. First, what happened. Be factual and precise: 'We detected 387 new threats in the past 24 hours, compared to an average of 47 over the previous two weeks.' Second, what you think happened. Did a malware campaign target your industry? Did you change a policy that increased detection volume? Did you enable a new detection engine? Third, what actions you have already taken. Have you isolated affected systems? Have you reviewed the verdicts? Have you adjusted policies? Fourth, what you are going to do next. What is the investigation plan? When will you have preliminary findings? When will you report again?

This structure is critical because it tells leadership that you are in control and that this is not chaos, it is a situation being managed. The spike is bad, but the fact that you immediately noticed it, investigated it, and developed a response plan is good. Leadership trusts you because you act like someone who has thought about this before.

The other part of bad-news reporting is managing expectations. If you discover a malware infection in a critical server, do not try to wait until the monthly report. Raise the alert immediately, escalate to incident response, and then use the report cadence to provide updates on remediation progress. But for metrics that are simply trending wrong, detection volume up, incident resolution time up, at-risk user count up, you can handle these in the regular report cycle if you contextualize them correctly.

The tone matters. Do not apologize for detections. Detections are literally the job of the security program. What you should be concerned about is undetected compromise. A report that says 'we had a bad month' is not as good as a report that says 'we detected an attempted compromise, contained it, and are using it to strengthen our controls.' The difference is that the second one is actually true, and it is also less likely to cause a panic.

9.8 Report Delivery and Distribution

SentinelOne can deliver reports in three ways. First, email. You configure a mailing list and SentinelOne generates and sends the report on schedule. Second, you can generate reports ad-hoc through the console and download them as PDF. Third, if you have an MSSP with a customer portal or if you want to integrate reports into an internal dashboard, you can use the SentinelOne API to pull report data and render it in your own interface.

Email delivery is the most common. You set up a scheduled report, specify the recipients, choose the interval (daily, weekly, monthly, first of month, every two weeks, custom), and SentinelOne handles the rest. When the schedule fires, the system generates the report, renders it as a PDF, and sends it to your list. One operational consideration: if you are an MSSP generating reports for many customers, do not pile all of them into a single scheduled job. Set up individual report schedules for each customer so each gets their own report at the right time. If you schedule twenty customer reports to all fire at midnight, you are going to create a performance spike on your SentinelOne instance.

If you need to customize a report on the fly, maybe you want to regenerate the previous month's report with different filters, or maybe an auditor asked for a specific date range, you can open the Reports section, select a template, adjust the parameters, and click 'Generate' to download it immediately as PDF. This is also how you validate that a scheduled report is going to look right before you send it to the whole organization. Generate one manually first. Make sure it contains what you think it contains. Then schedule it.

The API option is for power users. If you have a SIEM that ingests SentinelOne data, or if you have a dashboard platform like Splunk or Tableau, you can call the SentinelOne API to pull report data and visualize it in your own environment. This lets you build custom dashboards or mash up SentinelOne data with other security tools. It is also how you automate report distribution to a customer portal. You call the API daily, pull the latest metrics, update your portal's security-posture page, and customers log in to see their own trends. This is more work upfront but it gives you complete control over presentation and audience.

A final note on distribution: think about your email footprint. If you are sending daily reports to fifty people, that is 18,250 emails a year from your security tool. Some organizations have email retention policies that make this expensive. Some people manage their inboxes zealously and will unsubscribe. Start with weekly or monthly, measure whether stakeholders are actually reading the reports, and adjust frequency based on engagement. Reports that no one reads are not reporting, they are theater.

9.9 Archiving for Compliance

Once you start generating reports, you have a compliance obligation: you need to keep them. Regulators, auditors, and internal controls all require documentation that your security controls operated as designed during a given period. Reports are that documentation.

At minimum, you should retain monthly reports for the duration of your data-retention policy. If your organization maintains seven years of records for audit purposes, keep seven years of monthly reports. If you keep two years, keep two years of reports. Most organizations settle somewhere between two and five years depending on their regulatory environment.

The best practice is to set up an automatic archival process. When your scheduled reports generate, have them automatically copied to a dedicated folder or drive that is read-only and separately backed up. Some teams use Google Drive, some use SharePoint, some use an internal NAS. The key requirement is that the archive be immutable and durable. You cannot change a report once it is archived. Auditors will ask for the report that was generated on a specific date, and they want to see exactly what was sent, not a edited version created retroactively.

If you are generating reports for external customers, they also have archival obligations. Many service-level agreements require that you retain the customer's report for at least the life of the contract plus some period afterward (typically one to three years). Check your contracts and make sure your archival process supports customer retention periods independent of your own internal retention.

One technical note: if you are using the PDF download feature, the filename and metadata embedded in the PDF matter. SentinelOne automatically dates the PDF, but you should also keep a consistent naming convention so files are sortable and searchable. A file named 'Executive_Insights_2024_Q2_Acme_Corp.pdf' is infinitely easier to find three years later than 'Report (1).pdf.'

Tip: The Politics of Reporting Upward

Reports are not just documents. They are the primary interface between security and leadership. The message is the metric, and the metric you choose to highlight shapes the conversation your organization has about risk.

If you report only what is working, you will eventually be blindsided when something breaks and leadership finds out that you have been painting an incomplete picture.

If you report only what is broken, leadership will stop reading because everything looks catastrophic.

The path forward is to report the truth: what is working, what is not, what is being done about it, and what the trend is. Show good news as wins. Show bad news as problems being managed. Build credibility through honesty and through demonstrating that you have thought about the issues.

Your first report should not be perfect. Your first report should be honest. Iterate from there.

Chapter Summary

SentinelOne's reporting module is built to serve multiple audiences at once. The five core report types, Executive Insights, Executive Insights by Group, Mitigation and Response Insights, Application Insights, and Threat Insights, each surface different metrics and appeal to different stakeholders. Executive reports are shallow and trend-focused. Analyst reports are deep and detail-focused. The operational mistake is sending the wrong report to the wrong audience. Pair report type to recipient role: executives get Executive Insights, SOC teams get Threat Insights, program leads get Mitigation and Response Insights. Scheduling cadence should match the audience's ability to act. Daily reports work only for active incident response. Weekly reports are the standard for most operational teams. Monthly reports work for auditor-facing deliverables and low-threat environments. Avoid vanity metrics, numbers that look good but do not reflect actual security posture. Build a metrics narrative that puts each number into context: not just 'we detected X,' but 'we detected X, contained it, and here is what we learned.' When bad news comes, report it early, contextualize it, and show that it is being managed. Archive all reports for compliance, with immutable storage and clear naming conventions. Reports are how leadership understands security. Make them honest and make them count.

The organizations that do this well are not the ones with the fanciest dashboards. They are the ones where leadership trusts the security team because they have been honest about what is working and what is not, month after month. That trust is the most valuable output of your reporting.

Key Takeaways

- Executive Insights is for non-technical stakeholders. It shows trends, aggregate metrics, and deployment statistics. Threat Insights is for technical teams. It shows individual detections, verdicts, and indicators of compromise.
- Report only as frequently as your audience will act on the information. Weekly is the standard. Daily becomes spam. Monthly works for auditor-facing reports.
- Customize reports by audience. The same template can be filtered to different Sites, Groups, or customer profiles. Each audience should see only the metrics they need.
- Build a narrative, not just a list of numbers. Connect each metric to a decision or a trend. Explain what the number means and what you are going to do about it.
- Avoid vanity metrics. A metric is only valuable if it helps you understand security posture or guides a decision. If it just looks good, remove it.
- Bad news should be reported immediately in a separate communication, not hidden in a weekly report. Own the narrative. Provide context. Present the response plan.
- Archive all reports immutably for compliance. Most organizations need to retain reports for at least two to five years depending on regulations.

Hands-On Exercise

Before you continue to Chapter 10, do the following in your SentinelOne tenant.

- Generate an Executive Insights report for your entire Account (or your first Site if your Account is very large). Download it as PDF. Review the metrics and note which ones you think are most important for your leadership team to see.

- Generate a Threat Insights report for the same period. Compare it to the Executive Insights report. Notice how much detail is hidden in the executive version. Identify one metric from the Threat Insights report that you would add to the Executive Insights if you could customize it.
- Create a recurring scheduled report. Choose Executive Insights, set the frequency to weekly, and configure it to be delivered to your own email address. When you receive the first one, read it and imagine you are explaining the metrics to your leadership team. What context would you add? What would you say about the trend?

Review Questions

- 1. What is the difference between a Report Template and a Report Schedule?
- 2. You create a PDF report showing threats by detection engine over 30 days. The CISO receives it and says, "This doesn't match what I see in the Dashboard." What are three reasons the numbers might differ?
- 3. True or False: A Report can include data from multiple Sites simultaneously. Explain when this is useful and when it is problematic.
- 4. You want to send a monthly vulnerability remediation report to each customer showing only their own data. How would you accomplish this without creating 50 separate report schedules?
- 5. What is a Report Retention policy, and why should you set one?

Answer Key: Review Questions

1. A Template is a blueprint (which widgets, metrics, filters, layout). A Schedule is the recurring or one-time delivery (when to generate, to whom, in what format).

2. (1) Different Scope: Dashboard might be showing one Site while Report shows Account-wide. (2) Different Time Window: Dashboard might default to 7 days while Report might show 30. (3) Data Refresh Timing: Report might be generated at midnight while Dashboard refreshes in real time.

3. True, but with nuance. In an MSSP, a Report with Multi-Site scope shows aggregate data (useful for executive summary). But if you need customer-specific reports, create separate reports scoped to each Site. Mixing customer data in one report is a compliance risk.

4. Create a Template that filters by a variable or parameter (e.g., "Current Site"). Then create a Scheduled Report for each Site, applying the Template with that Site's filter. Some platforms allow a single schedule with parameterization; others require one schedule per Site.

5. A retention policy specifies how long reports are stored. If you don't set one, old reports accumulate and consume storage. Typical retention: 3 years for compliance, 7 years for audit holds.

Discussion Questions

- 1. Your CISO wants a single consolidated report showing all threats, all vulnerabilities, and all policy changes across all customers for executive review. As an MSSP, how would you explain why a single consolidated report is problematic, and what would you recommend instead?
- 2. Describe how you would design a report structure for three different audiences: (a) SOC daily operational review, (b) customer CISO monthly summary, (c) compliance auditor annual review. What metrics would each care about?
- 3. If a customer disputes a threat count reported in last month's report, how would you validate the number and investigate discrepancies?

Hands-On Lab Exercises

Lab 9.1: Create a Custom Report Template

Objective: Design and build a report template matching your team's operational needs.

Access to Reports; ability to add widgets, filters, and configure layout

Steps:

- Decide on your report's purpose (e.g., "Monthly Operational Summary for SOC Team" or "Quarterly Customer Threat Report").
- Select 4-5 widgets that answer key questions: total threats, threats by engine, endpoint health, remediation rate, rogue device count.
- Configure filters: Scope (Site or Group), Time Window (30 days), Threat Status (e.g., only unresolved threats if operational, only resolved if historical).
- Arrange widgets in a logical flow: summary metrics first, then details, then trend.
- Add a title, description, and footer with your team name and generation timestamp.
- Test the report: generate it once and review for clarity. Do the metrics answer your questions? Are any missing?
- Save the Template. Document its purpose and intended audience.

Expected Outcome: One working report template suitable for recurring distribution.

Reflection: Would this report be useful for your CISO, or does it need different metrics?

Lab 9.2: Schedule a Report and Monitor Delivery

Objective: Set up automated recurring report delivery.

Access to Report Scheduling; a completed report template

Steps:

- Select your template (from Lab 9.1 or use a built-in one).
- Configure Schedule: Daily, Weekly (e.g., every Monday at 8 AM), or Monthly (e.g., first day of the month).
- Select Recipients: email addresses of your team, CISO, or customer. Verify email addresses are correct.
- Choose format: PDF (most common), HTML, or native format if available.
- Set a retention policy: reports older than 90 days are automatically deleted.
- Save and activate the schedule.

- If possible, trigger a manual run to test. Verify the email arrives with the correct data.
- Document: "Report [Name] is scheduled [frequency] to [recipients]. Retention: [days]."

Expected Outcome: An operational scheduled report that delivers automatically.

Reflection: If a report fails to send, how would you troubleshoot?

Lab 9.3: Investigate a Report Discrepancy

Objective: Practice validating report numbers against live console data.

Access to a report and the SentinelOne console

Steps:

- Generate or obtain a recent report. Note a specific metric (e.g., "Threats Detected: 47").
- Go to the SentinelOne console and work through to the same view (Incidents, Applications, etc.). Apply the same filters the report used.
- Compare the number from the report to the live number. Do they match?
- If they differ, investigate: (a) Time window (is the report showing 30 days while the console shows 7?), (b) Scope (is the report showing one Site while the console shows multiple?), (c) Filters (is the report filtered by status or severity?), (d) Data lag (was the report generated before the latest data arrived?).
- Document your findings: "Report showed X, console shows Y. Discrepancy caused by [reason]. Resolution: [action]."

Expected Outcome: Confidence validating reports and explaining discrepancies to customers.

Reflection: If a customer claims the report is wrong, how would you respond?

What's Next

Chapter 10 covers Automation: using SentinelOne's RemoteOps surface to run PowerShell and shell scripts at scale across your endpoint fleet. This is where much of the operational efficiency of the platform lives, the ability to deploy a remediation to five thousand machines in minutes instead of weeks of manual work.

Mastering SentinelOne
Sample Expanded Chapter 10, Draft for Review
by Kendrick Washington, Technology Interpreters, Inc.

Chapter 10

Automation: STAR Rules and Response Playbooks

Learning Objectives

- Understand what STAR (Storyline Active Response) is and when automation makes sense versus when manual review is safer.
- Write a basic STAR rule from scratch, including trigger conditions, scope, and response actions.
- Test automation rules safely before deploying them to production endpoints.
- Design a response playbook that chains multiple actions together with proper controls.
- Recognize the guardrails that prevent runaway automation and what happens when you trigger them.
- Identify three common automations (auto-isolate, auto-quarantine, auto-tag) and the operational conditions under which each is appropriate.

Chapter Opener

Automation is where SentinelOne moves from observation to action at scale. Without it, every threat is a ticket, every alert requires a human click, and scaling security to tens of thousands of endpoints becomes a game of hiring faster than threats arrive. With it, a carefully tuned set of rules can isolate a compromised endpoint, quarantine a malicious file, gather forensic evidence, and page a human analyst, all in the seconds between detection and weaponization. The difference between having automation and not having it is the difference between defense and panic.

But automation is also where many teams create their biggest disasters. A rule that is too aggressive can lock endpoints out of the business. A playbook that does not account for false positives can quarantine critical applications. An automated response that nobody actually understands can hide the attack while you are busy patting yourself on the back for staying ahead of the threat. This chapter is about building automation you can trust: rules that have kill switches, guardrails that prevent cascades, and a habit of testing before you ship.

10.1 What STAR Is and Why It Matters

STAR stands for Storyline Active Response. It is SentinelOne's rule-based response automation engine. The core idea is simple: detect a condition using a SentinelOne threat or alert, and automatically execute one or more actions when that condition fires. Those actions can be local to the endpoint (kill a process, quarantine a file, isolate the network connection, clear an artifact), distributed across a group of machines (collect a memory dump from fifty workstations at once), or external (send a ticket to your SOAR, log an event to your SIEM, fire a webhook). STAR is what turns an alert from a data point into an orchestrated response.

The operational reality is that you will never have enough analysts to act on every alert individually, and you will never have enough bandwidth to tune detection engines perfectly. Some alerts are high-confidence, high-priority, and low-touch, an unsigned PowerShell script loading a suspicious DLL has a low false positive rate, and you want to kill it immediately. Other alerts are medium-confidence and high-touch, a process spawning an unusual child process might be legitimate custom software or it might be an attacker, and it needs human review before action. STAR lets you bucket these into high-confidence automations you ship and medium-confidence detections you funnel to the SOC. The result is that your team focuses on the 10 percent of alerts that actually need human judgment instead of drowning in the 90 percent that do not.

That said, there is no such thing as zero false positives. The second you automate a response, you are accepting some risk that the rule will fire on something you did not intend. The job of this chapter is teaching you to minimize that risk and to build confidence in the automations you do ship.

10.2 STAR Rule Anatomy

Every STAR rule has the same basic structure: a trigger, a scope, and one or more responses. Understanding each piece is essential before you write your first rule.

The trigger is the detection or alert that fires the rule. It can be a specific threat from one of SentinelOne's AI engines, a detection of a known malware family, a behavioral signature that matches ransomware-like activity, or a script-based detection. It can also be an alert you have written yourself using PowerQuery, which is SentinelOne's query language for describing patterns in telemetry. The trigger defines the condition: if X happens, the rule activates.

The scope is the boundary of where the rule applies. Most rules are scoped to a Group: they apply to all endpoints in that Group and nowhere else. Some rules are scoped more narrowly to a tag or a location. Some are scoped broadly to an entire Site. The scope answers the question: on which endpoints does this rule fire? A rule that auto-isolates on a specific malware detection might apply to your Production Servers group but not to your Pilot group, because you are still tuning detection in Pilot.

The response is the action the rule takes when the trigger fires and the scope matches. Responses can be local (kill process, quarantine file, isolate network, clear artifacts), distributed (collect memory, run a script), or external (send to SOAR, log event). Most rules have multiple responses that chain together: first collect evidence, then isolate the endpoint, then tag it for review, then send an alert. The order matters, because some actions depend on others completing first.

A mental model that helps: think of a rule as a machine in a factory. The conveyor belt brings you alerts (the trigger). You check whether the alert is the right one for your factory (the scope). If it is, you press the button (the response). Everything stops when something goes wrong.

10.3 Writing Your First STAR Rule

Let's build a simple rule from scratch. The scenario: you have a detection for a specific malware family called Emotet, which is a banking trojan that spreads aggressively across corporate networks. You want to isolate any endpoint that gets infected immediately, before it can spread. You also want to quarantine the malicious file and send an alert to your SOAR.

Step one: choose your trigger. In the SentinelOne console, you work through to Automation (or Playbooks, depending on your license tier) and create a new rule. You select the trigger as the Emotet threat: a specific threat ID or threat name that SentinelOne flags when it detects this malware. This is high-confidence detection, low false positive rate.

Step two: set your scope. You could scope this rule to your entire Account, but that is aggressive. Instead, you scope it to your Server Isolation group, a group where you have already decided that automatic network isolation is acceptable if an endpoint is compromised. You do not apply it to your Monitoring Only group, because that group is supposed to stay connected so you can investigate without disruption.

Step three: build your response chain. First, quarantine the malicious file. Second, isolate the endpoint from the network. Third, send a tag to the endpoint called 'emotet-isolated' so your SOC can find it in the console. Fourth, send a webhook to your SOAR with the endpoint ID, the threat details, and the timestamp. The chain runs in order, and if any step fails, the rule stops (most platforms do this by default, but verify).

Step four: test before you ship. In your test environment, trigger the rule manually or use a test detection. Watch the endpoint. Did it isolate correctly? Did it get the tag? Did the webhook reach your SOAR? Did anything unexpected happen? Once you are confident, you move the rule to production with a time-limited trial period, monitor it for one week, then make it permanent.

This four-step pattern, trigger, scope, response, test, should be your template for every rule you write.

10.4 Testing Automation Safely

The biggest mistake teams make is shipping automation without testing it. The second biggest is testing on production endpoints. Neither is acceptable.

If you have a staging environment, a group of test endpoints that you control and that do not host real business workloads, that is where rules get tested. You create the rule scoped to the test group, then you manually trigger a detection or an alert on a test endpoint and watch the rule execute. You verify that every response fired as expected. You also verify that nothing unexpected happened: the endpoint did not reboot, the network did not break, the SOAR webhook did not crash.

If you do not have a staging environment, create one. Two to five test machines running the same operating systems as your production fleet is the minimum price of admission to safe automation. Without staging, you are guessing.

Once a rule has been tested in staging, you have two options for production deployment. Option one is a phased rollout: ship the rule to a pilot group (maybe 5 to 10 percent of your endpoints), monitor it for a week, then expand it. Option two is a time-limited trial: deploy the rule production-wide but with a built-in expiration date (one to two weeks from now), so it automatically disables unless you manually extend it. Both approaches buy you time to catch unexpected behavior before it affects your whole environment.

Never, ever ship a rule without having a rollback plan. Know how you will disable it in an emergency. Know who has the permission to disable it. Know whether disabling it stops actions that are already in progress or only new detections. Get these answers before you are in a panic situation.

10.5 Building a Response Playbook

A STAR playbook is a collection of rules that work together to respond to a specific threat or class of threats. Where a single rule might isolate an endpoint, a playbook chains isolation, evidence collection, alerting, and external escalation into a coordinated workflow.

The classic playbook is ransomware response. When SentinelOne detects ransomware-like behavior (bulk file writes, file renaming, unusual entropy), you want to do several things at once: stop the process, isolate the endpoint from the network so it cannot spread to file shares, collect memory and logs for forensics, tag the endpoint for incident response, and send an alert to your SOAR with the full context. A well-designed playbook does all of this in parallel where possible, in sequence where order matters.

Building a playbook means thinking through the entire response flow before you write the first rule. What is the first thing you want to happen? (Usually: kill the malicious process or isolate the endpoint so it cannot do further damage.) What is the second thing? (Preserve evidence.) What is the third? (Alert the right person.) What are the failure modes? (What if the process cannot be killed? What if the network isolation fails?) What are the guardrails? (Can this playbook accidentally take down a file server?)

Most platforms do not call out playbooks explicitly, a playbook is simply a well-thought-out set of rules that trigger on the same conditions with complementary responses. The naming convention in SentinelOne and many others is to prefix rules with a category: 'ransomware-isolate', 'ransomware-quarantine', 'ransomware-collect-memory'. This naming makes it easy to find the set of rules that belong together and to audit the entire response chain.

A good playbook is also idempotent: if the same rule fires twice on the same endpoint, it should not cause problems. If you isolate an endpoint that is already isolated, nothing should break. If you tag an endpoint that is already tagged, the system should handle that gracefully. Think through these edge cases early.

10.6 Common Automations: Auto-Isolate, Auto-Quarantine, Auto-Tag

Three automations appear in almost every mature environment. Understanding when each is appropriate is key.

Auto-isolate means the endpoint loses network connectivity when a high-confidence threat fires. The endpoint is still powered on and the agent is still running, but it cannot reach the network, cannot reach file shares, cannot contact command-and-control servers. Use auto-isolate for threats you are very confident about (malware families, exploitation signatures with low false positive rates), for endpoints in groups where you have decided automatic response is acceptable, and only when you have verified that isolated endpoints can still be remediated remotely. If isolation breaks remote remediation, you have just painted yourself into a corner.

Auto-quarantine means the malicious file is moved to a secure location (a quarantine vault that the endpoint cannot access) or deleted entirely. Use auto-quarantine for suspicious files and for files that are easy to restore if you made a mistake (application installers, documents from the internet). Do not auto-quarantine critical system files or files whose loss would cause business disruption without human review first.

Auto-tag means the endpoint is labeled with a tag like 'ransomware-suspected' or 'malware-isolated' that makes it easy to find later and easy to scope subsequent actions to it. Tags are low-risk: they do not change endpoint behavior, they just make triage easier. Almost every automation should include a tagging action, because it gives you a paper trail and makes it easy for your SOC to find what the automation did.

The progression many teams follow is: start with auto-tag only (just mark detected endpoints), then add auto-quarantine for low-risk files, then add auto-isolate for high-confidence threats. This progression lets you build confidence in your automations before they take destructive action.

10.7 Guardrails: Preventing Runaway Automation

Runaway automation is the scenario where a rule fires, takes an action, that action changes the endpoint state in a way that triggers another rule, which triggers another, until you have a cascade that no human asked for and nobody knows how to stop. The classic example is a detection rule that kills a process, which causes a monitoring agent to restart, which looks like suspicious behavior, which triggers a malware rule, which isolates the endpoint, which makes it look like a compromised machine, and now your critical server is locked out of the network and nobody knows why.

Guardrails prevent this. The first guardrail is rule scoping: never write a rule that can recursively trigger itself or other rules. If you have a rule that kills a process, do not scope it to an endpoint type where killing that process would trigger another rule.

The second guardrail is rate limiting: cap the number of times a rule can fire on the same endpoint in a given time window. If a rule is firing more than once per hour on the same endpoint, something is wrong with either your detection or your rule logic. Most platforms allow you to set a firing limit: after five firings in one hour, the rule disables itself for that endpoint and sends an alert to your SOC.

The third guardrail is dry-run mode: before you ship a rule, test it in a mode where it logs what it would do without actually doing it. This gives you visibility into whether the rule would fire unexpectedly or fire too often.

The fourth guardrail is a kill switch: every rule should have a manual disable button that your SOC can hit in an emergency. If something is going wrong with automation, the ability to shut it off in under a minute is your safety net.

Build these guardrails into every rule from the start. They are not optional extras; they are how you avoid creating more problems than you solve.

10.8 When Not to Automate

This is the chapter's most important section, and the hardest to teach. Automation should not be your first instinct for every detection.

Do not automate if you do not fully understand the detection. If a threat name is unfamiliar, if the false positive rate is unknown, if the action is destructive (delete, isolate, quarantine), treat it as a detection that needs human review for now. Understand it first. Document your understanding. Build confidence over weeks or months. Then, and only then, write the automation. The cost of being wrong is too high to skip this step.

Do not automate if the detection is not specific enough. A rule that fires on 'suspicious behavior' is too vague. A rule that fires on 'PowerShell execution' is way too broad. Automation needs surgical precision. If your detection would fire on thousands of endpoints per day, do not automate the response; it is telling you the detection is not specific enough, and automating a low-precision detection is how you create havoc.

Do not automate if the response is not reversible without significant manual effort. If isolating an endpoint breaks critical business processes and requires a ticket, approval, and manual reactivation, isolation is not a good automation candidate. Consider a dry-run action first: tag the endpoint and alert your SOC, let them make the isolation decision.

Do not automate if you do not have visibility into what the automation did and whether it worked. Every automated response must be logged, auditable, and reviewable after the fact. If you cannot look at an isolated endpoint a week later and explain why it was isolated and what led to it, you should not have automated that response.

Do not automate your way out of a broken detection. If your alert rate is unsustainably high, if your false positive rate is too high, if your detection is missing attacks you know are happening, the answer is to fix the detection, not to automate a response and hope it helps. Automation does not replace tuning. It scales good tuning. It amplifies bad tuning.

10.9 RemoteOps and Script-Driven Responses

Beyond STAR rules, SentinelOne's Automation surface includes RemoteOps, which is the ability to push scripts (PowerShell, shell, Python) to endpoints and execute them at scale. RemoteOps is how you do custom remediation work that STAR rules do not handle natively.

The typical RemoteOps workflow is: you write a script that does something custom (clear an artifact, disable a service, restore a file, collect evidence). You upload it to SentinelOne's script library. You set parameters like execution timeout (SentinelOne defaults to 3600 seconds, which is 60 minutes), input requirements, and output handling. Then you target a set of endpoints or groups and execute.

RemoteOps is powerful but it requires discipline. Scripts can break things. They can hang. They can fail silently. Before you push a script to production endpoints, test it on a staging machine. Verify that it does what you think it does, that it handles errors gracefully, and that it does not leave the endpoint in an unusable state if something goes wrong.

Most teams treat RemoteOps scripts the way they treat code: version control, peer review, testing in staging first, and never pushing changes without a rollback plan. This is not paranoia. This is how you avoid taking down your entire production fleet with a typo in a batch script.

Warning: The Cost of Overly Aggressive Automation

Automation that is too aggressive is worse than no automation. A rule that isolates the wrong endpoint is a denial of service that came from inside. A rule that deletes files without human review will, at some point, delete something critical. A playbook that does not account for false positives will eventually waste days of incident response on something that was not real.

The safe path is to start conservative: tag and alert, nothing more. Measure the false positive rate over weeks. Only then add isolation or quarantine. Build confidence first, add power second.

Once you have shipped an automation, it becomes invisible. Your team stops noticing it is there. Months later, nobody remembers why the rule exists or what threat it was meant to catch. This is why every rule needs documentation, a clear name, and a scheduled review date. Once a quarter, sit down and review your automations. Are they still catching what they used to? Are the false positive rates still acceptable? Are there safer rules that would do the same job? This investment pays for itself the first time you catch a rule that became obsolete.

Chapter Summary

STAR rules and response playbooks are how you scale security from dozens of endpoints to tens of thousands. A STAR rule consists of a trigger (the detection or alert), a scope (the endpoints it applies to), and one or more responses (the actions to take). Testing in staging before production, phased rollouts, and built-in guardrails prevent runaway automation and cascading failures. The three most common automations are auto-isolate (for high-confidence threats), auto-quarantine (for suspicious files), and auto-tag (for tracking). Guardrails like rate limiting, dry-run mode, kill switches, and rule scoping prevent recursive triggering and cascades. Automation should not be your first instinct; it should be your second, after you have understood the detection, tuned it, verified it is low false positive, and built confidence over time.

Every automation you ship will eventually be invisible, which means it must be documented, logged, auditable, and reviewed regularly. The cost of overly aggressive automation is higher than the cost of doing things manually for a while longer.

Key Takeaways

- STAR rules automate the if-this-then-that workflow: when a threat or alert fires on a scoped set of endpoints, execute one or more responses.
- Every rule must have three parts: a specific trigger, a narrow scope, and one or more responses. Test all three before production deployment.
- Common automations are auto-isolate (network isolation for high-confidence threats), auto-quarantine (file removal), and auto-tag (marking for SOC triage). Tag first, escalate later.
- Guardrails prevent runaway automation: rate limit firing frequency, scope rules narrowly to prevent recursive triggers, test in dry-run mode, always have a kill switch.
- Do not automate what you do not understand, what you cannot reverse, or what you cannot audit. Automation should scale good tuning, not hide bad tuning.
- RemoteOps scripts are powerful but dangerous. Treat them like code: version control, peer review, test in staging, never ship without a rollback plan.

Hands-On Exercise

Before you continue to Chapter 11, do the following in your SentinelOne environment (or a test environment if you do not have Automation privileges in production).

- Write a single STAR rule on paper (not in the console yet) that would tag an endpoint if a specific low-risk suspicious behavior fires. Define the trigger, the scope, and the response. Have someone else review it for obvious issues.
- If you have access to a staging group, create that rule in the console, test it by manually triggering a detection on a test endpoint, and verify that the tag appeared.
- Review the existing automations in your environment (if any). For each one, write down: what trigger fires it, what is the scope, what are the responses, and how would you test it safely.
- Identify one detection or alert category in your environment that you do not yet understand well enough to automate. Plan to spend the next month collecting metrics on false positive rate, then revisit automation.

Review Questions

- 1. What is a RemoteOps task, and how does it differ from a manual Remote Shell command?
- 2. True or False: You can schedule a RemoteOps script to run automatically every Monday at 9 AM on all endpoints in a Group. If True, describe the use case. If False, explain why.
- 3. You have a PowerShell script that uninstalls a known-vulnerable piece of software from Windows endpoints. Before deploying it to 500 endpoints, what testing should you do?
- 4. A RemoteOps script fails on 10 out of 200 targeted endpoints. What could cause this failure, and how would you investigate?
- 5. List three examples of RemoteOps tasks that would save significant manual time in an MSSP or enterprise environment.

Answer Key: Review Questions

1. A RemoteOps task is a pre-built or custom script that SentinelOne stores and can run at scale. A manual Remote Shell command is a one-off command you type in real time. RemoteOps is scalable; Remote Shell is interactive and granular.

2. True (depending on platform capabilities). Use case: "Weekly patch-compliance check", run a script every Monday to verify installed software versions match standards, and report back. Another: "Friday disk-cleanup script", free up temp files on all laptops every week.

3. (1) Test on a single endpoint in a Dev or Pilot Group. (2) Verify the script uninstalls the software cleanly (no orphaned files or registry entries). (3) Confirm no dependent software breaks. (4) Test rollback: if the script fails halfway, can you manually undo? (5) Test on a small batch (10-50 endpoints) before the full 500.

4. Causes: script might depend on software not installed on all endpoints; file paths might differ between Windows versions; permission issues (script runs as SYSTEM but needs user context); endpoint offline or agent not responding; OS differences (script for Windows but some are Linux).

5. (1) Bulk uninstall of deprecated software. (2) Patch automated-patch failures (retry failed updates). (3) Collect forensic logs from suspected compromised endpoints. (4) Disable-enable services in bulk. (5) Compliance checks (verify firewall rules, antivirus status, etc. across the fleet).

Discussion Questions

- 1. You want to automate remediation of a critical vulnerability using a RemoteOps script. However, the patch sometimes causes reboots that interrupt user work. How would you balance automation and minimizing disruption to end users?
- 2. Describe the security risks of storing RemoteOps scripts in SentinelOne. What access controls would you recommend?
- 3. In an MSSP managing multiple customers, how would you govern RemoteOps script usage so that one customer's script does not accidentally run on another customer's endpoints?

Hands-On Lab Exercises

Lab 10.1: Explore Built-In RemoteOps Tasks

Objective: Familiarize yourself with pre-built automation capabilities.

Access to Automation or RemoteOps section; ability to browse available tasks

Steps:

- Work through to Automation > RemoteOps or equivalent. Browse the list of available pre-built tasks.
- Identify three tasks that would be relevant to your environment. For each, note: (1) Task name, (2) Supported OS(es), (3) What it does, (4) Required inputs or parameters.
- Read the task descriptions carefully. Are there any warnings or prerequisites?
- For one task, open its details. If a sample command or script is shown, review it for syntax and logic.
- Document: "Task [Name]: runs on [OS], does [action], would be useful for [business case]."

Expected Outcome: Inventory of useful pre-built tasks you could deploy.

Reflection: Which task would have the most impact on your MSSP's efficiency?

Lab 10.2: Design a Custom RemoteOps Script (Pseudocode)

Objective: Plan a custom automation task without necessarily building it.

Understanding of scripting concepts (even basic pseudocode)

Steps:

- Identify a recurring manual task in your environment (e.g., checking antivirus definitions, collecting a specific log file, patching a third-party app).
- Break the task into steps:
- - Step 1: [Check/collect/install X]
- - Step 2: [Verify success or log error]
- - Step 3: [Report back to console or send email]
- Identify what could go wrong and how to handle it: "If [condition], then [action]."
- Identify which endpoints would be safe targets: "Run on [Group], not on [Group]."
- Estimate time savings: "Doing this manually takes [X hours per week]. Automation saves [Y hours]."
- Document the pseudocode and the business case.

Expected Outcome: A documented design for a custom RemoteOps task.

Reflection: What would it take to actually build and test this script?

What's Next

Chapter 11 concludes the book with Settings: the control plane for users, notifications, integrations, and RBAC. This is where you operationalize everything you have learned, giving your team the right permissions to do the right jobs, making sure findings flow to the right people, and auditing who did what and when. Chapter 11 is about building trust in the system through transparency and control.

Mastering SentinelOne

Chapter 11, Final Chapter Draft for Review

by Kendrick Washington, Technology Interpreters, Inc.

Chapter 11

Settings: Tenant Configuration, Policy, and Governance

Learning Objectives

- Configure tenant-level, site-level, and group-level notification recipients and delivery mechanisms (email and Syslog).
- Understand the difference between site policy and group policy, and when to override at each level.
- Design and manage exclusions responsibly, including the security risks of broad exclusions and the audit trail required.
- Implement role-based access control (RBAC) across multiple sites and customer boundaries.
- Create service users and API tokens for integrations and automation workflows.
- Integrate SentinelOne with SIEM, SOAR, and identity providers (Okta, Entra ID) via Syslog and Single Sign-On.
- Use Locations to define network-aware endpoint groups and conditional policy application.

Chapter Opener

Settings is the chapter nobody loves to read, and everyone ignores until something breaks. This is where the boring work happens: who gets notified when a threat fires, who has permission to do what in the console, how alerts flow out to the SIEM, what happens when someone tries to add an exclusion to suppress a malware detection. It is governance, not detection. It is visibility and control for the team, not sophistication for the attacker. But this is also where MSSPs and large enterprises start to scale, and where small teams become chaotic. Get Settings right and the console stays usable even as you grow from one Site to one hundred. Get it wrong and you are managing exception requests, auditing mystery changes, and trying to figure out why alerts stopped flowing to your SIEM last month.

This chapter walks through the Settings menu end to end. We will cover notifications (who hears about detections), users and roles (who can do what), API keys and service accounts (how other systems talk to SentinelOne), integrations with SMTP and Syslog and SSO (how to plug SentinelOne into your existing infrastructure), and the governance mechanics you need to keep the console sane as a team scales. None of this is flashy. All of it is essential.

11.1 Notifications: Email and Syslog

SentinelOne can alert on dozens of events. Each event can go to email, to Syslog, or both. The notification system is where you decide what the team actually hears about, and how. Every event in the console that matters to the SOC or the customer CISO is a candidate for notification. The trick is avoiding alert fatigue: if you send too many notifications, the team ignores them. Send too few, and you miss something important.

Start by reviewing the notification categories in the Settings menu under Notifications. You will see sections for Malware (confirmed threats, benign verdicts, mitigated events), Device Control (USB allows, blocks, Bluetooth events), Custom Rules (when someone creates or modifies them), Exclusions (when someone adds an exclusion, deletes one, or modifies one), Endpoint Tagging (when tags are added or removed), Active Directory (if you have AD integration), Ranger (network discovery events, rogue device detection), and administrative actions (user logins, policy changes, API key creation). Each category is granular, and you can enable or disable each event type independently.

The starting recommendation: enable all malware-related events. A malware detection that nobody hears about is not a detection, it is a log entry. Enable Exclusions notifications, because an exclusion that suppresses malware detection is a governance risk and needs audit visibility. Enable administrative notifications (user actions, policy changes, API key creation) because you need to know who is doing what in the console. Everything else, tune by experience: add more as you encounter gaps, remove noise as your team discovers false-positive-heavy categories.

11.2 Email and Syslog Delivery

Notifications travel by two paths: email and Syslog. Email goes to a list of recipients you define in the Recipients tab. This is human-facing. Set up an email address like 'security-alerts@company.com' or a Slack bot email integration so the team sees notifications in Slack. Syslog goes to a machine (usually your SIEM or log aggregator like Splunk, ELK, or Elastic) and lets your monitoring system consume and correlate alerts alongside everything else the network is producing.

To configure email delivery, you need an SMTP relay. SentinelOne can use the relay provided by your upstream provider or MSSP, or you can point it at your own mail server. The configuration is straightforward: hostname, port (typically 587 for TLS), username, and password. Once configured, every email notification goes through that relay. To test it, trigger a notification manually (create a rule, modify an exclusion, log out and back in) and verify the email arrives.

To configure Syslog delivery, you specify the Syslog server IP address, port (typically 514 for UDP, sometimes 6514 for TLS), and optionally enable TLS encryption for security. SentinelOne will forward every enabled notification category as a Syslog message. Your SIEM must be listening on that port and must know how to parse SentinelOne's message format (check your SIEM's documentation). The beauty of Syslog is that once it is working, alerts flow into your existing SOC workflow: your SOAR can consume them, your ticketing system can ingest them, and your threat intelligence platform can enrich them, all in one place.

Pro tip: do not leave all notification categories enabled to Syslog. Syslog can create volume that overwhelms your SIEM or drowns out other important network traffic. Be selective: send malware detections, exclusion changes, user logins, and policy changes. Leave noisy categories (like endpoint tagging churn) out unless your SIEM can handle high volume or unless you have a specific use case for them.

11.3 Site and Group Policy Hierarchy

Policies in SentinelOne are not monolithic. They cascade down the hierarchy: a policy at the Site level is inherited by all Groups in that Site, unless a Group has its own policy that overrides it. Understanding where your policies live and which one is actually active is half the battle in troubleshooting SentinelOne misconfigurations.

A Site Policy is the default policy for the Site. When you create a new Site, you can assign it a policy at creation time, or use a copy of an existing policy as a template. This Site Policy is inherited by all Groups beneath it. The most common pattern is to leave the Site Policy as read-only and use it as a baseline, then override it at the Group level for custom requirements.

A Group Policy is a policy assigned to a specific Group. A Group can have its own policy, which overrides the Site Policy for all endpoints in that Group. This is how you end up with differentiated enforcement: a Monitoring Only group that alerts but does not auto-remediate, a Full Enforcement group that kills and quarantines, a Pilot group that stages policy changes before rollout to production. Each Group gets the policy it needs; endpoints inherit policies based on their Group membership.

To see which policy is actually active on an endpoint, work through to that endpoint's details, and check the Effective Policy section. This shows you the inherited policy, including any overrides. If the policy is not what you expected, walk the inheritance chain: check the endpoint's Group policy, then the Site policy, then (if you have Account or Global visibility) the Account or Global policy. Something along that chain is overriding what you thought was in effect.

A common mistake: creating a policy at the Account level expecting all Sites to inherit it. Policies at Account level are templates and visibility aids, not enforcement points. To enforce a policy across multiple Sites, you have to assign it at the Site level for each Site. This is by design: it prevents a global policy change from accidentally affecting all your customers.

Operator's Checklist: Diagnosing a Policy Mismatch

Open the endpoint detail page and note its Group assignment.

Work through to that Group and check if it has its own policy or inherits from the Site.

If the Group inherits from Site, open the Site policy and verify the settings.

If the Group has its own policy, open that policy and verify the settings.

If the policy looks correct but the endpoint is not behaving as expected, check the agent version: old agents sometimes do not support recent policy features.

11.4 Exclusions: Power and Peril

Exclusions are one of the most dangerous features in SentinelOne, because they are also one of the most necessary. An exclusion tells SentinelOne to ignore a specific process, file hash, file path, or executable. The legitimate use case is a custom-developed application that SentinelOne keeps flagging as suspicious because its behavior looks malware-like. You exclude it by hash or by full path, and SentinelOne stops inspecting it.

Here is where the danger lives: an exclusion can be used to suppress any detection, including detections of real malware. If someone with the right permissions adds an exclusion for a malware hash or a malicious file path, the platform will ignore it. This is not a backdoor, exactly, but it is an insider risk. Someone with administrative access can silence the security system.

The governance rule: never allow anyone to add an exclusion without review. Always enable Exclusions in your notification settings so that you are alerted the moment someone adds or modifies an exclusion. Document every exclusion in a central place (a spreadsheet, a wiki, a ticketing system), including who added it, when, why, and a review date. Set an expiration: many organizations require exclusions to be re-approved every 90 days. If the original reason for the exclusion has gone away (the problematic software was uninstalled or patched, the vendor fixed the issue), delete the exclusion.

The technical rule: prefer hash-based exclusions over path-based exclusions. A hash is immutable: if you exclude by MD5 or SHA256, you are excluding a specific binary. If you update that binary, the hash changes and the exclusion no longer applies. Path-based exclusions are broader and more persistent, which makes them riskier. If someone moves malware into that path, the exclusion will suppress it. Hash-based exclusions are harder to exploit.

The final rule: never exclude the SentinelOne agent itself from detection. SentinelOne adds exclusions for its own binaries automatically. Do not modify or delete them. If you think the agent is being detected as malware, contact SentinelOne support or add a policy override instead.

WARNING: Exclusion Abuse

Exclusions suppress detection. An attacker with admin access can use exclusions to hide malware.

Always monitor exclusion creation (enable Exclusions in notifications). Always document the reason for each exclusion. Always set an expiration date and re-approve regularly.

Hash-based exclusions are safer than path-based. Path-based exclusions can be exploited by placing malware in the excluded path.

Treat exclusion approvals the same way you treat privileged SQL statements: peer review, blast-radius assessment, and a rollback plan.

11.5 Users, Roles, and RBAC

Every person who logs into the SentinelOne console is a User. Every user has a Role that defines what they can do. The role system is fine-grained, allowing you to grant permissions down to the level of specific actions (create a new Site, run a report, delete an exclusion, update a policy). This is role-based access control (RBAC).

SentinelOne comes with several built-in roles: Global Admin (can do everything at Global level), Account Admin (can do everything within an Account), Site Admin (can do everything within a Site), Operator (can investigate and remediate threats), Analyst (can view threats but not remediate), Compliance Officer (can view and generate reports), and several others. Your organization may also have custom roles defined by your upstream provider. Check with them before trying to create new roles.

The hierarchy rule: a user created at a higher level (Account or Global) has access to everything below that level. A user created at the Site level can only see and act on that Site. This is how you enforce multi-tenant separation in an MSSP: create users at the Site level, and they cannot see other customers' data. Create a user at the Account level, and they can see all Sites in your Account. Create a user at the Global level (if you have Global access), and they can see everything.

Best practice for MSSPs: create a user for each customer Site at the Site level, and assign them a role that lets them see their data (usually Site Admin or Operator). Create a user for your own analysts at the Account level with a role that lets them investigate threats across all your customer Sites (usually Account Admin or a custom analyst role). Create a separate service user for API integrations (see below). This separation keeps customer data segregated and makes auditing easier.

To add a user, work through to Settings > Users. Click Add User, fill in the email address, select a Role, and optionally set an expiration date for the account. Expiration dates are useful for contractors, consultants, and temporary team members. Once created, the user receives an email invitation and can set their own password. They log in with email and password, or (if your organization has SSO enabled) they log in with their SSO provider.

11.6 Service Users and API Keys

A Service User is a special type of user account that does not represent a person. It represents another system: a SOAR, a vulnerability scanner, an automation script, an integration with your ticketing system. Service users can have API keys that last up to a year, whereas regular user accounts have API keys that expire after 30 days.

API keys are how external systems authenticate to the SentinelOne console. Instead of embedding a username and password (which is bad practice), you create an API key and embed that in the integrating system. The key is a token that the system presents on every API call. SentinelOne validates the token, checks what permissions the Service User has, and allows or denies the request.

To create a Service User, work through to Settings > Users, click Add Service User, give it a name (e.g., 'Splunk Integration', 'AWS Lambda Remediation'), select a Role (choose the most restrictive role that still allows it to do its job; a Splunk integration might only need Analyst permissions since it is just reading detections), and click Create. Then, click on the Service User and generate an API key. Copy the key to a secure location. You will need it to configure the external system. Once you paste it into the external system, you cannot retrieve it again from SentinelOne, so losing it means generating a new key.

Pro tip: set an expiration date on each API key. A key that lasts a year is a liability if it is ever compromised. Instead, set keys to expire after 90 days and rotate them quarterly. Add a calendar reminder to regenerate keys before they expire. When you rotate a key, update the external system to use the new key, wait for confirmation that it is working, then delete the old key.

Do not create API keys for regular user accounts if you can help it. The 30-day expiration becomes painful in production. Create a Service User instead, and you get a full year.

11.7 Integrations: SMTP, Syslog, and Single Sign-On

Beyond email and Syslog delivery (covered in 11.2), SentinelOne integrates with identity providers via Single Sign-On (SSO). If your organization uses Okta, Entra ID (Azure), Ping Identity, or similar, you can integrate SentinelOne so that users log in with their corporate credentials instead of maintaining a separate SentinelOne password.

SSO setup varies by provider, but the general flow is the same. SentinelOne acts as a service provider and your identity provider (Okta, Entra) acts as the identity provider. You go to Settings > Integrations > Single Sign-On, enable SAML 2.0, and follow the wizard. You will copy some values from SentinelOne into your identity provider's application settings, and then copy values back into SentinelOne. Once configured, users trying to log into SentinelOne are redirected to your identity provider, authenticate there, and land in SentinelOne without ever entering a SentinelOne password.

SSO is a big operational win for two reasons. First, users do not have to remember another password. Second, when someone leaves your organization and you disable their identity provider account, they automatically lose access to SentinelOne. You do not have to remember to delete the SentinelOne user manually.

Policy overrides are not something you configure in Settings every day, but they show up here and are worth understanding. A policy override is a rule that tells a specific detection engine to ignore a specific behavior pattern. This is different from an exclusion: where an exclusion says 'ignore this file hash', an override says 'ignore this behavioral pattern for this detection engine'. They are rare, specialized, and dangerous. You should never write a policy override without input from SentinelOne support. If you have one, it is because SentinelOne support identified a specific conflict (like the USB headset issue mentioned in the chapter opener) and provided you with the override rule to copy into the console.

11.8 Locations: Network-Aware Endpoint Groups

Locations allow you to define logical groups of endpoints based on network criteria. An endpoint can be a member of a Location if its IP address matches a range, if its DNS servers match certain addresses, if it resolves certain DNS host names, if it has a specific type of network interface, if a registry key exists on it, or if it is currently connected to the SentinelOne cloud. You can use these criteria to apply different policies based on where the endpoint is physically or logically located.

The classic use case: a Locations group for 'Corporate Network' that triggers when an endpoint is connected to the VPN or on the corporate IP range, and a Locations group for 'Remote or Public WiFi' that triggers when the endpoint is not on the corporate network. The Corporate Network group might have a looser USB policy (users can plug in USB devices), while the Remote WiFi group has a strict USB policy (no USB allowed). Same endpoint, different policy based on location.

To create a Location, go to Settings > Locations, click Add Location, give it a name, and define the criteria. If at least one criterion is true, the endpoint belongs to that Location. You can chain criteria with OR logic (if IP matches this OR DNS resolves that) or AND logic (if IP matches this AND interface type is wireless). Then, in a policy, you can make the policy behavior conditional on the endpoint's Location.

Locations are powerful but they add complexity. Do not overuse them. Stick to the high-level scenarios (on-network vs. off-network, managed vs. unmanaged, datacenter vs. remote office) and avoid creating dozens of overlapping Locations that are hard to understand six months later. Document each Location in a central place so that your team knows what each one means.

11.9 Sites and Account Management

Creating a new Site is something you do once per customer in an MSSP, or once per business unit in a large enterprise. When you create a Site, you choose the license model (trial or paid), the expiration date (when the Site's access should be revoked if the contract expires), the SKU (license type; usually 'Sentinel One Complete'), and the agent limit. You can also choose whether to enable specific features like Remote Script Orchestration or Ranger for that Site.

The agent limit is important: it caps the number of endpoints you can install the agent on at that Site. Set it conservatively. If you set it to 10 agents and a customer wants to install 20, they will hit the limit and get an error. Some organizations deliberately set low limits to prevent bill shock: they know a customer has a 10-license contract, so they set the agent limit to 10, and if the customer tries to install more agents than they paid for, the system stops them and forces a conversation. This prevents accidental billing surprises.

The Site Key is the most important piece. It is a unique identifier that the SentinelOne agent needs in order to register into the correct Site when installed. When you deploy agents, you embed the Site Key in the installation package. Without the right Site Key, the agent registers into the wrong Site and the endpoints appear in the wrong customer's console.

To view and manage Sites, go to Settings > Sites. Each Site shows its license consumption (how many agents are installed vs. the agent limit), the expiration date, the Site Key, and the policy assigned to it. You can also create new Sites, modify settings on existing Sites, and edit policies at the Site level.

11.10 Change Management and Console Governance

As your organization scales from a handful of endpoints to thousands, your console becomes a shared resource. Decisions made in Settings stop being personal preferences and start being organizational policies. You need governance to prevent chaos.

Here is a governance checklist: First, require approval before anyone adds an exclusion. Treat exclusions as risky exceptions and require written justification and a review date. Second, monitor all user and administrative actions via the Activity log. Review Activity weekly, looking for unexpected changes, new users, API key creation, or policy modifications. Third, maintain a change log or ticketing system for every console change: Site creation, policy updates, user creation, exclusion addition. If something is broken, you want to be able to trace it back to a specific change and a specific person. Fourth, implement separation of duties: do not give everyone admin access. Create roles and assign the most restrictive permissions that still allow people to do their jobs. Fifth, set expiration dates on users, API keys, and exclusions. Everything temporary should have an end date and a process to renew it or retire it.

For MSSPs specifically: the multi-tenant model is both a feature and a governance burden. Create users at the Site level so they cannot see other customers' data. Maintain a spreadsheet of all Sites, all customers, all contracts, all user accounts, and all API keys. When a contract expires, you need a process to decommission that Site, including revoking user access, invalidating API keys, and archiving data. Missing this step means customers can still access the console after their contract ends, or (worse) old users still have access to old customer data years after they left the organization.

Finally, treat your console like you would treat a production database. Do not let anyone make changes without a ticket. Do not roll out a policy change without testing it in a pilot group first. Do not delete an exclusion without checking Activity to see why it was created. Do not decommission a Site without auditing all its users, checking if any of them have access to other Sites, and making sure you have not orphaned any integrations or API keys. The 30 minutes you spend on governance today prevents hours of forensics and breach investigations later.

Chapter Summary

Settings is where you connect SentinelOne to the rest of your infrastructure. Notifications (email and Syslog) are how findings leave the console and reach the team or the SIEM. Users and Roles control access and enforce the principle of least privilege. Service Users and API keys are how external systems authenticate. Exclusions are a necessary evil that requires careful governance. Policy hierarchy (Site and Group) is how you differentiate enforcement across different groups of endpoints. Locations are how you make policies aware of network context. All of this is unglamorous, but it is the difference between a manageable console and one that devolves into chaos as the organization scales.

The final word on governance: you will be tempted to skip this work when you are busy. Do not. Every exclusion you add without documentation, every user you create without tracking, every policy change you make without a ticket is technical debt that compounds. Your future self will either thank you or curse you when incident response time comes and you have to trace who made what change, when, and why. Build governance first and grow into it. It is much easier to loosen governance later if it turns out you were too strict than it is to bolt it on after you have already created chaos.

Closing: What You Have Built

You have now completed this book. You have walked the entire SentinelOne console, from the Dashboard where you get situational awareness, through Sentinels where you deploy agents and configure policies, through Incidents where you respond to threats, through Reports where you show the board that the money they spent on EDR is working, and finally through Settings where you build the governance that keeps it all sane as you scale. SentinelOne is a big platform with a lot of moving parts, but they work together. The hierarchy flows top-down. The policies cascade through Groups. The threats land in Incidents and flow out through notifications. If you understand those patterns, the rest is configuration, not mystery. Go do something with it. Deploy an endpoint. Write an exclusion. Set up a Syslog integration. Join your organization's security team and start detecting and hunting. That is where the real work starts, and that is where this book stops.

Key Takeaways

- Notifications are the bridge out of SentinelOne. Choose email for humans and Syslog for machines (SIEM, SOAR, aggregators). Be selective; alert fatigue is real.
- Policies cascade top-down: Global to Account to Site to Group. If an endpoint is not behaving as you expected, walk the inheritance chain.
- Exclusions are powerful and dangerous. Govern them strictly: require approval, enable notifications, document each one, set expiration dates.
- Users and Roles enforce the principle of least privilege. Create users at the lowest level that makes sense; segregate customers at the Site level.
- Service Users and API keys are how external systems talk to SentinelOne. Rotate keys every 90 days; treat old API keys as security liabilities.

- SSO with Okta or Entra ID eliminates password management and automatically revokes access when employees leave.
- Locations make policies location-aware. Use them to differentiate enforcement on-network vs. off-network, but keep them simple.
- Governance is not optional. Monitor exclusions, track user actions, maintain a change log, and review the Activity audit log weekly.

Hands-On Exercise

Before you close this book, do the following in your SentinelOne tenant.

- Work through to Settings > Notifications and enable all malware-related notifications and administrative notifications. Set up email recipients for your security team.
- Create a test exclusion (exclude a safe binary by hash), then verify that an Exclusions notification reaches your email or Syslog destination. After confirming it works, delete the test exclusion.
- Review the Locations section and design one Location group for your network (e.g., "Corporate VPN" or "Remote Employees"). Document the criteria and what policy behavior should change for that Location.
- Audit your current users in Settings > Users. For each user, document their name, role, level (Site, Account, Global), and when they were created. Identify any users who should no longer have access.
- Work through to Settings > Sites and review the Site Key for your primary Site. Verify that you have stored it in a secure location and that your deployment processes use it correctly.

Review Questions

- 1. What are the two primary notification mechanisms SentinelOne supports, and when would you use each?
- 2. You configure a Notification rule to email the SOC team only when a threat with CVSS >= 8.0 is detected. Will the SOC receive emails for all detections, only Critical/High, or none?
- 3. True or False: A User created with role "Analyst" can create policies or change detection engine settings. Explain what an Analyst role typically permits.

- 4. What is a Location in SentinelOne, and why would you define one based on network criteria rather than just using Groups?
- 5. You want to integrate SentinelOne with your SIEM (Splunk). What SentinelOne feature would you configure, and what data would flow to Splunk?

Answer Key: Review Questions

1. Email (for human recipients) and Syslog (for machine recipients like SIEMs). Use Email for team notifications and alerts. Use Syslog for automated ingestion into a SIEM or log aggregator.

2. Only Critical and High (CVSS >= 8.0). Threats below 8.0 will not trigger an email, even if they are detected.

3. False. Analyst role typically allows incident investigation, threat analysis, and remediation actions, but not policy creation or engine configuration (which require Admin or similar). The role determines what settings changes are allowed.

4. A Location is a logical grouping of endpoints based on network criteria (IP range, DNS server, network interface type, connection state). Use Locations to apply different policies based on where the endpoint is (e.g., corporate LAN vs. public WiFi) without creating separate Groups.

5. Configure Syslog forwarding in Notifications. SentinelOne will send Activity logs, threat detections, alerts, and operational events to your Splunk instance in real time. This creates a permanent forensic record beyond SentinelOne's native retention.

Discussion Questions

- 1. You have 50 customers across an MSSP. Each customer's SOC wants different notification channels (email, Slack, PagerDuty) and different severity thresholds. How would you design a scalable notification strategy?
- 2. Your organization enforces strict RBAC (role-based access control). How would you configure SentinelOne users and permissions so that a Tier-1 analyst cannot accidentally break a production policy, but a senior analyst can?
- 3. Describe a scenario where using Locations would be more effective than using Groups, and explain the operational benefits.

Hands-On Lab Exercises

Lab 11.1: Configure Email and Syslog Notifications

Objective: Set up notification channels for operational alerts and SIEM integration.

Access to Settings > Notifications; email configuration and (optionally) Syslog endpoint details

Steps:

- Work through to Settings > Notifications > Email.
- Add a notification rule: "When threat classification = 'Malware', send to [SOC team email]."
- Add a second rule: "When threat detected AND endpoint status = 'Offline', send to [ops team email]." (This alerts when an endpoint goes offline during an active threat.)
- Test: Open Notifications > Test Email or trigger a test notification. Verify emails arrive.
- Work through to Settings > Notifications > Syslog (if available).
- Configure the Syslog endpoint: IP address and port of your SIEM or log aggregator.
- Enable forwarding of: Activity logs, Threats, Alerts, and any other relevant data.
- If your SIEM provides a test facility, send a test message and verify it arrives in Splunk/Elastic/etc.
- Document: "Email notifications configured for [rules]. Syslog forwarding enabled to [SIEM endpoint]."

Expected Outcome: Operational alerts reaching your team and SIEM integration live.

Reflection: If a SIEM is not available, what alternative would you use to retain Activity logs long-term?

Lab 11.2: Design an RBAC Policy for Your Organization

Objective: Map role permissions to job functions in your organization.

Understanding of your org structure (SOC analysts, tier levels, MSP roles if applicable)

Steps:

- List the roles your organization needs: (e.g., "Tier-1 Analyst," "Senior Analyst," "SOC Manager," "Admin").
- For each role, list what they should be able to do:

- - Tier-1: View incidents, mark as resolved, view Activity, but NOT change policies.
- - Senior Analyst: Everything Tier-1 + create exclusions, modify policies in test Groups, view all Sites.
- - Manager: Everything Tier-1 and Senior + manage users, view reports.
- - Admin: Everything.
- In Settings > Users, create users with these roles (or adjust existing users).
- Test: Log in as a Tier-1 user. Verify you cannot access Policy settings. Log in as Senior. Verify you can.
- Document your RBAC matrix in a table: Role | Can View Incidents | Can Modify Policies | Can Manage Users | etc.

Expected Outcome: An RBAC design that prevents accidental changes while enabling operational efficiency.

Reflection: How would you handle a request to give a Tier-1 analyst temporary elevated permissions?

Lab 11.3: Create and Apply Locations Based on Network Criteria

Objective: Define Locations to segment endpoints by network attributes.

Access to Settings > Locations; knowledge of your network segments (e.g., office LANs, VPN ranges, remote WiFi)

Steps:

- Identify three network segments in your organization: (e.g., "Corporate LAN: 10.0.0.0/8", "Remote VPN: 192.168.1.0/24", "Guest WiFi: 172.16.0.0/12").
- In Settings > Locations, create three Location definitions:
- - Location 1: "Corporate Office", IP range 10.0.0.0/8, DNS servers [your corporate DNS].
- - Location 2: "Remote VPN", IP range 192.168.1.0/24, VPN indicator enabled.
- - Location 3: "Guest/Public", IP range 172.16.0.0/12, Wireless interface type.
- Save each Location.

- Work through to a Policy (any Group's policy). Apply different Device Control settings: "Corporate Office: Allow USB drives. Guest/Public: Block USB drives."
- Verify the policy logic: when an endpoint in the Corporate Location attempts USB access, it is allowed. When the same endpoint roams to Guest WiFi and re-registers in the Guest Location, USB is blocked.
- Document: "Locations defined: [list]. Policies adapted per-location: [rules]."

Expected Outcome: Location-based policy differentiation, enabling adaptive security posture.

Reflection: How would this approach improve security for a company with field workers on public WiFi?

Mastering SentinelOne

Appendix A: Lab Setup Guide

For Academic Institutions and Faculty

by Kendrick Washington, Technology Interpreters, Inc.

Appendix A

Lab Setup Guide: Building a Three-Product Cybersecurity Lab

Introduction

A video lecture on SentinelOne can teach you what the interface looks like and why you would click each button. But a lab, a hands-on, working deployment where you and your students can install agents, generate detections, investigate incidents, escalate to a ticketing system, and document what you found, teaches you what it means to be on the job. This appendix is the operational guide for faculty at institutions like Palm Beach State College who want to stand up that lab.

The lab you will build has three commercial products working together: SentinelOne (endpoint detection and response), Tenable Nessus (vulnerability scanning), and ServiceNow (incident management). This topology mirrors real SOCs. A detection in SentinelOne generates an alert. The alert flows to ServiceNow, where a ticket is created and routed to an analyst. The analyst investigates in SentinelOne, then asks Nessus for vulnerability context to understand the blast radius. The analyst documents findings, closes the ticket, and the lab teaches your students the entire workflow.

What your students will learn from a properly-built lab versus a video-only course is the difference between knowing about a tool and knowing how to use it under time pressure. In the lab, a student who forgets what a policy override does cannot rewind the video; they have to read the documentation, think about the problem, and fix it. A student who misconfigures a policy and crashes detection will feel the weight of that mistake and learn not to repeat it. A student who successfully orchestrates SentinelOne, Nessus, and ServiceNow together will understand that EDR is not a solo act, it is part of a larger ecosystem.

This appendix differs from the book's chapters in one key way: it is written directly to you, the instructor, not to a student reading alone. We assume you have access to the book's main content and understand SentinelOne conceptually. What you need now is the practical roadmap: how to acquire licenses, build the infrastructure, schedule the curriculum, and handle the inevitable crises when something breaks. This guide walks you through three major phases: acquiring the three products for academic use (and how to ask vendors for licensing), designing the lab network so students cannot accidentally harm real endpoints, and running week-by-week labs that align with the chapters of this book. By the end of the semester, your students will have completed a capstone scenario where they detect, investigate, correlate, remediate, and report on a complete incident. That is what this appendix teaches you how to build.

One more note: this guide is current as of the publication date. Product features, vendor educational programs, and deployment best practices all evolve. Verify the details directly with vendors (SentinelOne, Tenable, ServiceNow) before you commit to a particular approach. Use this guide as a framework and a starting point for your own lab design, not as a static recipe.

Licensing Paths for Academic Programs

Before you buy hardware or stand up a lab network, you need to secure SentinelOne licenses for your student machines. The good news: SentinelOne recognizes educational value and has programs specifically for academic institutions. The better news: you have options, and they all work. The key is asking early, framing your request correctly, and being willing to explore alternatives if a preferred path does not materialize. This section walks you through three realistic acquisition paths, what to expect from each, and what questions to ask before you commit.

A word of caution: this book is current as of publication (2026), and vendor programs change frequently. SentinelOne's education team may modify licensing terms, trial duration, or endpoint limits. The structure and core questions described here will remain relevant, but verify the specific terms with SentinelOne directly before you plan your lab. Do not assume last year's education pricing applies this year.

Path 1: Direct Vendor Partnership (SentinelOne Education Program)

SentinelOne offers an education program designed specifically for accredited institutions. This is often the first place to look and the path most likely to yield a favorable outcome.

How to pursue this path: visit sentinelone.com and look for links to 'Education,' 'Academic Partnerships,' or 'University Programs.' If you cannot find a dedicated education page, contact SentinelOne's sales team and ask: 'Does SentinelOne have an education program for accredited colleges and universities?' Be specific about your institution (name, accreditation body, Carnegie Classification if applicable).

Typical outcomes: SentinelOne may provide a trial license (usually 30-90 days, free) to evaluate the product. This is useful for proof of concept but is too short for a full semester. If the trial is sufficient for your needs and you have a tight budget, this may be your path. If you need longer, explain your use case: 'We are running a semester-long cybersecurity course with X students, needing Y endpoints for hands-on labs.' Based on your institutional profile and timing, the vendor may offer an NFR (no-fee) license with a reduced endpoint limit (perhaps 50-100 agents instead of a full commercial count), valid for the academic year. Or, if your institution has a budget, they may offer an academic discount on a standard commercial license.

Path 2: MSP/MSSP-Brokered Tenants (Most Common for Community Colleges)

Many community colleges partner with Managed Service Providers (MSPs) or Managed Security Service Providers (MSSPs) who resell SentinelOne licenses under an aggregated agreement. This path is often more accessible than direct vendor partnerships, especially if your IT vendor already has a relationship with an MSSP.

How to pursue this path: contact your institution's primary IT vendor or managed services provider and ask if they offer SentinelOne licensing. Explain your use case: 'We need a SentinelOne lab for academic use with approximately X endpoints.' The MSSP will handle the negotiation with SentinelOne on your behalf, and you will receive a tenant provisioned at their account.

What to expect: MSP/MSSP licensing typically costs between $5-$10 per endpoint per month, depending on the bundle (base EDR only versus EDR with Vulnerability Management or XDR add-ons). A realistic model for a 16-student lab plus 5 server/sandbox machines (21 endpoints) might run $140-$210 per month ($1,700-$2,500 for a 12-month year). This is often significantly lower than a direct enterprise license. The trade-off: you lose some autonomy. Your tenant is managed by the MSSP, and they handle console access, user management, and support escalations. For academic purposes, this is a minor inconvenience and a fair trade for the cost savings.

Key questions to ask the MSSP before signing: (1) What is the price per endpoint per month, and are there volume discounts? (2) Is this a 12-month term, or can it be annual? (3) Are updates and support included? (4) What SentinelOne features are included (base EDR only, or does it include Vulnerability Management, XDR, Ranger)? (5) Can I request API access for student projects? (6) What happens if I exceed the endpoint count mid-semester? (7) Is there a setup/onboarding fee? (8) How long does provisioning take from contract signing to console access? (9) What is the process for requesting policy changes or exclusions? (10) If I need to end early (course discontinued, grant ends), what is the early termination penalty?

Path 3: Free/Trial Tenants (Capstone Use Only)

If your budget is zero and you cannot secure a partnership, you can still run a limited lab using free trial tenants. SentinelOne offers 30-day or 90-day trial licenses that require no payment.

Use case: This path works only if you plan to use the lab for a capstone exercise (final 2-4 weeks of the semester) rather than for the entire course. You cannot run a 16-week semester-long lab on trial licenses because the license will expire mid-semester and you will have no data continuity.

Limitations: Trial tenants typically cap at 25-50 endpoints. Trials are single-use; you cannot renew the same trial. If you run the lab in Fall, you will need a new trial for Spring. Trial tenants may have reduced data retention or feature limitations (e.g., no API access, limited reporting). Trial tenants are intended for evaluation, not production use, so there is no SLA or support guarantee.

Best practice if you choose this path: Use the trial for a single capstone exercise. Run it late in the semester so students have the full course context (chapters 1-10) before entering the capstone. Supplement the trial with documentation and recorded walkthroughs so students understand the workflow even if the trial license expires during their report-writing phase.

What to Ask the Vendor: A Checklist

- Before you agree to any licensing deal (Path 1, 2, or 3), get answers to these eight essential questions:
- What is the cost per endpoint per month, and how is 'endpoint' defined? (Is it per-agent or per-managed-device? Are servers counted the same as workstations?)
- What features are included in the base license, and what requires add-ons? (Specifically: Vulnerability Management, XDR, Ranger, API access, report exports?)
- What is the minimum term length (1 month, 12 months, 24 months)? Can you do month-to-month, or is there an early termination fee?
- How long from contract signature to console access and first agent deployment? (Ask for a written SLA.)

- What is the data retention policy? How long are incidents, logs, and telemetry kept? (For a semester-long course, you need at least 120 days minimum.)
- Who handles support and incident escalation? (Is there a dedicated support contact, or do you go through the MSSP/vendor?)
- Can I export data (incidents, reports, logs) from the console when the license expires? (You need audit trails for student records.)
- Are there any usage restrictions or audit rights clauses that limit what students can do with the lab? (Some education licenses prohibit commercial use or benchmarking; academic labs are fine, but read the terms.)

Faculty Checklist: Licensing Decision Timeline

At least 4 months before semester starts: Contact SentinelOne directly OR your IT vendor to inquire about education programs.

At least 12 weeks before: Receive quote or trial offer. Evaluate against your budget and course timeline.

At least 8 weeks before: Sign agreement and request onboarding to start. Request an SLA for console access.

At least 6 weeks before: Receive console access and begin lab environment setup and testing.

At least 4 weeks before: Validate that you can deploy agents, create test detections, and access reports.

At least 2 weeks before: Train your TAs and lab staff on the environment.

Week before semester: Final health check. Run a test detection to confirm everything works.

Hardware Bill of Materials: Starter Lab

A hands-on lab requires physical or virtual hardware. This section provides a concrete bill of materials for a starter 16-station classroom lab suitable for a class of 16-20 students. The BOM assumes you have access to a virtualization platform (such as VMware ESXi, Hyper-V, or KVM) on campus. If not, you can use a combination of physical machines and cloud instances. Prices are approximate as of 2026 retail and will vary by vendor, region, and discounts your institution may negotiate.

The lab consists of three tiers: (1) student workstations (16 machines), (2) infrastructure machines (1 instructor/faculty workstation), and (3) specialized lab sandbox machines (5 VMs for malware testing and network isolation). If budget is tight, you can reduce the number of student workstations and run the lab in rotating lab sessions. If budget allows, we suggest adding redundancy and higher specs for the faculty machine.

Bill of Materials: Detailed Breakdown

Item	Quantity	Specs/Notes	Approx. Cost per Unit	Subtotal
Student Workstations (Desktops or Thin Clients)	16	Intel i5/i7 or AMD Ryzen 5, 8GB RAM, 256GB SSD, Windows 10/11, RDP-enabled	$500-700	$8,000-11,200
Instructor Workstation	1	Intel i7 or AMD Ryzen 7, 16GB RAM, 512GB SSD, monitor(s), Windows 11 or Linux, for console access	$1,000-1,500	$1,000-1,500
Network Switch (Managed, PoE)	1	24-48 port Gigabit, managed, VLAN support, PoE for wireless APs	$300-600	$300-600
Firewall/Router (VLAN-capable)	1	Small business or campus firewall (Palo Alto, Cisco, Fortinet), VLAN tagging, 1Gbps+	$1,000-2,000	$1,000-2,000
Wireless Access Points (Optional)	2	802.11ax (Wi-Fi 6), PoE, VLAN-aware	$150-300/ea	$300-600
Hypervisor Server (if not using existing campus infra)	1	Dual-CPU server: 2x Intel Xeon or AMD EPYC, 64GB RAM, 2TB NVMe SSD, redundant PSU	$3,000-5,000	$3,000-5,000
	Bulk		Bulk discount	$500-1,000

Cabling and Patch Panels		Cat6/Cat6a cabling, wall plates, patch panel for 24-port switch		
UPS (Uninterruptible Power Supply)	1	5-10 kVA, 10-15 min backup for graceful shutdown	$1,000-2,000	$1,000-2,000
Spare Parts (RAM, SSDs, NICs)	Stock	For replacements during the semester	Varies	$500-800

Lab Total Hardware Cost: $15,600-$26,700 (assumes new hardware, no existing infrastructure). This is a one-time capital expenditure. Annual operational costs (utilities, network uplink, SentinelOne licensing, Tenable/ServiceNow subscriptions) are separate.

What You Can Skip (If Budget Is Tight)

- Managed firewall: if your institution has a campus firewall already, ask IT to carve out a lab VLAN instead of purchasing a separate device. This saves $1,000-2,000.
- Wireless access points: if all students have wired lab stations, APs are optional. This saves $300-600 but reduces flexibility for remote access.
- Redundant hypervisor: if you can tolerate a single-hypervisor failure (the lab goes down for a day or two for restart/rebuild), use a single powerful server instead of a clustered pair. This saves $3,000-5,000.
- UPS: if your institution has a data center with existing UPS infrastructure, and you can run the lab on that infrastructure, you do not need a dedicated UPS. This saves $1,000-2,000.
- Spare parts: buy spares only after you identify what fails. Start with a small buffer ($200-300) and replenish as needed.

What to Upgrade (If Budget Allows)

- Higher-spec student machines: 16GB RAM and NVMe SSD instead of SATA for faster lab responsiveness and better student experience. Cost increase: $100-200 per machine.
- Clustered hypervisors: two servers with shared storage (SAN or NAS) for fault tolerance. If one hypervisor fails, VMs migrate to the other. Cost increase: $3,000-5,000.
- Gigabit uplink from lab to campus core: 10 Gbps connection instead of 1 Gbps reduces latency during large scans (Nessus, vulnerability assessment). Cost increase: $500-1,000.
- Secondary Nessus scanner: run credential-based scans on one scanner while students run quick scans on another. Cost: $500-1,500 for Professional license.
- Dedicated logging infrastructure: a central syslog server or ELK stack (Elasticsearch, Logstash, Kibana) for long-term log storage and analysis. This is a bonus learning tool for students interested in SIEM. Cost: $1,000-3,000 (either licensing or cloud hosting).

Virtual vs. Physical Infrastructure Considerations

- The BOM above assumes a hybrid approach: physical student workstations in a classroom, plus virtual sandbox machines on a hypervisor. This is practical because students need a physical lab session experience, but simulation and malware testing benefit from being virtual (easy to snapshot and rollback).
- If you are constrained by space or prefer fully virtual, you can run everything on a cloud provider (AWS, Azure, GCP) or a campus OpenStack/vSphere cluster. The cost will differ: cloud instances run roughly $0.10-0.20 per hour (or $200-400 per month for a dedicated 16-machine lab). This may be lower total cost than buying hardware, especially if you can use existing campus cloud infrastructure.
- If you go fully cloud-hosted, ensure the cloud provider supports VLAN tagging or security groups that allow you to isolate the lab network from the production campus network. Test isolation before the semester starts.

Faculty Note: Procurement Timeline

Plan hardware procurement at least 4-6 months before the semester. Lead times for specialized equipment (firewalls, servers) can be 6-8 weeks.

Request IT department help early. They often have spare hardware or can speed up procurement if it is academic.

If you are budget-constrained, ask IT if they have decommissioned but still-functional machines you can repurpose for the lab.

Once hardware arrives, budget 2-4 weeks for setup, VLAN configuration, and testing before the semester starts.

Network Topology

Your lab network must be isolated from your institution's production network, while still having controlled access to the internet for updates and threat intelligence. This section describes a realistic topology in prose, showing how the pieces fit together. Imagine this layout:

At the core, your lab VLAN lives on a dedicated subnet: 192.168.100.0/24 (or another private range chosen by your IT team). This VLAN is separated from campus by a firewall or layer-3 switch that blocks any traffic between the lab subnet and production subnets. No lab machine can reach the campus Active Directory, student file shares, or critical infrastructure.

Within the lab VLAN, you have four logical zones: (1) the student workstation zone (192.168.100.10-192.168.100.80, 16 machines), (2) the faculty/instructor zone (192.168.100.5, 1 machine with console access), (3) the sandbox zone (192.168.100.110-192.168.100.114, 5 machines for malware and attack simulation), and (4) the network services zone (192.168.100.200-192.168.100.210, including Nessus, ServiceNow VM if not cloud-hosted, optional syslog server).

Internet egress from the lab VLAN flows through a single gateway (192.168.100.1, typically your managed firewall or router). This gateway has two critical rules: (1) Allow outbound traffic to SentinelOne cloud (for console communication, telemetry, threat intelligence feeds), Tenable cloud (for vulnerability data), and ServiceNow cloud (for incident tickets). (2) Block all other outbound internet traffic, and block all inbound traffic from the internet to the lab. This prevents students from accidentally (or intentionally) downloading actual malware from the internet, and prevents the lab network from being probed by external attackers.

Within the lab VLAN, all machines have full network visibility to each other (so students can simulate lateral movement and students can use Nessus to scan lab endpoints). However, students cannot directly route traffic to the campus network or the internet except through the controlled gateway. This configuration allows students to intentionally attack their lab machines without risk of hitting production systems.

Network Isolation: Validation and Testing

- Before the semester starts, test isolation. From a student lab machine, try to reach: (1) a production campus server (ping the faculty file server, RDP to a campus machine, DNS query to campus Active Directory), (2) the internet (ping 8.8.8.8, curl a public URL). Both should fail with 'network unreachable' or 'timeout.' If you can reach production systems or the internet from a lab machine, your isolation is incomplete. Work with IT to add firewall rules or VLAN segmentation until traffic is blocked.
- Next, verify that students can reach the SentinelOne console and deploy agents. From a student machine, open a browser and work through to your SentinelOne tenant URL (e.g., https://sentineloneconsole.company.com or a cloud-hosted instance). The console should load. If it does not, check: (1) is the firewall rule allowing traffic to SentinelOne cloud in place? (2) is there a proxy on the lab network that requires authentication? (3) is DNS working? (test by pinging SentinelOne's domain).
- Finally, run a test Nessus scan of a lab machine from the Nessus server. The scan should complete without hitting network boundaries. If the scan hangs or times out, debug: is the Nessus server on the same subnet as the target? If not, are there firewall rules allowing the Nessus traffic? If Nessus is outside the lab VLAN (on campus network), you will need a firewall rule allowing traffic from Nessus server to lab subnet for scanning.

Network Access Options: Wired vs. Wireless

- Student machines can connect to the lab VLAN via wired Ethernet or wireless. Wired is more reliable for lab work (less packet loss, more consistent throughput); wireless is more flexible if students want to bring their own laptops.
- Recommended approach: Provide wired lab stations (desktops with Ethernet in the classroom). Set up wireless access points (optional) for flexibility, but make it clear to students that wired is the supported configuration. If a student chooses wireless, they are responsible for debugging connectivity issues.

- If you support wireless, ensure the VLAN is properly configured on the APs (VLAN 100 or your chosen lab VLAN ID) and the access point is isolated from the campus wireless network. Use a different SSID for the lab VLAN (e.g., 'Lab-Cybersecurity') so students know which network to connect to.

Remote Access to Lab Machines (For Hybrid or Online Classes)

- If students are remote (or a mix of in-person and remote), they need RDP or VPN access to their lab machines. Two models:
- Model 1 (VPN + RDP): Students connect to a VPN gateway (Cisco AnyConnect, Palo Alto, FortiClient) that gives them access to the lab VLAN. Then they RDP to their assigned lab machine. This is secure and clean but requires VPN infrastructure and client software on student devices.
- Model 2 (RDP Jump Host): Set up one faculty machine in the lab as an 'RDP jump host' (visible to the internet with hardened security: strong passwords, MFA, IP whitelisting). Students RDP to the jump host, then RDP from there to their lab machine (nested RDP). This is slower but requires no VPN infrastructure.
- Recommendation: Model 1 (VPN) is preferred if your IT department can support it. It is more secure and performs better. If VPN is not available, use Model 2 but be very careful with the jump host (it will be a target). Restrict who can log in, change the default RDP port, and monitor for failed login attempts.

Classroom Topology

For in-person labs, each student gets a virtual machine running Windows 10 or 11, installed with the SentinelOne agent. All student machines connect to the lab VLAN. The faculty machine runs the SentinelOne console (web browser), Tenable Nessus Manager, and a ServiceNow Developer Instance (free, time-limited). One additional VM serves as a target for Nessus scanning and for intentional malware simulations.

For hybrid classrooms (in-person and remote), students remote in via RDP to their lab machines, or they install a lightweight VPN client that gives them access to the lab VLAN. Do not give students direct internet access from the lab machines; all outbound traffic should pass through a lab gateway you control. This prevents students from accidentally (or intentionally) exfiltrating data or downloading actual malware.

Network bandwidth: a typical lab of twenty machines generating detection telemetry, scanning traffic, and vulnerability scans can sustain on 100 Mbps shared internet uplink. For larger cohorts, upgrade to 1 Gbps. In-lab traffic between student machines and the SentinelOne cloud (your management console) is light, you are only sending heartbeats and telemetry summaries, not raw logs.

Workstation and Network Specifications

- Student machine specs (minimum): 2 vCPU, 4 GB RAM, 40 GB disk, Windows 10 or 11, RDP enabled.
- Faculty/admin machine: 8 vCPU, 16 GB RAM, 200 GB disk, capable of running web browser and lightweight services.
- Target/demo machine: 2 vCPU, 4 GB RAM, 50 GB disk, Windows Server 2019 or later, for intentional detections and scanning.
- Lab network: isolated VLAN, 192.168.100.0/24 or similar private range, no access to production network.
- Internet egress: lab traffic exits through a single gateway you monitor and control. Students cannot access external networks directly.
- RDP/SSH: faculty machine accessible via RDP from student machines for demonstrations. No SSH between student machines (prevent lateral movement practice beyond the scope of the lab).

Faculty Note: Network Isolation is Non-Negotiable

Do not run the lab on a shared campus network. A misconfigured policy or a simulated attack can spread to production systems.

If you do not have VLAN infrastructure, use a dedicated physical network segment with a firewall that blocks all outbound traffic except to your designated lab gateway.

Test isolation by trying to reach a production system from a lab machine. If you can reach it, your isolation is incomplete.

SentinelOne Tenant for Education

As of publication, SentinelOne offers academic and educational partnerships, though the program details, licensing terms, and availability may change. Your starting point is the SentinelOne education partner program. Reach out to the company's education team (look for 'academic partnerships' or 'education program' on sentinelone.com) and describe your use case: a cybersecurity course at an accredited institution with X students, needing a deployment for hands-on labs.

How to frame your request to SentinelOne: be specific about your institution's accreditation status (they are more likely to help accredited schools), the number of students, the expected number of endpoints you will deploy, and your timeline (e.g., 'We will be running this course starting Fall 2024'). Mention if this is part of a degree program (two-year or four-year) versus a standalone course; degree programs are often more attractive to vendors because they lead to student familiarity and future customer relationships. If your institution has existing vendor relationships (with Microsoft, Cisco, etc.), mention those, it shows you are serious and integrated.

Common outcomes: SentinelOne may provide a trial license (usually 30 or 90 days, free) to evaluate the product. If the trial is insufficient, they may offer an educational/NFR (no-fee) license with reduced agent limits (maybe 100 agents instead of 5,000). If you have a budget, they may offer an academic discount on a standard license. There is no single answer, the program varies by region and by institutional profile. The key is asking early and framing the ask as an educational investment, not a cost reduction.

Once you have a license, you will receive a tenant provisioned at SentinelOne. As an MSSP or educational deployment, you will be Account-level or Site-level (you probably will not be Global). This is fine; you will have full control over your own Site and Groups. You will receive credentials (username and password, or SSO instructions if your institution supports it) and a URL to your console. From that point forward, you can create Sites, Groups, policies, and manage users entirely on your own.

Multi-Tenant vs. Single-Tenant Lab Patterns

You have two design choices. In a single-tenant pattern, all students operate in the same Site and the same Groups. This is simpler to manage: one Site Key, one policy structure, all students see and investigate the same detections. The downside is that one student's misconfiguration can affect everyone else's experience. A student who deletes the main detection policy will break detection for twenty others.

In a multi-tenant pattern, you create one Site per section or cohort, with each Site having its own Site Key, its own policies, and its own incident queue. This gives students isolation and is more realistic (they are managing their own tenant), but it quadruples your operational burden: more Site Keys to track, more policies to maintain, more notification setup.

Recommendation: start with single-tenant. One Site, one Group per section (if you teach multiple sections, use Group names like 'Section A' and 'Section B'). This keeps the initial complexity low. As you scale to multiple cohorts or multiple departments sharing the lab, migrate to multi-tenant per section.

Recommended Tenant Structure

- In your SentinelOne Account, create a structure like this:
- Site: 'Cybersecurity Lab - [Academic Year]' (e.g., 'Cybersecurity Lab - 2024-2025'). This is your primary lab Site.
- Group: 'Section A' (contains student machines for first class period)
- Group: 'Section B' (contains student machines for second class period)
- Group: 'Faculty Demo' (contains the target machine and faculty machines used for demonstrations)
- Group: 'Staging' (used for testing new policies before rollout to Section A or B)

With this structure, you can apply different policies to different sections (maybe Section A runs the full lab curriculum, while Section B is a catch-up section with more monitoring and less autonomous remediation). The Staging group lets you test policy changes without affecting student experience. The Faculty Demo group isolates your demonstrations from student machines.

Sample Policy Hierarchy for Student-Safe Operations

SentinelOne policies control what the agent does when it detects something. You need to carefully configure policies so that students can learn incident response without accidentally breaking detection or creating unintended harm.

Create two site-level policies: (1) 'Detect Only' and (2) 'Controlled Remediation'. The 'Detect Only' policy enables all detection engines (Static AI, Behavioral AI, Script AI, Fileless, Anti-Exploitation, Intrusion Detection) but sets all actions to 'alert only',SentinelOne will flag something suspicious but will not automatically kill, quarantine, or remediate. This is the default policy for student machines. It is safe: detection happens, the student can investigate, but nothing is automatically destroyed.

(2) 'Controlled Remediation' enables the same detection engines but allows SentinelOne to kill or quarantine when a detection fires. However, do NOT enable automatic rollback or file recovery in the student lab. Rollback is a powerful feature but it is also complex, and a misconfigured rollback can corrupt a student's machine. Keep it disabled in the lab.

Assign 'Detect Only' to Group 'Section A' and Group 'Section B'. In the Staging group, use 'Controlled Remediation' so you can test what autonomous action looks like before teaching students about it in a later chapter.

Detection Engines and Baseline Configuration

- Enable these detection engines in your baseline policy:
- Static AI, Behavioral AI, Script AI, Fileless Malware Detection, Anti-Exploitation, Intrusion Detection, all enabled. Set actions to 'Alert Only' (no auto-remediation).
- Device Control: Enabled. Set to alert only on USB drive insertion (do not block, just alert). This teaches students about device control without disrupting lab flow.
- Network Controls: Disabled by default in student labs (students will enable it later in the curriculum when they understand firewall rules). Enable it only in the Faculty Demo group.
- Applications (Vulnerability Management): Enabled. This lets students see the built-in vulnerability scanner results on their machines.

Student Account Creation and RBAC

- Do not create student user accounts in SentinelOne. Students do not log into the console individually; you log in as the instructor and guide them through what they should look at. This prevents students from making administrative mistakes (like accidentally deleting a policy or disabling detection).
- Instead, set up one or two faculty/TA accounts with different roles:
- Instructor account: Account Admin or Site Admin role. This is you. You can create policies, manage exclusions, view all incidents, and modify settings.
- TA/Teaching Assistant account: Operator or Analyst role. This is your TA if you have one. They can investigate incidents and run queries but cannot modify policies or create/delete exclusions. This gives them hands-on experience while protecting critical configuration from accidental changes.

For API access (if students will write scripts to query SentinelOne), create a Service User account named 'Student Scripts' with read-only Analyst permissions. Generate an API key and share it with students. They can use it in scripts to query incidents and endpoints, but they cannot change policies or modify configuration.

Lab Console Access Patterns

- You have three options for how students access the SentinelOne console during lab time. Choose based on your classroom infrastructure and teaching goals.
- Option 1 (Instructor-Led): You project the SentinelOne console on a shared screen. Students follow along on their own machines (RDP into their lab VM) and see what you are clicking. You guide students through investigations, show them where to look, and ask them to identify key details. This is the safest approach early in the semester and requires minimal student access setup.
- Option 2 (Guided Lab): Students log into a read-only SentinelOne account (you create separate read-only operator accounts for each student or pair of students). They can work through the console independently but cannot change anything. They are guided by a written

lab worksheet that asks specific questions: 'How many endpoints are showing infected status?', 'Find the most recent threat and identify the detection engine that flagged it.' They take screenshots and annotations as evidence.

- Option 3 (Open Lab): Advanced students in later weeks can have Operator role accounts (or you supervise them one-on-one) where they can run certain operations: create Deep Visibility queries, initiate remediation actions, add endpoints to groups for simulations. This requires careful scoping and supervision but gives the most authentic experience.
- Recommendation: use Option 1 for weeks 1-4 (chapters 1-3), transition to Option 2 for weeks 5-10 as students build confidence, and move to Option 3 only for the capstone (week 15) with close supervision.

Provisioning Workflow and Console Navigation

- When you set up the lab, here is the one-time provisioning workflow:
- Log into your SentinelOne Account. Go to Settings > Sites and create a new Site called 'Cybersecurity Lab - [Year]'. Optionally, add a description like 'Academic lab for cybersecurity coursework at [Institution Name]'. This helps if you ever need to reach out to SentinelOne support and reference the lab.
- Set the agent limit conservatively (e.g., 100 agents for a class of 20 students, plus 10-20 buffer for testing machines and future cohorts). Go to the Site and note the Site Key. Save this key in an encrypted file or password manager, you will need it every time you deploy a new agent.
- Create Groups within the Site: 'Section A' (students in first time slot), 'Section B' (students in second time slot, if applicable), 'Faculty Demo' (faculty/TA machines used for live demonstrations), 'Staging' (test group for policy changes). If you only teach one section, you can skip Section B.
- Go to Sentinels > Packages and download the Windows agent installer. Use the Site Key to generate a deployment package (either a standalone installer or a silent-install script, depending on your preferences). Store this package in a shared location: your institutional GitHub repository (if IT allows), a shared drive (like OneDrive or Google Drive), or your course LMS (Blackboard, Canvas, etc.). Include clear instructions:

students should open a PowerShell window as Administrator on their lab machine, download the installer, and run it. The agent will register to your Site automatically once the installer runs.

- Create the baseline policies at the Site level: 'Detect Only' and 'Controlled Remediation' (as described above). Assign 'Detect Only' to Section A and Section B Groups. Assign 'Controlled Remediation' to Staging. Test each policy on a non-student VM first to make sure the settings are correct.
- Go to Settings > Notifications and enable malware, exclusion, and administrative alerts. Set up email recipients (your security team email or a shared classroom email) so you are notified when things happen in the lab. Send a test notification to confirm the SMTP relay is working.
- Go to Settings > Users and create your faculty and TA accounts. Create yourself as Site Admin. Create your TA (if you have one) as Operator. If students will work with APIs, create a Service User called 'Student Scripts' with read-only Analyst role and generate an API key.
- Take a screenshot of the entire console after setup is complete. Store this as a 'baseline' screenshot so you can compare the current state to the baseline if something gets misconfigured.

Figure A.1: SentinelOne Site Key Location (described: Settings > Sites > [Site Name] > copy Site Key)

Figure A.2: Group Creation Workflow (described: Sentinels > [Group icon] > Create New Group > assign policy > save)

Tenable Nessus Lab Deployment

Tenable Nessus is the industry standard for vulnerability scanning. For academic use, you have two options: Nessus Essentials (free, single-user, up to 16 IP addresses, good enough for a lab) or Nessus Professional (paid, multiple users, unlimited IP addresses). As of publication, Nessus Essentials is free to use, though Tenable may require registration and agree to their terms. Reach out to Tenable's education program (similar to your SentinelOne request) if you want Professional licensing.

For the lab, Nessus Essentials is usually sufficient. You are scanning a small lab network (maybe 25 machines), and Essentials can handle that. Download Nessus from tenable.com, register for a free activation code, and install it on the faculty machine or on a dedicated scanning machine within the lab VLAN.

Nessus Architecture: Manager vs. Scanner

Nessus comes as a single application: you install it, start the web UI, and run scans. For a lab, this is fine. You do not need the full Nessus Manager + multiple Scanner architecture (that is for enterprises). Install Nessus on the faculty machine or on a dedicated lab server.

Once installed, browse to https://localhost:8834 and log in. The default account is 'admin' with a password you set during installation. From here, you can create scan policies, define scan targets, and launch scans.

Lab Scanning Patterns

- Define scan policies and targets for your lab:
- Scan Policy 'Student Lab Network': Basic Network Scan of the 192.168.100.0/24 range, daily schedule, credential-based scanning (add a lab service account credential so Nessus can log into target machines and check patches). This discovers all machines on the network and identifies missing patches. Credential-based scanning requires you to create a local lab service account on all student machines (you can do

this via group policy or via SentinelOne RemoteOps). The service account should have local administrator rights so Nessus can enumerate installed patches and services.

- Scan Policy 'Target Demo Machine': Authenticated scan of the target machine (192.168.100.50 or your equivalent). Run this weekly. This machine will deliberately have old, vulnerable software installed (older versions of Java, Adobe Reader, 7-Zip, Firefox). Students will use this scan to understand what Nessus output looks like and what remediation looks like. Keep this machine offline except during scanning to preserve the vulnerable state.
- Scan Policy 'Spot Check': Ad-hoc scan of individual student machines when you want to show what vulnerabilities they might have. Run manually during class demonstrations. Only scan a single machine at a time during class to avoid overwhelming the network.
- Scan Policy 'Credential Scan (Weekly)': Full credential-based scan of all student machines. Schedule this for Friday evening after classes end. Results will be available Monday morning. This gives students actual vulnerability data to work with without disrupting class time.
- Configure all scans to output results in multiple formats: PDF (for reports), CSV (for analysis and comparison), and NESSUS native format (for archival). Store all scan results in a shared location with timestamps so you can show students how vulnerability counts change over time.

Vulnerability Remediation Workflow in the Lab

- Use Nessus scans to create a mini vulnerability-management workflow that students can execute:
- Each week, a Nessus scan identifies new vulnerabilities. You export the results and present them to students in a weekly 'vulnerability briefing' (10 minutes, during class).
- Students, working in groups or individually, select one or two Critical or High severity vulnerabilities and propose a remediation approach: patch the software, uninstall the vulnerable application, or isolate the affected machine.

- Once you approve the proposal, the student executes the remediation (or you do it for them if it requires admin privileges). Most patches can be installed by students themselves; some require SIEM or firewall rule changes that you handle.
- After remediation is applied, students re-run the Nessus scan on that machine to verify the vulnerability is gone. This teaches the important lesson that remediation should be validated, not just executed.

Integration with SentinelOne

- SentinelOne's Applications section (Chapter 7 of this book) includes built-in vulnerability scanning. This overlaps with Nessus functionality. The lab uses both because they serve different purposes:
- SentinelOne Applications: agent-based, lightweight, covers installed software on endpoints. Available to all students, no configuration needed. Students see risk scores in the console.
- Nessus: network-based, comprehensive, checks for network misconfigurations, open ports, weak protocols, patch compliance. More detailed but slower. A valuable learning tool for students to understand the breadth of what vulnerability scanning can detect.
- In the capstone lab (Section 7 below), students will use both: SentinelOne to see what the agent knows about vulnerabilities, Nessus to see what an external network-based scanner would find during an assessment. Comparing the two outputs teaches students that security tools give different views of the same problem.

ServiceNow Integration

ServiceNow is the industry standard for incident and change management. For academic use, Tenable and ServiceNow both offer free Developer Instances for educational purposes. A Developer Instance is a full-featured ServiceNow environment that expires after a period of inactivity (usually 30 days of no login). It is perfect for a lab: you get the real product to learn on, no license cost, with the understanding that it is temporary.

To request a ServiceNow Developer Instance, visit developer.servicenow.com, create an account, and request an instance. Within minutes, you will have a sandbox environment with full ServiceNow functionality. The instance URL will be something like 'dev12345.service-now.com'. You log in with credentials you set during creation.

ServiceNow Incident Management Workflow

- Create a basic incident-management workflow in ServiceNow that mirrors real SOC processes. Here is the minimal setup:
- Create a Service called 'Cybersecurity Lab' with a Catalog Item called 'Security Incident'. This is what tickets will be created under.
- Create an Incident Table that includes fields: Incident Number (auto-generated), Title, Description, Priority (Critical, High, Medium, Low), Status (New, In Progress, Resolved, Closed), Assigned To, Created By, Created Date, Updated Date.
- Create a workflow/automation rule: when a new incident is created with Priority 'High' or 'Critical', send an email to the security team (your instructor email).
- Set up a user group called 'Lab Security Team' and make it the default assignee for new incidents. You can be the only member for now, but later you can add TAs or advanced students.

SentinelOne to ServiceNow Integration

- The integration works via a webhook or middleware. When SentinelOne detects a threat with High or Critical severity, you want a ServiceNow ticket to be created automatically. This integration can be built two ways:
- Method 1 (Recommended for labs): Use SentinelOne's Syslog export to send detections to a lightweight middleware (a Python script, Node.js app, or a no-code platform like Zapier or Make) that translates the Syslog message into an HTTP POST to ServiceNow's REST API. This is more hands-on and educational.
- Method 2 (Simpler but less flexible): Manually create ServiceNow tickets when SentinelOne detects threats, so you can show students the entire workflow. In a real SOC, ticket creation is automatic; in a teaching lab, sometimes manual is better because students understand each step.
- For simplicity, start with Method 2: you detect a threat in SentinelOne, you manually create a ticket in ServiceNow, students investigate both and learn the process. Later, add the webhook automation if you have a developer helping or if students code the middleware themselves (a great capstone project).

Incident Lifecycle in the Lab

- Walk students through the entire incident lifecycle:
- SentinelOne detects a threat (malware, suspicious behavior, or intentional simulation). The detection appears in SentinelOne Incidents.
- You (or a student, if they have Operator role) create a ServiceNow ticket with the threat details: 'Malware detected on endpoint [name]: [threat name]'.
- The ticket is assigned to the Lab Security Team. The assigned analyst (a student or TA) begins investigation. They gather context: what process was running, what file was detected, did the detection fire on other endpoints?
- The analyst asks Nessus: does this endpoint have vulnerabilities that would explain how it got compromised? They correlate Nessus findings with SentinelOne investigation.

- The analyst documents findings in the ServiceNow ticket. They recommend remediation (patch, block, isolate, rebuild).
- Once remediation is complete and confirmed, the analyst marks the ServiceNow ticket as 'Resolved' or 'Closed'.
- Students review the ticket and the investigation for completeness, accuracy, and compliance.

Sample 16-Week Lab Schedule

Here is a semester-long outline mapping each chapter of 'Mastering SentinelOne' to weekly labs. Adjust timing based on your institution's calendar and your teaching pace.

Week	Topic	Chapter(s)	Lab Activities
1	Course Introduction & Lab Orientation	1	Faculty walks students through the SentinelOne console, Nessus, ServiceNow environments. Students create accounts (if multi-tenant) or verify they can log in. Review the lab VLAN and student machine assignments.
2	Dashboard Customization	2	Students log into SentinelOne console as read-only observers. Faculty guides them through Dashboard widgets, scope filters, and threat summary cards. Students screenshot their dashboard and annotate each widget.
3-4	Ranger Network Discovery	3	Ranger product overview. Students install SentinelOne agent on their lab machines. Ranger begins discovering devices on the network. Students use Ranger to identify all machines in the lab and confirm isolation (no unexpected

			devices). Document findings.
5-6	Sentinels: Fleet Management & Policies	4-5	Students review their endpoint details in Sentinels. Faculty explains policy inheritance and Group assignment. Lab activity: understand how a policy is inherited from Site to Group to endpoint. Trace the effective policy on their machines.
7	Midterm: Incident Triage Exercise	6	Faculty simulates or injects a detection into the lab (low-risk malware simulation). Each student investigates the incident, answers guided questions: what process? what behavior? was it blocked? Triage the incident in SentinelOne. Create a ServiceNow ticket.
8	Spring Break / Catch-Up Week	-	Students review Chapters 1-6 materials. Faculty holds optional office hours. Students who missed earlier labs catch up.
9-10	Applications & Activity Logs	7-8	Students review Applications tab on

			their machines and identify vulnerabilities. Faculty demonstrates Activity logs: login records, policy changes, remediation actions. Students audit their own machines' activity.
11	Reports & Metrics	9	Faculty creates a sample PDF report in SentinelOne showing threat summary, infected endpoints, remediation status. Students review the report and discuss what metrics are valuable for different audiences (C-suite vs. SOC analysts).
12-13	Automation & STAR Rules	10	Faculty demonstrates a custom detection rule (STAR rule) in SentinelOne. Students propose a detection rule for a behavior they want to flag. Faculty reviews and guides implementation. Lab activity: run a simulation to test the rule.
14	Settings & Governance	11	Faculty reviews Settings menu: notifications, users,

			API keys, exclusions, integrations. Lab activity: create a test API key, configure an exclusion (with documentation), verify notifications work.
15	Capstone Lab: End-to-End Scenario	All	Multi-day scenario: detect, investigate, correlate, remediate, document. See Section 7 below for full details.
16	Capstone Presentations & Course Wrap-Up	-	Student groups present their capstone findings. Faculty reviews key takeaways from the book and the lab. Course evaluation and feedback.

Day-1 Troubleshooting Playbook

Despite careful planning, something will go wrong on the first day you attempt to deploy the lab. An agent will fail to install, the console will not respond, Nessus will time out, or a student machine will not connect to the network. This section is a reference guide: for each of the ten most common day-1 issues, you will find a symptom, the likely cause, a diagnostic procedure, and a fix. Print this section and keep it near your desk during the first few lab sessions.

Issue 1: Agent Install Fails on Windows (Error: "Unable to Open Log File" or Install Hangs)

Symptom: Student runs the SentinelOne installer on a Windows machine. Installation starts but fails with an error code, or the installer hangs without completing.

Likely Causes: (1) A third-party antivirus (Windows Defender, Norton, Kaspersky) is blocking the installer. (2) Missing Windows prerequisites (Visual C++ runtime, .NET Framework). (3) Insufficient disk space or insufficient user permissions.

Diagnostic Steps: (1) Have the student open Task Manager and check if the SentinelOne installer process (sentinelctl.exe) is running and consuming CPU. If it hangs at 100% CPU, the installer is likely stuck waiting for file I/O. (2) Check disk space: 'C:\> wmic logicaldisk get name,freespace' should show at least 1 GB free. (3) Temporarily disable Windows Defender (Settings > Windows Security > Virus & Threat Protection > Manage Settings > toggle off Real-Time Protection). Run installer again. (4) Check Windows event logs: Event Viewer > Windows Logs > System, look for errors from the SentinelOne installer service.

Fix: (1) If antivirus is blocking: add the SentinelOne installer to the AV's exclusion list before running it again. (2) If prerequisites are missing: run 'wmic product list brief | find /I "Visual"' to check for Visual C++ runtime. If missing, download from Microsoft and install. (3) If disk space is low: free up space (delete old temp files, empty Recycle Bin), or use a different drive (USB external drive if necessary). Restart the installer. (4) If installer still hangs: uninstall any previous SentinelOne versions (Control Panel > Programs > Uninstall), clean the registry (use reg delete for SentinelOne keys if you are comfortable), and reboot before re-attempting installation.

Issue 2: Agent Install Fails on macOS (System Extension Not Approved)

Symptom: Student installs SentinelOne on a Mac. Installation completes without errors, but the agent never becomes 'online' in the console. System Settings shows 'Unidentified Developer' or 'System Extension Not Allowed.'

Likely Cause: macOS requires user approval for system extensions. The SentinelOne agent installs but does not run until the user approves the system extension.

Diagnostic Steps: (1) On the Mac, open System Settings > Privacy & Security > scroll down to 'System Extensions' or 'Security'. (2) Look for a SentinelOne entry that says 'Not Allowed' or 'Not Verified.' (3) Check the Console app (Applications > Utilities > Console) for messages like 'SentinelOne: system extension denied.'

Fix: (1) Have the student open System Settings > Privacy & Security and click the 'Allow' button next to the SentinelOne system extension. (2) The system will ask for the admin password or biometric confirmation. Student provides it. (3) The agent becomes active within 30 seconds. (4) Verify in the SentinelOne console that the machine now shows 'Online.'

Issue 3: Agent Install Fails on Linux (Missing Kernel Module Dependencies)

Symptom: Student runs 'dpkg -i SentinelOne-agent.deb' or equivalent on Ubuntu/CentOS. Installation fails with error 'Unmet dependencies' or 'Kernel module failed to load.'

Likely Cause: The Linux agent requires specific kernel development packages (linux-headers, build-essential) to compile the kernel module. If these are not installed, the agent cannot load.

Diagnostic Steps: (1) Have the student check installed packages: 'apt list --installed | grep linux-headers' (Ubuntu) or 'rpm -qa | grep kernel-devel' (CentOS). (2) If linux-headers are missing, run 'apt update && apt install -y linux-headers-$(uname -r)' (Ubuntu) or 'yum install -y kernel-devel' (CentOS). (3) Check dmesg for kernel module errors: 'dmesg | grep -i sentinel.'

Fix: (1) Install missing dependencies: 'apt install -y build-essential' (Ubuntu) or 'yum groupinstall -y 'Development Tools'' (CentOS). (2) Re-run the agent installer. (3) Verify the agent is loaded: 'lsmod | grep sentinel' should show SentinelOne kernel module. (4) Check agent status: 'sudo /opt/sentinelone/sentinel-agent ctl status' should show 'Connected.'

Issue 4: Agent Installs but Shows Offline in Console (Firewall/Proxy Blocking)

Symptom: The SentinelOne agent installs successfully (no errors), but the endpoint never appears 'Online' in the console, or it appears Online briefly then goes Offline repeatedly.

Likely Causes: (1) Lab network firewall is blocking outbound traffic to SentinelOne cloud. (2) An HTTP proxy on the lab network requires authentication; agent cannot connect. (3) DNS is not resolving SentinelOne's console domain. (4) Agent is trying to connect to the wrong console URL (misconfigured during deployment).

Diagnostic Steps: (1) On the student machine, test DNS resolution: 'nslookup sentineloneconsole.company.com' (or your tenant URL). Should return an IP address. If it returns 'Non-existent domain,' DNS is failing. (2) Test network connectivity: 'ping 8.8.8.8' to verify internet connectivity. If it fails, the student's machine has no internet access. (3) Check the agent log: 'C:\Program Files\SentinelOne\Sentinel\log\agent.log' (Windows) or '/var/log/sentinel/agent.log' (Linux). Look for 'Connection refused,' 'Timeout,' 'Proxy authentication failed,' or 'Certificate error.' (4) From the lab gateway, try 'telnet sentineloneconsole.company.com 443' to verify firewall rule is allowing the connection.

Fix: (1) If DNS is failing: check lab DHCP server configuration. Ensure students' machines have correct DNS servers (usually 8.8.8.8 or your institution's DNS). Manually set DNS if needed: 'ipconfig /setdnsservers Ethernet 8.8.8.8' (Windows) or edit /etc/resolv.conf (Linux). (2) If firewall is blocking: work with IT to add a rule allowing outbound traffic on port 443 (HTTPS) from the lab subnet to SentinelOne cloud IP ranges. SentinelOne publishes these in their docs. (3) If proxy authentication is required: configure agent to use the proxy. For Windows, create a registry key or use group policy. For Linux, set HTTP_PROXY environment variable. Contact SentinelOne support for agent-specific proxy configuration. (4) If console URL is wrong: verify the deployment package was generated with the correct Site Key for your lab tenant. If the Site Key is wrong, the agent will connect to the wrong console. Re-generate the deployment package and re-deploy agents.

Issue 5: Console Login Fails (SSO Misconfiguration or MFA Lockout)

Symptom: Faculty tries to log into the SentinelOne console. Login fails with error 'Invalid Credentials' or 'SSO Configuration Error.' Or, faculty is locked out after multiple failed login attempts.

Likely Causes: (1) SSO (Single Sign-On) is enabled but not properly configured in your institution's identity provider (Okta, Entra ID, etc.). (2) Password is incorrect or cached credentials are stale. (3) MFA (Multi-Factor Authentication) is enabled but the second factor is not being presented. (4) Account is locked due to too many failed login attempts.

Diagnostic Steps: (1) Try logging in with a local (non-SSO) account. Go to the SentinelOne login page and look for a 'Sign in with username/password' option separate from SSO buttons. If local login works, the SSO configuration is broken. (2) Check your institution's identity provider (Okta/Entra dashboard) to verify that SentinelOne is configured as a trusted application and that the faculty user is assigned to the SentinelOne application. (3) If MFA is enabled, check: do you have access to the second factor (SMS, authenticator app, hardware token)? Is the second factor device registered for the user account? (4) Check SentinelOne's server logs (contact support) for SSO error details.

Fix: (1) If SSO is broken: temporarily disable SSO and switch to local username/password login. (This may require contacting SentinelOne support or using a management API.) Log in, and then reconfigure SSO correctly via Settings > Users > SSO Settings. Follow SentinelOne's official SSO setup guide for your IdP. (2) If password is incorrect: use the 'Forgot Password' link on the login page. Enter your email and follow the reset link. (3) If MFA is preventing login: contact your MSSP or SentinelOne support to temporarily disable MFA, reset credentials, and re-enable MFA with the correct device. (4) If account is locked: wait 15 minutes (lock timeout) and try again, or contact SentinelOne support for account unlock.

Issue 6: Ranger Shows Zero Devices (Not Discovering Anything)

Symptom: Ranger is enabled and has been running for an hour, but it shows 'Discovered: 0 devices.' You know there are at least 16 student machines on the lab network.

Likely Causes: (1) No SentinelOne agent is on the lab network yet; Ranger requires at least one agent to begin passive discovery. (2) Ranger active scanning (ICMP, SNMP, SMB) is not enabled. (3) Network segmentation or firewall rules are preventing Ranger from seeing broadcast traffic.

Diagnostic Steps: (1) Check if at least one SentinelOne agent is online: go to Sentinels tab, and verify that you have at least one endpoint showing 'Online' status. (2) Check Ranger settings: Settings > Ranger > Status. Is Ranger enabled? Are active scans (ICMP, SNMP, etc.) toggled on? (3) From the lab gateway, verify network traffic is not being filtered. Run 'tcpdump' or Wireshark on the gateway interface and check for broadcast/multicast traffic from the lab subnet.

Fix: (1) If no agent is online: deploy at least one agent to a lab machine first. Once that agent comes online, Ranger will begin passive discovery. (2) If Ranger settings are off: enable Ranger and enable active scanning methods (ICMP, SNMP, mDNS, SMB). Start with ICMP (safest) and add others as needed. (3) If firewall is blocking: work with IT to ensure Ranger's port ranges are not blocked. SentinelOne uses multiple ports for scanning; consult their Ranger documentation. (4) Give Ranger 30-60 minutes to run a full discovery cycle. Device discovery can be slow on large networks.

Issue 7: Activity Logs Show No Recent Actions (Retention or Timezone Issues)

Symptom: Faculty logs into SentinelOne and navigates to Activity > Logs. The log is empty, or shows only old data from months ago. No recent policy changes, user logins, or admin actions are recorded.

Likely Causes: (1) Activity log retention is set to a short period (e.g., 7 days) and old logs have been purged. (2) Timezone is misconfigured; logs are being written in UTC but the console is displaying in a different timezone, so recent logs are not visible in the current date range. (3) No activity has actually occurred since the lab was set up.

Diagnostic Steps: (1) Check the date/time filter at the top of the Activity log. Is it set to 'Last 24 hours,' 'Last 7 days,' or 'Custom'? Try changing it to 'Last 30 days' or 'All time' to see if older logs appear. (2) Check Settings > Notifications > Activity Log Retention. Note the retention period. (3) Verify the console timezone: Settings > Preferences or Account Settings. Check if it matches your lab's timezone. (4) Perform a test action (create an exclusion, change a policy, add a user) and immediately check if it appears in the Activity log within 2-3 minutes.

Fix: (1) If date range is too narrow: expand the range in the filter. (2) If retention is too short: change retention policy if possible (Settings > General > Activity Log Retention). Some editions allow customization; others have fixed retention. If fixed, this is a licensing limitation. (3) If timezone is wrong: change it in Preferences. (4) If no activity is showing: ensure you are filtering by the correct scope (Site, Group, or Global) and date range. Use the 'export' feature to download the full activity log as CSV for deeper analysis.

Issue 8: STAR Rules Not Firing (Rule Not Matching Threats)

Symptom: Faculty creates a custom STAR (Storyline Active Response) rule to detect a specific behavior (e.g., process named 'malware.exe'). The rule is deployed to a test group. A student intentionally triggers the behavior, but the rule does not fire and no incident is created.

Likely Causes: (1) Rule scope is wrong; the rule is deployed to the wrong Group, or the endpoint is in a Group where the rule is not assigned. (2) Rule syntax or logic is incorrect; the condition does not match the actual threat data. (3) The threat engine or detection type required by the rule is disabled in the policy.

Diagnostic Steps: (1) Verify rule scope: go to Settings > STAR > select the rule. Check which Groups the rule is assigned to. Verify your test endpoint is in one of those Groups. (2) Manually trigger the detection again (run the malware simulator or process on the test machine). Check the Incidents tab to see if ANY incident fires (even if it is from a different detection engine, like Behavioral AI). (3) Check the agent policy: go to the endpoint's Group and review the policy. Are the detection engines required for your rule enabled? (e.g., if your rule depends on 'memory detection,' is Behavioral AI enabled in the policy?). (4) Review the rule syntax: open the rule in the editor. Step through each condition and verify it uses correct field names and values. Check SentinelOne's STAR rule documentation for syntax examples.

Issue 9: Reports Show No Data (Date Range or Scope Filter Wrong)

Symptom: Faculty generates a report (e.g., 'Threats Detected This Week' or 'Patch Compliance'). The report comes back with no data, or data from the wrong time period.

Likely Causes: (1) Report scope is set to a Site or Group that has no endpoints or no activity. (2) Date range is set incorrectly (e.g., report is querying last month, but the lab was just set up this week). (3) Report type is not compatible with the current license or SentinelOne version.

Diagnostic Steps: (1) Before generating the report, verify that your scope has active endpoints: go to Sentinels tab and count endpoints. Is it greater than zero? (2) Verify that there has been recent activity: go to Dashboard and look for recent threats or incidents. If the Dashboard is also empty, the lab has no activity, not a reporting problem. (3) Check the report date range setting. If the lab was deployed last week, a report for 'last 90 days' may include your data. Try a custom date range starting from the lab deployment date. (4) Check SentinelOne release notes to confirm the report type you are using is available in your version and license tier.

Fix: (1) Change the scope filter to a Group or Site that you know has active endpoints. (2) Adjust the date range to cover when the lab was deployed and when activity occurred. (3) If the report is still empty and other tabs (Dashboard, Incidents) show data, the report type may be unavailable in your edition. Check documentation or contact support. (4) As a workaround, export raw data from Incidents or Deep Visibility and build a report manually in a spreadsheet.

Issue 10: API Token Returns 401 Unauthorized (Token Expired or Malformed)

Symptom: A student or faculty tries to use the SentinelOne API to query incidents or endpoints. The API call returns HTTP 401 Unauthorized or 'Invalid API Token' error.

Likely Causes: (1) API token is expired (tokens expire after a set period, typically 30 or 90 days). (2) API token is revoked or deleted. (3) API request is missing the Authorization header or the header format is incorrect. (4) API is not enabled in the license, or the user account does not have API permissions.

Diagnostic Steps: (1) Check if the token is still valid: go to Settings > API Tokens and verify the token exists and has an 'Expiration Date' in the future. (2) Verify the API request format. The Authorization header should be: 'Authorization: APIToken [your-token-here]'. Check that the token is spelled correctly and there are no extra spaces. (3) Test with a simple API call: 'curl -H "Authorization: APIToken [token]" https://your-sentinel-console/api/v2.0/agents' (adjust URL for your tenant). (4) Check if API is available in your edition: Settings > Users > API section. Some education licenses have limited API access.

Fix: (1) If token is expired: generate a new token in Settings > API Tokens > Create Token. Copy the new token and use it in the API request. (2) If token format is wrong: ensure the Authorization header follows the exact format above. Use a tool like Postman or curl to test with -v flag to see the exact headers being sent. (3) If API is not available in the license: contact SentinelOne support or your MSSP to request API access, or upgrade to a license tier that includes API. (4) As a temporary workaround, use the web console to manually query the data students need, and have them document findings from screenshots instead of automated scripts.

Lab Exercises by Chapter: A Cross-Reference

This table maps each chapter of the book to the hands-on labs students will complete. Use this to plan your 16-week syllabus, estimate workload, and identify prerequisites. Each row represents one chapter; columns show the number of labs in that chapter, what infrastructure they require, and typical time per lab.

Chapter	Topic	Num. Labs	Required Infrastructure	Time/Lab (min)	Prerequisites
1	Console Overview	1	Console access (faculty-led demo)	45-60	None (intro)
2	Dashboard	1	Student console access (read-only)	45-60	Chapter 1
3	Ranger	1	Ranger-enabled site, lab network	60-90	Chapter 1; network basics
4	Sentinels: Fleet Mgmt	1	Sentinels tab, 5+ deployed agents	45-60	Chapters 1-3
5	Sentinels: Remediation	1	Live malware simulation, policy test	60-90	Chapter 4
6	Incidents: Investigation	2	Live threat or EICAR simulation, Deep Visibility	90-120 each	Chapters 1-5
7	Applications: Vulns	1	Vulnerable software on test machine	60-90	Chapter 6; Nessus access
8	Activity Logs	1	Admin action (create exclusion/ policy change)	45-60	Chapter 6
9	Reports	1	Data available for report	45-60	Chapters 1-8 activity

			(requires prior labs)		
10	STAR Rules & Automation	2	Staging group, malware simulation, monitoring	90-120 each	Chapters 4, 6, 9
11	Settings & Governance	1	API key creation, exclusion documentation	60-90	Chapters 1, 8, 10
Capstone	End-to-End Scenario	1 (multi-day)	All infrastructure: console, Nessus, ServiceNow	240-360 total (4-6 hours)	All chapters

Using This Table to Plan Your Semester

- Total hands-on lab hours (excluding capstone): approximately 13-16 hours of student lab time spread across 15 weeks. With two 75-minute lab sessions per week, you have roughly 22.5 hours per semester. This means labs consume about 65% of available lab time, leaving 35% for lecture, review, and buffer.
- Cumulative labs: Chapters 1-5 build foundational skills (console navigation, agent deployment, policy basics). Chapters 6-7 deepen investigation skills. Chapters 8-11 focus on operations, governance, and automation. By the time students reach the capstone (week 15), they should be comfortable with all major console sections.
- Prerequisite considerations: Students cannot start Chapter 6 (Incidents) labs without deployed agents and live threats (requires Chapters 1-5). Students cannot start Chapter 10 (STAR Rules) labs without understanding Chapter 4 (policies). Plan your pacing so prerequisites are met before the chapter is assigned.

- Flexibility: If your semester is shorter (12 weeks) or your class meets once per week instead of twice, you may need to compress labs or assign some as homework (asynchronous). Chapters 2, 8, and 9 are good candidates for asynchronous completion since they focus on reading reports and logs, not real-time interactions.
- Assessment: Use the lab exercises as formative assessment during class. Assign the capstone (Chapter 12) as the major summative assessment. Each chapter's lab should result in a deliverable (a screenshot, a report, a query result, a documented exclusion) that you collect and review for evidence of learning.

Capstone Lab: End-to-End Incident Scenario

The capstone is a multi-day, multi-step lab where students simulate a complete incident from detection through remediation and reporting. This is where all the pieces come together.

Scenario Brief

- Your organization's security team receives an alert: a user on the Sales team has clicked a link in a phishing email and downloaded a suspicious executable. The malware has been contained, but you need to investigate the full scope and impact. Questions to answer:
- What process was running when the malware was detected?
- Did the malware execute? Did it do anything suspicious (network connections, file modifications, privilege escalation)?
- Are there other endpoints in the organization that are running the same malware? (lateralization check)
- Does the affected endpoint have any unpatched vulnerabilities that could have been exploited?
- What is the recommended remediation? (patch, isolate, rebuild, monitor)
- How should you report this incident to management?

Learning Objectives

- Investigate a malware detection in SentinelOne, understand the threat chain (process tree, network connections, file activity).
- Correlate threat data from multiple sources: SentinelOne threats, SentinelOne Deep Visibility queries, Nessus vulnerability scans.
- Create and manage an incident ticket in ServiceNow.
- Recommend and execute remediation actions.
- Document findings and prepare a presentation for a non-technical audience.

Capstone Deliverables

- Incident Investigation Report (2-3 pages): summary of findings, timeline, root cause, impact, recommendation.
- Detailed Technical Analysis (Appendix): process tree screenshots, network connection data, file hashes, YARA rule or hash-based exclusion recommendation.
- ServiceNow Ticket: fully documented, including all investigation notes, status updates, and final resolution.
- Presentation (10-15 minutes): students present findings to faculty and peers. Presentation should be understandable by non-technical stakeholders.

Capstone Rubric

Criterion	**Excellent**	**Good**	**Needs Improvement**
Threat Investigation	Student identified all key details: process tree, parent-child relationships, suspicious behaviors, network connections, file hashes. Used Deep Visibility queries effectively.	Student identified most key details. Deep Visibility queries present but incomplete.	Student missed key investigation steps. Little or no Deep Visibility usage.
Correlation & Context	Student correlated SentinelOne findings with Nessus vulnerability scan, explained how vulnerabilities could have led to compromise.	Student referenced Nessus data but connection to threat was unclear or incomplete.	Student did not consult Nessus data or failed to correlate findings.
ServiceNow Ticket	Ticket is complete, professional, includes investigation notes, remediation recommendation, and status updates. Ready for real SOC handoff.	Ticket covers main points but lacks detail in some areas. Status updates present but sparse.	Ticket is incomplete or disorganized. Missing key investigation details.
Remediation Recommendation	Student recommended specific, actionable remediation (patch specific CVE, isolate endpoint, add exclusion). Explained rationale and trade-offs.	Student recommended remediation but lacked detail or reasoning.	Student did not provide clear remediation recommendation or recommendation was vague.
Presentation	Clear, well-organized, appropriate for non-	Presentation covered main points but was somewhat	Presentation was difficult to follow or too technical /

	technical audience. Student fielded questions confidently.	disorganized or technical level was mismatched.	not technical enough for the stated audience.

Role Assignments

- Divide the class into small groups (3-4 students per group). Within each group, assign roles:
- Incident Analyst: leads investigation in SentinelOne, runs Deep Visibility queries, documents findings.
- Correlation Lead: cross-references SentinelOne findings with Nessus scan data, vulnerability database lookups, threat intelligence.
- ServiceNow Owner: creates and maintains the incident ticket, updates status, coordinates with other roles.
- Communicator/Presenter: synthesizes findings into a clear report and presentation for non-technical stakeholders.

Rotate roles if you have multiple capstone scenarios, so each student gets to lead investigation at least once.

Capstone Timeline

- Day 1 (In-class): Faculty injects the malware simulation onto a target student machine (or reveals that a machine is 'infected'). Students begin investigation. Faculty is available for guidance but should resist giving answers. By end of day, each group should have initial findings documented. A good checkpoint at the end of Day 1 is that students have identified the suspicious process, the parent process, and at least one suspicious behavior (network connection, file write, registry modification).
- Day 2 (Homework / out-of-class): Groups continue investigation, run Nessus scans on the affected machine, consult threat intelligence (VirusTotal, MITRE ATT&CK), draft reports. Faculty should be available via email for quick questions but not doing the investigation for them.

- Day 3 (In-class): Groups finalize reports and presentations. Faculty reviews findings with each group to ensure accuracy and completeness. This is a 1-on-1 or small-group review session (not the full class). Faculty checks: are the findings technically correct? Is the remediation recommendation justified? Does the report tell a clear story?
- Day 4 (In-class): Presentations. Each group presents findings (10-15 min) followed by Q&A from faculty and peers. Other students should have read copies of each group's report before presentation so they can ask informed questions.
- Optional Day 5 (Debrief): After all presentations, do a full-class debrief. Discuss what was hardest about the investigation. Compare how different groups approached the same problem. Highlight excellent work and learning moments.

Grading and Feedback on the Capstone

- The capstone should be worth a significant portion of the course grade (20-30%). Each deliverable contributes to the grade:
- Investigation Report (40% of capstone grade): Accuracy, completeness, clarity. Deduct points for factual errors, missed investigation steps, or unclear reasoning.
- Technical Analysis Appendix (20% of capstone grade): Quality of screenshots, hash analysis, log excerpts. Are the technical details correct and relevant?
- ServiceNow Ticket (20% of capstone grade): Professionalism, detail, documentation of the investigation process. Is it a ticket a real SOC analyst would be proud to hand off?
- Presentation (20% of capstone grade): Clarity for a non-technical audience, confident delivery, ability to field questions. Did the student explain findings in terms a manager would understand?

Provide detailed rubric feedback on each group's work within one week of presentations. Students should leave the course knowing exactly what they did well and where they should focus in future coursework or on the job.

Faculty Notes: Common Pitfalls and Operational Tips

Running a lab at this scale is more complex than running a video-based course. Here are the pitfalls you will likely encounter and how to handle them.

Pitfall 1: SentinelOne Tenant Gets Misconfigured

Someone (often you, when testing) disables the main detection policy or sets all endpoints to 'Exclude All'. Suddenly, no detections are firing.

Solution: Before each class, do a 10-minute health check. Log into SentinelOne, check the Dashboard to verify threats are coming in. If detection is silent, walk the inheritance chain: Go to one student endpoint, check its Group policy. Go to that Group, check the assigned policy. Go to the Site policy. Is detection enabled? Is the policy assigned to the right Group?

Prevention: use the Staging group for all your experimentation. Never modify the Section A or Section B policies unless you are intentionally teaching a lesson about policy changes. Document any temporary overrides (e.g., 'Week 12: Disabled Behavioral AI in Staging group to demonstrate policy override') and restore them afterward.

Pitfall 2: Student Machines Stop Checking In

A student machine loses network connectivity or the agent crashes. The endpoint drops off the console and students panic.

Solution: keep a running list of 'expected endpoints'. Before class, screenshot the Sentinels view showing all expected machines. If one is missing, immediately check: does the machine have network connectivity? Can you RDP into it? Is the SentinelOne agent service running (check Services or Task Manager on the student machine)? If the agent is not running, restart it. If the machine has no network, check VLAN and DNS configuration.

Prevention: do a connectivity test at the start of each lab session. Have students ping the lab gateway and verify they can reach the SentinelOne cloud (a simple telemetry check in the agent console).

Pitfall 3: Malware Simulation Does Not Trigger Detection

You run a simulation file (a EICAR test or benign malware simulator) expecting SentinelOne to detect it. Detection does not fire.

Solution: this is usually a policy issue. Verify the target machine is in the right Group and has the right policy assigned. Verify the detection engines you expect to fire (e.g., Static AI, Behavioral AI) are enabled in the policy. Check the Activity log on the agent: did it even see the file? Sometimes the simulation is too well-known and whitelisted. Try a different simulation or contact SentinelOne support to request a test file that will trigger reliably in your environment.

Prevention: test your simulation ahead of time in the Staging group. Once you find a simulation that works, document it and reuse it for every capstone.

Pitfall 4: Students Forget Lab Credentials or Lock Themselves Out

A student forgets the password to their lab machine or the ServiceNow Developer Instance password.

Solution: have a master password list (stored securely, encrypted, in a password manager or encrypted file on your faculty machine). Reset the password for the student. For ServiceNow Developer Instances, reset is easy: log out, click 'Forgot password', and reset via email. For student lab machines (if they are VMs), you can also reset via hypervisor snapshotting or VM cloning.

Prevention: at the start of the semester, have each student write down their credentials in a secure notebook and keep it locked away. Provide a password reset procedure in the syllabus.

Pitfall 5: Nessus Scan Takes Too Long or Overwhelms the Network

A student launches a full vulnerability scan of all 20 lab machines. The scan takes hours and generates so much traffic that other lab activities slow down.

Solution: educate students about scan scope and scheduling. Run full scans outside of class time (overnight or over the weekend). During class, run quick scans on a single machine or use a pre-saved scan snapshot. Most importantly, document scan SLAs: 'Nessus full network scans run on Friday evenings, results available by Monday morning.'

Prevention: create Nessus scan policies with time-of-day restrictions. Set scans to run only after 5 PM or on weekends.

Pitfall 6: ServiceNow Developer Instance Expires

ServiceNow Developer Instances expire after 30 days of inactivity. If you go on spring break and do not log in, the instance disappears.

Solution: set a reminder in your calendar to log in to the instance every 28 days, even if you are not actively using it. A 30-second login resets the inactivity timer. Alternatively, request a second Developer Instance as a backup, so you have a hot spare if one expires.

Prevention: document the ServiceNow instance URL and credentials prominently in your syllabus and course management system. Add a standing calendar event: 'Log in to ServiceNow to prevent expiration.'

Faculty Checklist: Weekly Lab Health Check (Before Class)

Log into SentinelOne and verify all expected endpoints are showing in Sentinels. If any are missing, investigate.

Check the Dashboard for recent threats or detections. If no recent activity, verify policies are enabled.

Log into ServiceNow and verify the environment is responsive.

Log into Nessus and verify the last scan completed without errors.

Test one student machine: can you RDP into it? Can it reach the lab gateway and SentinelOne cloud?

Review the Activity log for any unexpected changes made since your last session.

Maintenance and Updates

Your lab will not remain static. SentinelOne, Tenable, ServiceNow, and the threat landscape will all evolve. Here is how to stay current without spending all your time on maintenance.

SentinelOne Product Updates

SentinelOne releases agent updates and console updates regularly. As of publication, the update cycle is roughly every 2-4 weeks for agent updates and monthly for console updates.

For the lab: you do not need to update agents immediately. SentinelOne maintains backward compatibility; older agents work with newer consoles. However, roughly every semester (spring and fall), plan a 'lab maintenance week' where you push agent updates to all student machines. Schedule this during a week with lighter lab activities (e.g., during the catch-up week in Week 8).

Subscribe to the SentinelOne release notes (check sentinelone.com/blog or release-notes for your region). If a critical security fix is released, apply it immediately. If a major new feature lands (e.g., a new detection engine), plan a faculty-only exploration session to understand it before teaching it to students.

Chapter Updates and Curriculum Sync

As SentinelOne evolves, so will the chapters of this book. Check Kendrick Washington's website or the publisher's companion materials for updated chapters and supplementary guides. Roughly once per year, re-read the chapters most relevant to your lab (Chapters 1, 4, 5, 11) to ensure your lab practices still align.

If a chapter is significantly updated (e.g., 'Chapter 10: Automation' has a new STAR rule engine), take time to understand the changes yourself before teaching it. Use your lab's Staging group to test any new techniques before deploying them to student machines.

Threat Landscape and Vulnerability Data

The vulnerabilities and threats you use in your lab should stay current. Every year, new CVEs are published and old ones fade. For your capstone scenario or your simulations, keep a curated list of recent vulnerabilities (Critical and High severity) that are relevant to your student environment.

Use resources like: NVD (nvd.nist.gov) for CVE data, CISA.gov for current advisories, and the CVE Details website for trending vulnerabilities. Every semester, pick a couple of new CVEs to include in your Nessus scans or capstone scenario. This keeps the lab relevant and teaches students that vulnerability management is an ongoing practice.

Seasonal Refresh

At the start of each academic year: create a fresh SentinelOne Site for the new cohort (do not reuse last year's Site; start clean). Archive old logs and incidents from the previous year for reference. Verify that your Nessus license (Essentials or Professional) is still active. Provision a fresh ServiceNow Developer Instance. Run a full health check on all lab infrastructure: hypervisor, network, virtualization platform, firewall rules.

Documentation and Knowledge Sharing

- Document your lab as you build it. Keep a faculty wiki or shared document with:
- Lab network topology (IP ranges, VLAN IDs, gateway IP, DNS servers)
- SentinelOne Site Key and credentials for your lab Site (encrypted)
- Nessus admin credentials and scan policy templates (encrypted)
- ServiceNow Developer Instance URL and admin credentials (encrypted)
- List of known good malware simulations and where they are stored
- Common troubleshooting steps and solutions (what you learned from Pitfalls 1-6 above)
- Contact information for SentinelOne, Tenable, and ServiceNow support (if you have support relationships)

Share this documentation with co-faculty, TAs, and (in encrypted form) with your institution's IT department. If you leave the institution or retire, your successor will be able to stand up and run the lab without starting from scratch.

Best Practices for Lab Sustainability

- After you run the lab once, you will have insights for running it better the second time. Here are practices that help labs remain sustainable over years, not just one semester.
- Version Your Lab Configuration: Keep your lab topology, network diagram, and policy templates in version control (GitHub, GitLab) or a shared wiki. When you make a change (e.g., update a detection policy, add a new Group), document it with a date and a brief note. This makes it easy to understand why a decision was made and to revert if necessary.
- Record Lab Sessions (with Consent): If possible, record your lab demonstrations (screen capture + audio) so students can review them asynchronously. This helps students who miss a class and provides a reference for future cohorts. Use a platform like Zoom, OBS, or your institution's video capture tool. Always get written consent from students before recording.
- Build a Lab FAQ: After the first run, you will have answered the same questions ten times. Compile them into a FAQ document: 'How do I RDP into my lab machine?', 'What do I do if SentinelOne is not detecting anything?', 'How do I export a Nessus scan as PDF?' Distribute this to students at the start of the semester.
- Establish Lab Office Hours: Dedicate one or two hours per week (during a time that works for most students) for open lab office hours. Students can drop in with questions, show you their work, and get real-time feedback. This is where you catch students who are stuck early, before they fall behind.
- Rotate Lab Machines: Every academic year, rebuild all student lab machines from scratch. This prevents configuration drift (where one machine gradually becomes different from others) and ensures a clean starting point. Script the VM creation if possible so you can spin up a fresh cohort in an afternoon.

- Annual Review: Once per year, review the entire lab design. Ask: What worked? What frustrated students? What new features in SentinelOne or Nessus should we include? What labs took too long? Too short? Use this feedback to iteratively improve the curriculum.

Lab Assessment and Learning Outcomes

As you design labs and assignments, align them to measurable learning outcomes. Here are outcomes your students should achieve by the end of the semester, organized by chapter.

Chapter-by-Chapter Learning Outcomes

Chapter	Learning Outcome	Assessment Method
1	Work through the SentinelOne console and identify all ten left-nav capability areas	Lab exercise: screenshot and annotate each area
2-3	Design a custom Dashboard and explain why each widget is relevant to the SOC	Lab: create custom dashboard, written justification
4-5	Understand policy inheritance and the impact of Group-level policy overrides	Lab: trace policy for an endpoint, identify inheritance chain
6	Investigate a live threat in SentinelOne using process trees and Deep Visibility	Lab: mini-incident investigation with guided worksheet
7	Correlate endpoint vulnerability data with known CVEs and risk scores	Lab: analyze Applications tab output, map to CVSS data
8	Read and interpret the Activity audit log to answer "who did what when"	Lab: audit log review exercise with specific questions
9	Create a PDF report appropriate for a C-level executive audience	Lab: generate report, peer review on clarity
10	Write a custom detection rule (STAR rule) and test it on a simulated behavior	Lab: propose rule, faculty reviews and deploys for testing
11	Configure exclusions and API keys with appropriate governance	Lab: create exclusion with documentation, generate API key
All	Orchestrate SentinelOne, Tenable, and ServiceNow in an end-to-end workflow	Capstone lab: detect, investigate, remediate, report

Formative vs. Summative Assessment

Formative assessment happens during the lab: you observe students working, ask them questions, and provide immediate feedback. 'What do you think this process is doing?' 'Why do you think SentinelOne flagged it?' These moments are teaching opportunities, not evaluations. Do formative assessment every class.

Summative assessment happens at the end of units or the course: graded assignments, quizzes, the capstone. These measure whether students met the learning outcomes. Use the lab deliverables (investigation reports, screenshots, presentations) as summative evidence.

The balance: 70% of student grades should come from formative assessment and active participation in labs. This reflects the reality that cybersecurity is a hands-on discipline and mistakes in a lab are valuable learning opportunities. 30% should come from summative assessment (capstone, written exam if you give one). This incentivizes students to show up and engage.

Closing: The Journey Ahead

You now have the blueprint for a hands-on cybersecurity lab that will give your students experience that video lectures alone cannot provide. The lab is not perfect; it will have hiccups. A student will misconfigure something, a tool will have an unexpected downtime, a simulation will not behave as expected. That is the point. Your students will learn not just what SentinelOne is, but what it means to operate and troubleshoot it under real conditions.

Start small. Run the lab with one section before scaling to multiple sections. Build the capstone gradually: the first time you run it, have a TA or colleague present so there is a safety net. By the third semester, you will have refined the lab, documented the common problems, and streamlined the setup so that it takes far less faculty time than it does the first time.

Finally, feed back what you learn into the community. Share your lab design with other faculty teaching cybersecurity. Contribute improvements to open educational resources. Your students will be grateful, and the entire field benefits when educators share what works.

Mastering SentinelOne

Academic Edition, Appendix B

by Kendrick Washington, Technology Interpreters, Inc.

Appendix B

MITRE ATT&CK Mapping for SentinelOne Operators

Why ATT&CK Matters for the Operator

The MITRE ATT&CK framework has become the de facto common language for describing and sharing threat intelligence across the security industry. A threat intelligence analyst, a forensic investigator, a red-team operator, and an SOC analyst can all reference the same technique ID,say, Execution T1106: Native API,and immediately understand the attack step being discussed, without ambiguity or regional interpretation. This shared vocabulary is now expected in federal procurement, in breach reporting, in threat intelligence feeds, and in academic research.

For a SentinelOne operator, understanding how SentinelOne's detection capabilities map to ATT&CK techniques serves three practical purposes. First, it lets you communicate findings in the language your threat intelligence team and incident-response peers understand. Second, it helps you answer gap-analysis questions: "Which ATT&CK techniques do we have visibility into?" and "Which do we have the capability to detect or block?" Third, it drives detection-engineering decisions: when you design detection rules, alerts, or STAR automation rules, you are effectively writing coverage for specific ATT&CK techniques, and knowing which techniques matter most to your threat model keeps you focused on high-value work.

This appendix maps the major ATT&CK tactics and techniques that SentinelOne is designed to detect or contain, and ties each to the corresponding chapter in this book where you will find the operational detail. The mapping is not exhaustive,ATT&CK contains hundreds of techniques,but it covers the ones that matter most for endpoint detection and response. Throughout this book, when a chapter addresses a particular class of attack, you will find ATT&CK references in sidebars, callouts, and references sections that anchor the discussion to the framework.

How This Appendix Is Organized

This appendix is structured around the ATT&CK Enterprise tactics,the broad categories of adversary behavior, such as Initial Access, Execution, Persistence, and so on. For each tactic, we list the most relevant techniques that SentinelOne operators encounter in practice, provide a brief description of why that technique matters, and map it to the chapter(s) where you will find operational guidance.

A critical note: ATT&CK is a living framework, maintained by MITRE and updated quarterly. This appendix was written against ATT&CK v15, released in April 2025. If you are reading this in April 2026 or later, some technique IDs and descriptions may have shifted. Before you commit to building detection logic around a specific technique, verify that it still exists and that its definition has not been refined or deprecated. You will find the canonical ATT&CK matrix at attack.mitre.org.

The techniques listed here represent the techniques that SentinelOne's detection engines, behavioral analysis, network monitoring, and response capabilities are most directly suited to addressing. Not every technique is equally visible on an endpoint; some require network-level sensors or supply-chain intelligence. Where that matters, we have noted it.

ATT&CK Tactics Covered in This Book

- Initial Access: T1189 (Drive-by Compromise), T1566 (Phishing), T1195 (Supply Chain Compromise)
- Execution: T1059 (Command and Scripting Interpreter), T1106 (Native API), T1053 (Scheduled Task/Job), T1204 (User Execution)
- Persistence: T1547 (Boot or Logon Autostart Execution), T1547.001 (Registry Run Keys / Start Folder), T1098 (Account Manipulation), T1098.003 (Additional Cloud Credentials)
- Privilege Escalation: T1548 (Abuse Elevation Control Mechanism), T1548.002 (Bypass User Account Control), T1547 (Boot or Logon Autostart Execution)
- Defense Evasion: T1548 (Abuse Elevation Control Mechanism), T1140 (Deobfuscate/Decode Files or Information), T1027 (Obfuscated Files or Information), T1222 (File and Directory Permissions Modification)

- Credential Access: T1187 (Forced Authentication), T1056 (Input Capture), T1056.004 (Credential API Hooking), T1110 (Brute Force)
- Discovery: T1087 (Account Discovery), T1010 (Application Window Discovery), T1217 (Browser Bookmark Discovery), T1526 (Cloud Service Discovery)
- Lateral Movement: T1570 (Lateral Tool Transfer), T1570 (Lateral Movement via Network Device), T1550 (Use Alternate Authentication Material)
- Collection: T1557 (Man-in-the-Browser), T1115 (Clipboard Data), T1123 (Audio Capture), T1119 (Automated Exfiltration)
- Command and Control: T1071 (Application Layer Protocol), T1008 (Fallback Channels), T1571 (Non-Standard Port)
- Exfiltration: T1020 (Automated Exfiltration), T1048 (Exfiltration Over Alternative Protocol), T1537 (Transfer Data to Cloud Account)
- Impact: T1531 (Account Access Removal), T1561 (Disk Wipe), T1491 (Defacement), T1561.002 (Encrypted Data Impact)

Tactic-by-Tactic Mapping

TA0001: Initial Access

Initial Access techniques describe how an attacker first gets a foothold on a target system or network. From an endpoint perspective, the initial access moment is often a user action: clicking a phishing link, opening a malicious attachment, or interacting with a compromised website. SentinelOne's initial-access defenses center on preventing that foothold from executing code or gaining persistence.

Drive-by Compromise (T1189) occurs when a user navigates to a compromised website that exploits a browser vulnerability or uses social engineering to trick the user into installing malware. SentinelOne's Static AI and Anti-Exploitation engines detect the resulting executable before it runs, and Browser Isolation (if enabled) prevents the initial compromise entirely by sandboxing untrusted web content. Chapter 4 walks the detection of unsigned or suspicious executables that result from drive-by attacks.

Phishing (T1566) is the most common initial-access vector: a user receives an email with a malicious link or attachment. SentinelOne does not control email gateways, but once the user downloads the attachment or clicks the link, SentinelOne's agent on the endpoint detects the resulting child process, script execution, or file creation. Chapter 6 covers triage of phishing-origin threats and how to correlate the user, the email sender, and the resulting detection into a coherent incident story.

Supply Chain Compromise (T1195) is harder to detect at the endpoint level because the malicious code comes from a legitimate software vendor. However, once the compromised software executes, SentinelOne's Behavioral AI and Static AI detect unusual behaviors: unexpected registry modifications, suspicious child processes, or network connections to command-and-control infrastructure. Chapter 3 (Ranger) can help identify when a compromised third-party tool has begun propagating laterally across your network.

TA0002: Execution

Execution techniques describe how an attacker runs code on a target system. SentinelOne's primary defense against execution is real-time behavioral analysis: watching process creation, file writes, registry modifications, and network connections in the instant they happen, and blocking or alerting on suspicious patterns before the attack progresses.

Command and Scripting Interpreter (T1059) encompasses executing code via cmd.exe, PowerShell, or shell scripts. This is an attacker favorite because it requires no compilation and uses legitimate system tools. SentinelOne's Script AI and Behavioral AI detect unusual script executions: PowerShell launch with obfuscated arguments, wmic.exe spawning child processes, or shell scripts writing to unexpected directories. Chapter 5 covers policy configuration for script-execution monitoring; Chapter 6 walks the incident-response workflow when a script-origin threat fires.

Native API (T1106) involves directly calling Windows API functions to perform malicious actions, bypassing some traditional defenses. SentinelOne's Behavioral AI detects common API abuse patterns: CreateRemoteThread, SetWindowsHookEx, and other injection vectors. These are covered in detail in Chapter 5 under Anti-Exploitation defenses.

Scheduled Task/Job (T1053) uses the Windows Task Scheduler or cron jobs to ensure persistence. SentinelOne's agent logs all scheduled task creation and modification, and Behavioral AI detects suspicious patterns: tasks that launch scripts from unusual paths, or tasks created with System privilege by non-system processes. Chapter 4 walks endpoint inventory and lifecycle; Chapter 5 covers policy tuning for task-creation alerts.

TA0003: Persistence

Persistence techniques make sure that once an attacker gains access, they can maintain that access even after reboot or credential changes. These are often the most dangerous techniques because they represent commitment: an attacker investing time to ensure they can return later.

Boot or Logon Autostart Execution (T1547) uses startup folders, registry keys, or run keys to execute code during boot or login. SentinelOne's agent detects registry modifications in HKCU\Software\Microsoft\Windows\CurrentVersion\Run and similar locations, and Behavioral AI flags suspicious startup persistence. This is one of the highest-confidence threat signals in Chapter 6's triage workflow. Chapter 5 covers policy configuration for detecting and remediating persistence.

Account Manipulation (T1098) involves compromising user accounts or creating new ones to maintain access. SentinelOne's Identity module (Chapter 1's Identity section) detects unusual account creation, privilege escalation, and lateral movement via credential abuse. This is especially critical in MSSP environments where account manipulation could affect multiple customer Sites.

Web Shell (T1505.003) is a common persistence technique in web-facing environments: an attacker uploads a malicious script to a web server. SentinelOne's agent detects unusual file creation in web directories (e.g., C:\inetpub\wwwroot) and suspicious web process behavior. Chapter 4 covers managing web servers with SentinelOne; Chapter 6 walks response workflows.

TA0004: Privilege Escalation

Privilege Escalation techniques allow an attacker to go from user-mode execution to system or admin privileges. This is often a critical turning point in an attack: once an attacker has system privilege, they can bypass many defenses, create persistence mechanisms, and move laterally across the network.

Abuse Elevation Control Mechanism (T1548) includes exploiting UAC (User Account Control) bypass vulnerabilities. SentinelOne's Anti-Exploitation engine detects known UAC-bypass patterns and process behaviors consistent with privilege escalation. Chapter 5 details the policy configuration for elevation monitoring.

Exploitation of Vulnerability (T1068) involves using an unpatched OS or application flaw to gain privilege. SentinelOne's Vulnerability Analytics (Chapter 7) gives you an inventory of vulnerable software on each endpoint;

Chapter 5's remediation workflows show how to coordinate patching. The endpoint agent also detects behaviors consistent with exploitation, such as unusual API calls or exception handling that follows a crash, and can block them before privilege is gained.

Access Token Manipulation (T1134) involves stealing or reusing access tokens to impersonate other users. SentinelOne's Behavioral AI detects suspicious token access patterns and unusual impersonation attempts. Chapter 6 walks the incident-response workflow when credential abuse is detected.

TA0005: Defense Evasion

Defense Evasion techniques allow attackers to avoid or disable detection mechanisms. They are among the most sophisticated and varied attacks, and they matter intensely to an operator: a good evasion technique can blind your platform to the attack that follows.

Obfuscated Files or Information (T1027) includes code obfuscation, encrypted payloads, and encoded scripts. SentinelOne's Static AI detects behavioral signatures of obfuscated code, and Behavioral AI detects the deobfuscation process itself (when the obfuscated code is unpacked and executed in memory). Chapter 5 covers the policy settings that control how aggressively SentinelOne hunts for obfuscation.

File and Directory Permissions Modification (T1222) involves changing file permissions to hide malware or prevent detection. SentinelOne's agent logs all permission changes and Behavioral AI detects suspicious patterns: bulk permission modifications by non-admin processes, or hiding of system files. Chapter 5 walks policy tuning for this detection class.

Indicator Removal (T1070) includes deleting event logs, clearing browser history, or overwriting audit trails. SentinelOne's Activity log (Chapter 8) captures these attempts before they succeed, because the agent logs the attempt itself. This is a high-confidence indicator of active response to detection.

Disable or Modify Tools (T1562) involves disabling antivirus, Windows Defender, or endpoint detection agents. SentinelOne's Exploit Prevention blocks many of the known techniques for disabling Windows Defender and other tools. Chapter 5 covers policy settings for detecting disable attempts.

TA0006: Credential Access

Credential Access techniques involve stealing or cracking credentials to move laterally or access sensitive data. These techniques are often the pivot point between an initial breach (phishing, malware) and true compromise of the environment.

Input Capture (T1056) includes keylogging and screen capture. SentinelOne's Behavioral AI detects keylogger patterns: process hooks into user input APIs, or processes that poll keyboard state repeatedly. Chapter 5 covers policy tuning for input-capture detection. Chapter 6's incident response section walks the communication needed when a keylogger is detected.

Forced Authentication (T1187) uses file shares or other protocols to coerce a system into sending its credentials. SentinelOne's network monitoring (via Ranger, Chapter 3) can identify suspicious SMB activity or NTLM coercion attempts, and SentinelOne's Identity module detects forced-authentication patterns.

Brute Force (T1110) attempts to guess credentials by trying many passwords. SentinelOne's Behavioral AI detects brute-force patterns: many failed login attempts in rapid succession, or unusual authentication patterns outside normal business hours. Chapter 6 covers incident response for suspected brute-force attacks.

Credentials from Password Stores (T1555) involves stealing credentials from browsers or password managers. SentinelOne's Static AI and Behavioral AI detect process behaviors consistent with credential theft from known password-storage locations.

TA0007: Discovery

Discovery techniques allow an attacker to learn about the environment: what systems exist, what software is running, what credentials are available, and how systems are connected. These are often the first steps an attacker takes after gaining initial access.

Account Discovery (T1087) involves querying the system to identify user accounts and admin accounts. SentinelOne's Behavioral AI detects unusual process behaviors consistent with account discovery: PowerShell commands querying Active Directory, or net.exe commands enumerating local accounts. Chapter 6 walks incident response for suspected reconnaissance.

System Information Discovery (T1082) involves running tools like systeminfo.exe or wmic.exe to inventory the environment. SentinelOne's Behavioral AI detects the execution of these system-discovery tools, especially when run by non-standard processes. Chapter 5 covers policy tuning for system-discovery detection.

Network Service Discovery (T1046) involves scanning for services. SentinelOne's Ranger module (Chapter 3) detects unusual network scanning behavior by endpoints, and Deep Visibility queries (Chapter 6) can isolate network discovery attempts after the fact.

Peripheral Device Discovery (T1120) and Browser Bookmark Discovery (T1217) involve gathering information about connected devices and the user's browsing patterns. SentinelOne's agent logs these activities, and Behavioral AI flags unusual enumeration patterns.

TA0008: Lateral Movement

Lateral Movement techniques allow an attacker to move from one system to another within the network, deepening their foothold and expanding the scope of compromise. For an operator, detecting lateral movement is critical because it signals that the attacker is moving beyond reconnaissance and toward long-term persistence or data theft.

Remote Services (T1021) involves using legitimate remote-access tools: RDP, SSH, WinRM, or Psexec. SentinelOne's Behavioral AI detects unusual remote-access patterns: RDP connections during off-hours, or RDP launched by non-user processes (often a sign of lateral movement automation). Chapter 3 (Ranger) and Chapter 6 cover lateral-movement detection workflows.

Lateral Tool Transfer (T1570) involves copying attack tools from one system to another. SentinelOne's agent detects suspicious file copies, especially across network boundaries, and Behavioral AI flags executables being copied to network paths. Chapter 3 (Ranger) helps map the network impact of suspected lateral movement.

Use Alternate Authentication Material (T1550) involves using stolen credentials or tokens. SentinelOne's Identity module and Behavioral AI detect unusual authentication patterns: logins from unusual locations, unusual times, or with unusual privilege levels. Chapter 1's Identity section covers this in detail.

Taint Shared Content (T1080) involves poisoning shared folders to infect other users. SentinelOne's agent detects suspicious modifications to shared folders and Behavioral AI flags executables being written to shared network paths.

TA0009: Collection

Collection techniques involve gathering data from endpoints or the network. This is often the true objective of an attack: exfiltration comes after collection.

Clipboard Data (T1115) involves reading data that a user has copied. SentinelOne's Behavioral AI detects processes that repeatedly access clipboard content. This is a common technique in data-theft attacks and is flagged in Chapter 6's incident-response workflow.

Audio Capture (T1123) and Screen Capture (T1113) involve recording audio or screenshots. SentinelOne's Behavioral AI detects process patterns consistent with screen capture, especially if the screen capture is being exfiltrated or saved to unexpected locations. Chapter 5 covers policy configuration for capture-activity detection.

Email Collection (T1114) involves exfiltrating email. SentinelOne's agent detects unusual process access to email client data and Behavioral AI flags data being copied from email stores. Chapter 6 walks incident response for suspected data theft.

Data Staged (T1074) involves collecting data into a staging area before exfiltration. SentinelOne's Deep Visibility queries (Chapter 6) can identify large file movements and unusual data aggregation patterns.

TA0011: Command and Control

Command and Control (C2) techniques allow an attacker to maintain communication with compromised systems. C2 is where an attack shifts from autonomous (malware running pre-programmed logic) to interactive (attacker issuing commands).

Application Layer Protocol (T1071) uses HTTP, HTTPS, DNS, or other application protocols to hide C2 traffic in normal-looking network activity. SentinelOne's Behavioral AI detects suspicious network connections: connections to newly registered domains, connections at odd hours, or connections with unusual data patterns. Chapter 3 (Ranger) covers network monitoring; Chapter 6 covers incident response for C2 detection.

Non-Standard Port (T1571) involves using unusual ports for C2. SentinelOne's network-monitoring capabilities (Ranger, Chapter 3) can flag outbound connections on unusual ports, especially to external IP addresses.

Protocol Tunneling (T1572) involves tunneling traffic through an innocent protocol to hide C2. SentinelOne's Behavioral AI detects common tunneling patterns and the data exfiltration that often follows C2 establishment.

Proxy (T1090) involves routing C2 traffic through intermediate systems. SentinelOne's network monitoring can identify these patterns, especially when combined with Deep Visibility queries (Chapter 6) that trace network behavior.

TA0010: Exfiltration

Exfiltration techniques involve removing data from the target network. For many attackers, this is the true objective: the previous steps (access, persistence, collection) are all in service of stealing data.

Exfiltration Over Alternative Protocol (T1048) uses protocols other than HTTP to steal data: DNS tunneling, email, or custom protocols. SentinelOne's network monitoring (Ranger, Chapter 3) detects suspicious data volumes over unusual protocols, and Behavioral AI can flag processes generating unusual amounts of network traffic.

Transfer Data to Cloud Account (T1537) involves exfiltrating data to a cloud storage service (AWS S3, Azure Blob, Google Drive, etc.). SentinelOne's Behavioral AI detects unusual access to cloud-storage APIs and credential use by non-user processes. Chapter 5 covers policy configuration for this detection.

Automated Exfiltration (T1020) involves malware automatically stealing data without user interaction. SentinelOne's Behavioral AI flags processes that read large amounts of sensitive data and immediately send it over the network, or processes that compress and upload data to external systems.

Exfiltration Over C2 Channel (T1041) involves using the established C2 connection to steal data. SentinelOne's network monitoring (Chapter 3) can identify spikes in C2 traffic that suggest data is being sent over the C2 channel.

TA0040: Impact

Impact techniques represent the final stage of an attack: actions that degrade or destroy the target's systems or data. These range from data destruction (wiper malware) to ransom demands (ransomware) to service disruption (worms).

Ransomware (T1486) or Disk Wipe (T1561) involve encrypting or destroying data. SentinelOne's Behavioral AI detects the process patterns associated with ransomware: bulk file access, encryption operations, and file-extension changes. Chapter 5 covers Anti-Ransomware policies; Chapter 6 covers incident response and recovery.

Data Destruction (T1561) involves overwriting or deleting files. SentinelOne's agent logs all file deletions and Behavioral AI flags bulk-deletion patterns, especially of files with specific extensions (databases, documents, backups).

Service Stop (T1489) involves disabling critical services. SentinelOne's Behavioral AI detects service-stop commands and unusual process terminations, and can block them before they take effect if configured in Enforce mode.

Defacement (T1491) involves modifying the appearance of systems or websites. SentinelOne's agent can detect file modifications in web directories and important system folders, and Chapter 4 covers web-server monitoring.

Building an ATT&CK-Driven Detection Catalog

As a SentinelOne operator, you can use the ATT&CK framework as a gap-analysis tool. Start by listing the tactics and techniques that matter most to your threat model. If you are an MSSP protecting financial services customers, Lateral Movement, Credential Access, and Exfiltration are high-priority. If you are protecting critical infrastructure, Impact techniques like ransomware and service disruption are top-of-mind. If you are an academic institution, Research and Development data theft (Collection and Exfiltration) is the target.

Once you have identified your priority techniques, walk through this appendix and Chapter 5's policy-tuning section. For each priority technique, note whether SentinelOne has a built-in detection (usually in Static AI or Behavioral AI), whether that detection is enabled in your current policy, and whether it is in Detect-Only or Enforce mode.

Create a gap matrix: columns are ATT&CK tactics/techniques, rows are your detection methods (SentinelOne Behavioral AI, Static AI, Deep Visibility queries, Identity module, Ranger network monitoring, third-party EDR or SIEM integrations). For each cell, mark Green (covered), Yellow (partially covered), or Red (no coverage). The Red cells are your detection-engineering priority: these are the gaps where you need to write custom rules, alerts, or STAR automation rules.

Finally, document your ATT&CK coverage in your playbooks and runbooks. When an incident comes in, triage it against ATT&CK. This accomplishes two things: it gives you a shared vocabulary with your IR team and your threat intelligence partners, and it lets you retroactively improve your detection posture. When you detect an attack against technique T1486 (Ransomware), ask whether your current detection would have caught the first T1486 attempt. If not, that is a detection gap you should close before the next incident.

Operator's Checklist: ATT&CK Gap Analysis

Identify the top 10 ATT&CK techniques relevant to your threat model.

For each technique, verify that SentinelOne has a detection (Chapter 5's policy section lists them all).

Check whether that detection is enabled in your current policy and set to Enforce or Detect-Only.

For any technique with gaps, design a custom detection rule (Chapter 10 covers STAR rules) or a Deep Visibility query (Chapter 6).

Document your coverage in your IR playbooks and runbooks, tied to technique IDs.

Monthly, review incident data and ask: "Which ATT&CK techniques did we see, and did we detect them?" Close the gaps.

References for Further Study

- MITRE ATT&CK Official Matrix: https://attack.mitre.org. This is the canonical source for all tactics and techniques. Visit this site to verify the latest technique IDs, definitions, and sub-techniques.
- ATT&CK for Enterprise: https://attack.mitre.org/matrices/enterprise/. This is the primary matrix for this book. It covers Windows, macOS, Linux, and cloud platforms.
- MITRE Threat Intelligence Integration: Many threat intelligence feeds now include ATT&CK mappings. When you receive a report about a malware family or attack group, cross-reference it against ATT&CK to understand their behavior patterns.

- SentinelOne Detection Mappings: SentinelOne maintains mappings of its detection engines to ATT&CK techniques. Check your vendor documentation and SentinelOne's Ranger threat-intelligence feeds for the latest coverage claims.
- Cyber Threat Coalition and MITRE ATT&CK-driven Threat Intelligence: Organizations like the Cyber Threat Coalition (https://cyberthreatcoalition.org) publish threat intelligence using ATT&CK mappings, allowing you to benchmark your detection coverage against known adversary behaviors.
- This book: Every chapter in this book references relevant ATT&CK techniques in sidebars and references sections. Use the Table of Contents to jump to techniques that matter to your investigation or detection engineering.

Mastering SentinelOne

Academic Edition, Appendix C

by Kendrick Washington, Technology Interpreters, Inc.

Appendix C

NIST Cybersecurity Framework 2.0 Mapping for SentinelOne Operations

Why NIST CSF 2.0 Matters

The National Institute of Standards and Technology (NIST) Cybersecurity Framework is the de facto standard for cybersecurity risk management in the United States and increasingly worldwide. Originally released in 2014, NIST CSF has been adopted by federal agencies, critical infrastructure operators, defense contractors, and enterprises of all sizes as the core language for articulating security strategy, building governance programs, and demonstrating regulatory compliance.

In 2024, NIST released Cybersecurity Framework version 2.0 (NIST SP 1271), which marked a significant evolution: the addition of a sixth function called GOVERN. Where CSF 1.1 comprised Identify, Protect, Detect, Respond, and Recover, CSF 2.0 added GOVERN to explicitly address organizational security strategy, planning, and governance. This addition reflects the growing recognition that technical controls (the heart of the other five functions) cannot succeed without strategic oversight, accountability, and alignment with business objectives.

For a SentinelOne operator, understanding how SentinelOne capabilities map to NIST CSF 2.0 serves multiple purposes. First, if your organization is subject to federal procurement requirements (if you are a federal contractor, operate critical infrastructure, or work in defense), CSF compliance is mandatory. Second, if you are building a security program or reporting to a compliance officer, CSF 2.0 is likely the framework your governance team uses to organize and audit the program. Third, CSF 2.0 helps you build a more mature security architecture: it forces you to think beyond detection (Detect) and response (Respond) to include preparation (Protect), understanding (Identify), and recovery (Recover). This appendix maps SentinelOne's capabilities to each CSF 2.0 function and category, and anchors each to the relevant chapter in this book.

The Six Functions of NIST CSF 2.0

- GOVERN (GV): This new function in CSF 2.0 addresses organizational structures, policies, procedures, and processes that support cybersecurity decision-making. GOVERN includes activities like establishing roles and responsibilities, developing cybersecurity policies and procedures, and implementing compliance and risk-management programs.
- IDENTIFY (ID): Understanding assets, risks, and vulnerabilities. This function includes asset inventory, risk assessment, vulnerability management, and threat modeling. For SentinelOne, this means knowing what endpoints you have, what software they run, and where they are vulnerable.
- PROTECT (PR): Safeguarding against threats through defensive measures. This includes access control, encryption, segmentation, vulnerability remediation, and security monitoring. For SentinelOne, Protection is realized through detection policies, exclusions, remediation policies, and enforcement controls.
- DETECT (DE): Identifying unauthorized or anomalous activity. This function includes event logging, network monitoring, anomaly detection, and threat hunting. This is SentinelOne's primary strength: Behavioral AI, Static AI, and Deep Visibility are all Detect function capabilities.
- RESPOND (RS): Taking action when a security event is detected. This includes incident analysis, containment, eradication, and communication. SentinelOne's Incidents module, response automation, and activity logging all support this function.
- RECOVER (RC): Restoring systems and data to normal operations after a security incident. This includes recovery planning, system restoration, and post-incident analysis. SentinelOne's remediation and rollback capabilities support this.

Function-by-Function Mapping

GOVERN (GV): Organizational Governance

NIST CSF 2.0's new GOVERN function requires organizations to establish cybersecurity governance: roles, responsibilities, policies, and oversight mechanisms. Unlike the other five functions which are primarily technical (Protect, Detect, Respond, etc.), GOVERN is strategic and organizational. It asks: Who owns cybersecurity? What is the policy framework? How are decisions made? How are we complying with regulations?

For SentinelOne operators, GOVERN manifests through several capabilities. First, Chapter 1's hierarchy discussion (Global, Account, Site, Group) maps directly to organizational governance: it shows how policies flow down from strategic (Global) to tactical (Group). Chapter 11 (Settings) covers user roles and RBAC (Role-Based Access Control): who can do what in the console is a governance question. Activity logging (Chapter 8) is explicitly a GOVERN capability: audit trails prove to regulators and auditors that controls are in place and working.

Specific CSF 2.0 categories under GOVERN that SentinelOne addresses:

- GV.PO: Policy and Oversight. Chapter 11 covers how to design and enforce policies across your hierarchy. Chapter 8's Activity logs demonstrate that policies are being followed.

- GV.RM: Risk Management. Chapter 7 (Applications: Software Inventory) and Chapter 3 (Ranger) contribute to understanding and managing risk: inventory of software and network devices is foundational risk data.

- GV.RO: Roles and Responsibilities. Chapter 11 (Settings > Users and RBAC) covers how to assign roles and ensure accountability.

Your GOVERN posture in SentinelOne is strongest when (1) you have documented policies at the Site level, (2) you have clearly assigned RBAC roles to team members, (3) you review Activity logs regularly to ensure policy compliance, and (4) you conduct quarterly reviews of your Group-level overrides to ensure they are still justified and not turning into accumulated technical debt.

IDENTIFY (ID): Asset, Risk, and Vulnerability Understanding

The IDENTIFY function requires organizations to understand what they have, where it is, and what risks it faces. This is foundational: you cannot protect what you do not know about, and you cannot detect threats if you do not understand your baseline.

SentinelOne provides multiple IDENTIFY capabilities. The Sentinels section (Chapter 4) is primarily an inventory tool: it lists every endpoint you have, what OS and version they run, when they last checked in, and their health status. The Applications section (Chapter 7) goes deeper: it inventories every piece of software installed on every endpoint and cross-references it against CVSS vulnerability data, giving you a risk score for every endpoint. Ranger (Chapter 3) extends this to network discovery: it identifies devices on your network (including unmanaged devices) and flags anomalies like rogue endpoints.

Specific CSF 2.0 categories under IDENTIFY that SentinelOne addresses:

- ID.AM: Asset Management. Chapter 4 (Sentinels) shows you every endpoint; Chapter 7 (Applications) shows you software inventory.

- ID.RA: Risk Assessment. Chapter 7 (Applications) uses CVSS data to assign risk scores. Your Deep Visibility queries (Chapter 6) can identify risky behaviors and usage patterns.

- ID.GV: Governance. Chapter 1 and Chapter 11 cover RBAC and access control to sensitive data.

Your IDENTIFY posture is strongest when (1) you are confident about endpoint inventory (Sentinels), (2) you know what software is installed and which packages are vulnerable (Applications), (3) you have identified critical assets or high-risk groups and are monitoring them closely, and (4) you are using that data to inform threat modeling (which techniques matter most to your environment) and detection tuning.

PROTECT (PR): Defensive Safeguards and Prevention

The PROTECT function encompasses defensive controls: access management, encryption, segmentation, patching, and hardening. PROTECT activities prevent attacks from succeeding. In a well-designed security program, PROTECT is stronger than DETECT: if you prevent attacks, you do not have to detect and respond to them.

SentinelOne's PROTECT capabilities come primarily from its policy framework. Chapter 4 and Chapter 5 cover policy design and enforcement: which detection engines are enabled, whether remediation is automatic or manual, which files or processes are excluded, how aggressive the platform should be in blocking suspicious activity. The Anti-Exploitation engine (Chapter 5) is explicitly a PROTECT control: it prevents exploitation attempts from succeeding. The Anti-Ransomware policies (Chapter 5) are PROTECT controls: they prevent file encryption before it happens rather than waiting to detect it in progress. USB device control, network isolation, and browser isolation (all Chapter 5) are PROTECT controls.

The Policy Inheritance discussion in Chapter 1 and the detailed policy tuning in Chapter 5 show how to systematically build PROTECT into your environment. A location-based policy that imposes stricter controls on endpoints connecting from untrusted networks (Chapter 11) is a PROTECT strategy.

Specific CSF 2.0 categories under PROTECT that SentinelOne addresses:

- PR.AA: Account and Authentication. Chapter 11 covers RBAC and access control.

- PR.AC: Access Control. Policies that restrict what users can do are PR.AC controls.

- PR.AT: Awareness and Training. SentinelOne supports this indirectly: the console can surface training prompts and policy notifications.

- PR.DS: Data Security. Anti-ransomware policies and file-protection policies are PR.DS.

- PR.PT: Protective Technology. All of SentinelOne's AI engines, Anti-Exploitation, and behavior blocking are PR.PT controls.

Your PROTECT posture is strongest when (1) you have carefully tuned policies that block known-bad behaviors (Malware, Ransomware, Exploitation, Fileless, etc.), (2) you have location-based policies that enforce stricter controls in riskier network segments, (3) you have tested your remediation policies to ensure they work correctly without breaking legitimate applications, and (4) you are continuously evaluating new threats and updating your policies to block them.

DETECT (DE): Monitoring and Anomaly Detection

The DETECT function requires organizations to implement continuous monitoring and anomaly detection to identify security events. DETECT acknowledges that despite PROTECT controls, some attacks will succeed, and the system must be able to see them.

SentinelOne is primarily a DETECT platform. The Dashboard (Chapter 2) provides situational awareness: you see at a glance how many threats are active, which endpoints are unhealthy, and whether detection engines are talking. The Incidents section (Chapter 6) is where threats land: every detection from SentinelOne's AI engines (Static AI, Behavioral AI, Document AI, Script AI, Anti-Exploitation, Fileless, Intrusion Detection) creates a threat in Incidents. Deep Visibility (Chapter 6) allows hunters and analysts to query endpoint telemetry in detail to hunt for threats that evaded automated detection. Chapter 6's triage workflow walks the entire process of categorizing a threat, understanding its scope, and determining severity.

Ranger (Chapter 3) provides network-level DETECT capabilities: monitoring for lateral movement, detecting C2 communications, identifying rogue endpoints. The Identity module (Chapter 1) provides DETECT capabilities for credential abuse and lateral movement across Active Directory.

Specific CSF 2.0 categories under DETECT that SentinelOne addresses:

- DE.CM: Monitoring and Detection. Every AI engine, every alert, every query is a DE.CM control. Chapter 5's policy section lists which engines to enable for which threats.
- DE.AE: Anomalies and Events. Chapter 6 walks triage and how to distinguish important anomalies from noise.
- DE.CH: Detection Processes. Chapter 6's incident-response workflow is a DE.CH capability.
- DE.DP: Detection Data Sources. Ranger provides network data; Deep Visibility queries provide telemetry data.

Your DETECT posture is strongest when (1) you have a clear policy for which detection engines to enable and at what sensitivity level, (2) you understand the false-positive rate for each engine and have tuned them appropriately, (3) you have defined custom alerts via PowerQuery or STAR rules that catch organization-specific threats, (4) you have a triage workflow documented (Chapter 6) so that when a threat fires, your team responds consistently, and (5) you are regularly hunting for threats in Deep Visibility to catch things that evaded automated detection.

RESPOND (RS): Incident Response and Remediation

The RESPOND function encompasses incident analysis, containment, eradication, and communication. When a threat is detected, RESPOND is the process by which you understand it, contain it, remove it, and recover from it.

SentinelOne supports RESPOND through several capabilities. The Incidents module (Chapter 6) provides the interface for triaging and understanding a threat: what is it, which endpoints are affected, how many endpoints, what is the risk, what actions have been taken. SentinelOne's one-click remediation actions (kill, quarantine, rollback) are RESPOND capabilities: they allow you to contain and eradicate a threat at scale. The Automation/STAR rules section (Chapter 10) allows you to automate response actions: when a threat fires, automatically take a set of actions (isolate the endpoint, kill the process, collect forensic data, notify the team).

The Activity log (Chapter 8) is crucial for RESPOND: it documents every action taken, who took it, and when. This is essential both for incident documentation and for regulatory proof that you responded.

Specific CSF 2.0 categories under RESPOND that SentinelOne addresses:

- RS.RP: Response Planning. Chapter 10 (Automation) walks how to build response playbooks. Your STAR rules and alert definitions are RS.RP controls.
- RS.IM: Improvements. Chapter 8's Activity-review section walks post-incident analysis.
- RS.AN: Analysis. Chapter 6's investigation workflow and Deep Visibility queries are RS.AN capabilities.
- RS.MI: Mitigation. Quarantine, kill, and rollback actions in the Incidents module are RS.MI.
- RS.CO: Communications. Chapter 11 (Settings > Notifications) covers how to alert stakeholders. Automated notifications via STAR rules make sure that critical incidents trigger immediate alerting.

Your RESPOND posture is strongest when (1) you have tested your remediation actions in a non-production environment to ensure they work correctly, (2) you have automation rules for high-confidence threats so that containment happens in minutes rather than hours, (3) you have a documented triage and response workflow so that when an incident happens, everyone knows what to do, (4) you are reviewing Activity logs regularly to verify that response actions are being executed, and (5) you have post-incident review procedures that ask whether the threat should have been caught earlier and whether your detection posture needs to improve.

RECOVER (RC): System Restoration and Resilience

The RECOVER function encompasses restoring systems to normal operations, validating that restoration is complete, and improving resilience to prevent recurrence. RECOVER is what happens after containment and eradication: you have killed the malware, now you need to make sure that the system is clean and that you can trust it again.

SentinelOne's primary RECOVER capability is the Rollback feature (Chapter 5): if an endpoint is compromised, SentinelOne can reverse all changes made by the malware (file writes, registry modifications, service installations) back to a known-good state without requiring a full endpoint rebuild. This is a transformative capability for recovery: instead of wiping and rebuilding an endpoint (which can take hours or days), you can restore it to pre-attack status in minutes.

The Remediation actions (Chapter 5) support RECOVER: you can uninstall unwanted software, remove malicious files, and reset compromised configurations. The Applications section (Chapter 7) helps with RECOVER: once you have remediated a malware infection, Applications tells you what software was installed or modified, so you can verify that the endpoint is clean.

Specific CSF 2.0 categories under RECOVER that SentinelOne addresses:

- RC.RP: Recovery Planning. Chapter 10 (Automation) walks building recovery playbooks. Your STAR rules can trigger automated rollback and remediation.

- RC.IM: Improvements. Post-recovery, review what went wrong (Chapter 8: Activity logs) and ask how to prevent recurrence.

- RC.CO: Communications. Chapter 11 (Notifications) ensures stakeholders are informed when recovery is complete.

Your RECOVER posture is strongest when (1) you have tested the Rollback feature with representative malware samples to ensure it works and does not break legitimate system functionality, (2) you have documented which types of compromises can be recovered via Rollback and which require a full rebuild, (3) you have backup and recovery plans documented so that if rollback does not work, you have a fallback procedure, and (4) you are tracking mean time to recovery (MTTR) for incidents and using that to guide improvements to your automation and response procedures.

Implementation Tier Considerations

NIST CSF 2.0 defines four Implementation Tiers that describe the maturity level of an organization's cybersecurity program. These tiers, Partial, Risk-Informed, Repeatable, and Adaptive, reflect the degree to which an organization's cybersecurity activities are managed, integrated, and aligned with business strategy.

Partial (Tier 1): Reactive, ad hoc. Processes are not formalized. SentinelOne is deployed but policies are minimal, alerts are not being monitored closely, and incident response is manual and slow.

Risk-Informed (Tier 2): Beginning to formalize. Policies are documented and enforced. SentinelOne policies are tuned for known threats in your environment. Alerts are monitored and triaged manually. Incident response is documented but not automated.

Repeatable (Tier 3): Formalized and consistent. Policies are regularly reviewed and updated. Detection rules are tuned and regularly refined. Incident response is largely automated via STAR rules. Post-incident analysis is conducted and used to improve detection.

Adaptive (Tier 4): Proactive and continuous improvement. SentinelOne deployment is mature. Policies are continuously updated based on threat intelligence. Automation rules are comprehensive and regularly tested. Threat hunting is ongoing. The platform is integrated with the broader security ecosystem (SIEM, SOAR, threat intelligence feeds).

In academic environments, Tier 2 (Risk-Informed) is a reasonable starting point: students and faculty are important assets, sensitive research data needs protection, but the deployment is smaller than an enterprise. Chapter 11's guidance on policy design helps move from Tier 1 to Tier 2. In operational (non-academic) settings, Tier 3 (Repeatable) is the goal: if you are protecting customer data or critical systems, your incident response and detection engineering need to be repeatable and documented.

SentinelOne supports all four tiers. The basic agent and console functionality map to Tier 1 and Tier 2. The advanced features, Behavioral AI tuning, Deep Visibility queries, STAR automation rules, and Ranger integration, enable the jump to Tier 3 and Tier 4.

Operator's Checklist: CSF 2.0 Maturity Assessment

GOVERN: Do you have documented policies and RBAC? Are Activity logs reviewed regularly?

IDENTIFY: Do you have a complete endpoint inventory (Sentinels)? Do you know what software is running and which packages are vulnerable (Applications)?

PROTECT: Are your detection policies tuned for your threat model? Are location-based policies in place? Have you tested your remediation?

DETECT: Are your detection engines enabled and monitored? Do you hunt regularly (Deep Visibility)? Do you have custom alerts for organization-specific threats?

RESPOND: Is your incident-response workflow documented? Do you have automation rules for high-confidence threats? Are you conducting post-incident analysis?

RECOVER: Have you tested Rollback? Do you know your mean-time-to-recovery? Do you have a rollback plan for incidents that cannot be auto-remediated?

Assess yourself in each category: are you Partial, Risk-Informed, Repeatable, or Adaptive? The gaps are your roadmap for the next quarter.

References

- NIST Cybersecurity Framework 2.0 (NIST SP 1271): https://nvlpubs.nist.gov/nistpubs/csf/NIST.SP.1271.pdf. This is the official reference document. It defines all six functions, 23 categories, and 81 outcomes. Use this to dive deep into specific categories or to align your program with the official guidance.
- NIST Cybersecurity Framework Documentation and Guidance: https://www.nist.gov/cyberframework. NIST maintains supplementary resources, implementation guides, and tools.
- This book: Every chapter maps to specific CSF 2.0 categories. Chapters 1, 4, and 11 address GOVERN; Chapter 7 addresses IDENTIFY; Chapter 5 addresses PROTECT; Chapters 2 and 6 address DETECT; Chapter 6 also addresses RESPOND; Chapter 5 addresses RECOVER.
- Your Organization's CSF Self-Assessment: If your organization has a security program, it likely has a CSF maturity assessment. Request a copy and use it to understand where SentinelOne deployment can close gaps.

- Sector-Specific CSF Guidance: Different industries (financial services, critical infrastructure, healthcare) have sector-specific CSF guidance. If you operate in a regulated industry, your sector's CSF implementation guidance is mandatory reading.

Mastering SentinelOne
Appendix D, Academic Edition Draft for Review
by Kendrick Washington, Technology Interpreters, Inc.

Appendix D

CIS Critical Security Controls v8 Mapping

Why CIS Controls Matter

The CIS Critical Security Controls (CIS Controls, formerly CIS Top 20) represent a prioritized set of defensive safeguards that have proven effective at stopping the most common attack patterns. Unlike framework documents that provide a vocabulary and structure (such as NIST's Cybersecurity Framework), CIS Controls are prescriptive: they tell you what to do, not just how to think about it. The v8 edition organizes these defenses into eighteen controls, each mapped to implementation groups (IG1, IG2, and IG3) that allow organizations to stage their adoption based on maturity and risk tolerance.

CIS Controls have become the de facto standard for mid-market and SLED (state, local, and education) organizations because they distill decades of incident-response data into a focused, actionable list. When a CISO says, 'We follow the CIS Controls,' they are committing to a specific, verifiable set of practices. The Endpoint Detection and Response (EDR) capabilities in SentinelOne align strongly with these controls, particularly in the areas of asset management, detection, and incident response.

This appendix maps SentinelOne's core features to each of the eighteen CIS Controls. The goal is to show which chapters in this book teach you how to implement the SentinelOne portion of each control, and to acknowledge where SentinelOne provides strong support and where additional tools or processes are required.

How This Appendix Is Organized

The CIS Controls v8 are organized into three groupings based on their scope and audience: Governance, Risk Management, and Compliance Controls (1-4); Supply Chain Risk Management Controls (5-8); and Implementation Groups that stage the adoption of controls based on organizational size and risk tolerance.

Each of the eighteen controls addresses a specific security objective. Controls 1-4 focus on governance: knowing what assets you have, maintaining an inventory, establishing policies, and managing change.

Controls 5-8 focus on supply chain security: managing access, protecting data, and securing software. Controls 9-18 focus on detection and response: securing accounts, protecting the network, defending against malware, controlling admin access, maintaining system integrity, detecting and responding to incidents, and understanding the threat landscape.

For each control, this appendix provides a brief description of what the control requires, identifies the SentinelOne capabilities (if any) that directly support it, references the chapter in this book where you will learn to implement those capabilities, and notes the Implementation Group level where the control becomes important (IG1 = essential for all organizations, IG3 = mature, resource-intensive organizations).

Within each control description, you will see language like 'SentinelOne provides strong support' when SentinelOne alone is sufficient for that control, 'SentinelOne provides partial support' when the platform contributes meaningfully but other tools are required, and 'SentinelOne does not directly address this control' when the control requires technology or processes outside the EDR domain.

Control-by-Control Mapping

Control 1: Inventory and Control of Enterprise Assets

Control 1 requires that every hardware and software asset in your organization be inventoried, kept up to date, and managed through a formal lifecycle (acquisition, deployment, maintenance, decommissioning). You cannot protect what you do not know you have.

SentinelOne provides strong support through the Sentinels interface and the Applications module. Sentinels shows you every endpoint with an agent installed, reports agent versions and hardware configuration, and lets you tag and organize assets. Applications extends this to software inventory, identifying every installed application, its version, and its vulnerability status. Together, these give you the hardware-software bill of materials that Control 1 requires.

The limitation: SentinelOne can only inventory endpoints where the agent is running. For unmanaged devices or devices without agents, you will need separate asset-discovery tools (such as Ranger, included in SentinelOne, for network-based discovery). Chapter 4 covers Sentinels in depth; Chapter 7 covers Applications. Chapter 3 covers Ranger, which identifies rogue and unmanaged devices on the network.

Implementation Group: IG1. Every organization, regardless of size, must know what assets it has.

Control 2: Software Asset Management

Control 2 requires that software (both commercial and in-house custom applications) be inventoried, authorized, and kept up to date with security patches. Like Control 1, you need to know what is installed, who authorized it, and whether it is vulnerable.

SentinelOne's Applications module provides the inventory and vulnerability-assessment portion of Control 2. It queries every endpoint for installed software, checks versions against CVSS data, and produces risk scores. The platform does not provide license-compliance auditing or approval workflows (those typically require a separate Software Asset Management tool or commercial license-tracking service), but it gives you the telemetry to feed such a system. Chapter 7 walks Applications in detail.

For patch management and authorization workflows, SentinelOne can trigger notifications and integrate with ticketing systems, but the actual patch deployment and approval governance usually flows through your IT operations tools (WSUS, Jamf, Intune, or equivalent). SentinelOne reports what is vulnerable; you use another tool to authorize and apply the fix.

Implementation Group: IG1. Small organizations often merge this with basic IT operations. Larger organizations separate it into a formal Software Asset Management function.

Control 3: Address Unauthorized Software

Control 3 requires that you block or remove software that is not authorized. The classic targets are malware, potentially unwanted programs (PUPs), unauthorized remote-access tools, and cryptominers. The goal is to allow only known-good software to run.

SentinelOne provides strong support through its detection engines and policy system. The Static AI engine identifies known malware by file signature and behavior patterns. Behavioral AI detects zero-day and polymorphic malware by watching for malware-like activity even when the file is new. The policy system lets you create allowlists (defining what is permitted to run) or blocklists (defining what is explicitly forbidden). Exclusions, covered in Chapter 4, let you carve out legitimate custom applications that the detection engine might flag incorrectly. Chapter 5 details policies and detection engines. Chapter 6 covers incident response when unauthorized software is detected.

The limitation: SentinelOne cannot block software at install time on all operating systems (kernel-mode blocklist on Windows is strong, but some Mac and Linux workloads may require kernel or OS-level control in addition). For air-gapped or offline devices, you may need supplementary tools.

Implementation Group: IG1. This is a foundational control; all organizations should implement it.

Control 4: Secure Configuration Management

Control 4 requires that systems be hardened: unnecessary services disabled, default credentials changed, security settings tightened. Configuration management means having a baseline, tracking deviation, and remediating drift.

SentinelOne contributes to this through the Activity log (Chapter 8) and the policy system (Chapter 5). The policy system can enforce settings; the Activity log shows who changed what and when, giving you the audit trail. However, the majority of hardening work, disabling services, setting file permissions, hardening the OS, happens through your endpoint-management platform (Active Directory Group Policy, Intune, MDM, or Configuration Management tools like Ansible). SentinelOne is the visibility layer, not the configuration layer.

Where SentinelOne shines for this control is in detecting configuration drift. If an attacker or a misconfigured script changes a critical setting, SentinelOne's Behavioral AI or custom alerts can detect the anomalous activity and alert you. This ties into Chapter 6 (incident response) and Chapter 8 (activity logging).

Implementation Group: IG1. Configuration hardening is a fundamental practice.

Control 5: Access Control Management

Control 5 addresses identity and access: only authenticated, authorized users should be able to access resources. This spans privileged access management (PAM), role-based access control (RBAC), multi-factor authentication (MFA), and the principle of least privilege.

SentinelOne's role in Control 5 is visibility and incident detection rather than direct enforcement. The Identity module (Chapter 3 and referenced in Chapter 1) provides Ranger AD (detecting AD compromises), AD Secure EP (deception-based defense against AD attacks), and Threat Path (showing attack paths through your network). These detect when an attacker tries to abuse access, but they do not configure the access controls themselves. Access control enforcement happens through your directory service (Active Directory, Okta, Entra ID) and PAM tools.

Where SentinelOne adds critical value is in post-breach detection: if someone with legitimate credentials is abusing access (lateral movement, privilege escalation), the Behavioral AI and Identity module can detect it. Chapter 6 covers incident response for credential-related threats.

Implementation Group: IG1. Access control is non-negotiable.

Control 6: Secure Access to Assets

Control 6 requires that access to sensitive data be restricted and monitored. This includes data encryption in transit and at rest, data classification, and audit logging of access.

SentinelOne provides strong visibility into data access through the Activity log and Deep Visibility. Chapter 6 (Deep Visibility) explains how to hunt for suspicious file-access patterns. Chapter 8 (Activity) shows the audit trail of administrative actions. However, SentinelOne does not enforce data encryption or classification. Those are responsibilities of your encryption tools (BitLocker, FileVault, disk-level encryption), your DLP platform, and your data-governance process.

For monitoring, SentinelOne is excellent: you can see which processes accessed which files, when, and from what remote source. This telemetry is what an auditor wants to see. The enforcement (blocking unauthorized access, encrypting at rest) is handled by other tools.

Implementation Group: IG2. Data protection becomes important once you have identified your sensitive assets; IG1 organizations focus on visibility, IG2+ add enforcement.

Control 7: User Access Management

Control 7 requires discipline around user accounts: remove accounts when people leave, revoke unnecessary permissions, disable shared accounts, and enforce strong authentication. This is a process control more than a technical one.

SentinelOne does not directly manage user accounts on endpoints (that is handled by your directory service and endpoint-management tools), but it provides the audit trail. Activity (Chapter 8) shows when accounts are created, modified, or deleted. Deep Visibility and Behavioral AI (Chapters 6) detect when an account is behaving suspiciously (a user accessing files they have never touched before, or logging in from an impossible location). This detective capability is Control 7's enforcement mechanism in SentinelOne's domain.

SentinelOne's Ranger AD module can detect when a dormant account has been reactivated, or when a disabled account is still being used, both red flags for post-breach attacker behavior.

Implementation Group: IG1. User hygiene is fundamental.

Control 8: Audit Logging and Event Monitoring

Control 8 requires that all meaningful security events be logged and reviewed. This spans system logs, security logs, application logs, and access logs. The logs must be protected from tampering and retained for sufficient time to support incident investigation and compliance audits.

SentinelOne provides exceptionally strong support for Control 8. The Activity log (Chapter 8) records every meaningful action on the platform itself. The Incidents interface (Chapter 6) creates timestamped records of every threat and alert. Deep Visibility (Chapter 6) logs every process, network connection, file access, and registry change on every endpoint. Reports (Chapter 9) aggregate this telemetry for compliance review.

The limitation: SentinelOne logs agent behavior and platform actions, but not necessarily everything your organization needs to log. Operating-system-level audit logs (Windows Event Log, syslog, auditd) are still the responsibility of your OS or SIEM. However, SentinelOne's logs are among the richest available from any EDR platform.

Implementation Group: IG1. Auditing is required by virtually every compliance framework.

Control 9: Email and Web Browser Protections

Control 9 requires that email and web traffic be monitored and filtered to block phishing, malware, and other threats. This includes both gateway controls (filtering at the perimeter) and endpoint controls.

SentinelOne provides endpoint-level protection complementary to gateway solutions. Behavioral AI can detect when a user clicks a malicious link or downloads a suspicious file. Script AI detects malicious PowerShell or JavaScript running from a browser. Document AI detects exploits in Office documents. However, SentinelOne is not a mail gateway or a web-proxy; those are separate purchases. SentinelOne is the backup: if a malicious email got past your gateway, SentinelOne catches it when it is opened on the endpoint. Chapter 4 (policies for detecting file-based attacks) and Chapter 6 (incident response) cover this.

For true defense-in-depth, you need both a secure email gateway and endpoint EDR. SentinelOne is the latter.

Implementation Group: IG1. Email is the primary attack vector for most organizations.

Control 10: Malware Defenses

Control 10 requires that malware be detected and removed. This includes both signature-based detection (known bad files) and heuristic/behavioral detection (files that act like malware even if they are new).

SentinelOne provides exceptionally strong support for Control 10. The Static AI engine identifies known malware. Behavioral AI identifies polymorphic and zero-day malware. Fileless AI detects in-memory attacks that never touch disk. Anti-Exploitation detects code-injection and memory-corruption exploits. Together, these engines form a multi-layered defense that is among the most comprehensive in the market. Chapter 4 covers detection engines in depth. Chapter 5 covers remediation and rollback when malware is found.

SentinelOne's advantage for this control is that it does not rely on file signatures alone; the behavioral and behavioral engines catch new malware that traditional antivirus would miss.

Implementation Group: IG1. Malware defense is non-negotiable.

Control 11: Data Protection

Control 11 requires that sensitive data be protected: classified, encrypted, and monitored. The control spans data at rest and data in transit, and includes DLP (data loss prevention) and encryption-key management.

SentinelOne provides visibility into data movement. Deep Visibility lets you see which processes are accessing sensitive files. Activity logs show which administrators accessed what data. However, SentinelOne does not classify data, encrypt it, or block exfiltration. Those functions are provided by dedicated DLP tools, encryption tools (BitLocker, FileVault, third-party solutions), or cloud access security brokers (CASBs). SentinelOne is the eyes; the policy and enforcement come from elsewhere.

For a data breach investigation, SentinelOne is invaluable: you can reconstruct what data was accessed, by whom, and where it was sent. Chapter 6 covers forensic investigation using Deep Visibility.

Implementation Group: IG2. Data protection becomes important once you have identified where sensitive data lives and how it flows.

Control 12: Network Segmentation

Control 12 requires that the network be logically or physically divided so that compromise of one segment does not automatically compromise others. This includes isolating sensitive systems, creating DMZs, and controlling traffic between segments.

SentinelOne supports network segmentation detection and enforcement. Ranger (Chapter 3) discovers network topology and unmanaged devices. Threat Path (part of the Identity module, referenced in Chapter 1) shows attack paths through your network given current access controls. Behavioral AI can detect lateral movement (an attacker moving from one segment to another) and alert you. However, SentinelOne does not build or manage the firewalls and network policies that enforce segmentation; that is your network team's responsibility. SentinelOne is the detective, not the enforcer.

When combined with a proper network segmentation strategy, SentinelOne's detection of lateral movement adds critical enforcement: an attacker who crosses a network boundary will be caught by behavioral detection even if the network firewall is misconfigured.

Implementation Group: IG2. Network segmentation is a maturing practice; it requires coordination across network, security, and operations teams.

Control 13: Protective Monitoring

Control 13 requires continuous monitoring of the network and endpoints to detect and respond to attacks. This includes both real-time alerting and forensic investigation.

SentinelOne is nearly synonymous with Control 13 for the endpoint domain. The eight detection engines (Static AI, Behavioral AI, Document AI, Script AI, Fileless, Anti-Exploitation, Intrusion Detection, and Ransomware) provide continuous monitoring. Behavioral AI is especially relevant for this control because it detects novel attacks in real time. Chapter 4 covers detection engines. Chapter 2 covers the Dashboard, which surfaces these detections. Chapter 6 covers investigation and response once a threat is detected.

The SentinelOne advantage: you get both real-time detection and the ability to retroactively hunt for similar activity across your entire fleet. If a zero-day is disclosed, you can query all historical telemetry to see if it was ever active in your environment.

Implementation Group: IG1. Continuous monitoring is foundational.

Control 14: Secure Access to Network Resources

Control 14 requires that access to network resources (file shares, databases, web applications) be authenticated, authorized, and monitored. This includes multi-factor authentication, credential protection, and session monitoring.

SentinelOne's role is detection and audit. The Identity module detects credential-based attacks (Kerberoasting, password spraying). Behavioral AI detects suspicious access patterns once an attacker has obtained credentials. Activity logs (Chapter 8) audit all administrative access to the platform itself. However, SentinelOne does not enforce access policies to file shares or databases; that is the job of your directory service and resource-level RBAC.

For post-breach detection, SentinelOne is strong: if an attacker uses stolen credentials to access resources, the behavioral detection and identity module will likely catch the anomalous activity. Chapter 6 covers this.

Implementation Group: IG2. Secure access governance is more important in organizations with sensitive shared resources.

Control 15: Wireless Access Control

Control 15 requires that wireless networks be secured with encryption, authentication, and monitoring. This includes preventing rogue access points and detecting unauthorized devices.

SentinelOne provides wireless detection through Ranger. The endpoint agent can report what wireless network the endpoint is connected to, and Ranger can identify rogue access points (unauthorized APs broadcasting known SSIDs). However, SentinelOne does not configure or control the wireless network itself; that is your network team's responsibility. The platform detects when an endpoint connects to a suspicious wireless network and can alert you. Chapter 3 covers Ranger in detail.

A key SentinelOne use case for Control 15: detecting when a laptop connects to a personal or untrusted wireless network while traveling, and triggering a policy change or notification to the user.

Implementation Group: IG2. Wireless security becomes important in organizations with significant mobile-device deployment.

Control 16: Account Monitoring and Control

Control 16 requires that administrative accounts be monitored for suspicious activity and that account-management processes be enforced. This includes privileged-account auditing, periodic access reviews, and detection of account misuse.

SentinelOne provides strong auditing through the Activity log. Every login, policy change, Remote Shell session, and agent decommissioning is logged with timestamp and user. This is the raw material for a privileged-access audit. For detection, Behavioral AI can flag when an administrative account is used from an unusual location or device, or when it accesses files it normally would not. Chapter 8 covers Activity logging. Chapter 6 covers behavioral detection of suspicious activity.

The limitation: SentinelOne does not enforce password policies or multifactor authentication on the platform itself (those are handled by your identity provider or PAM tool). SentinelOne is the audit trail and the anomaly detector.

Implementation Group: IG2. Account monitoring is increasingly important as privileged-account abuse becomes a common attack path.

Control 17: Threat Intelligence

Control 17 requires that your organization understand the threats it faces: who is attacking, what tactics they use, and what artifacts (malware hashes, IP addresses, domains) belong to known threat actors. This intelligence should inform your detection rules and response procedures.

SentinelOne integrates threat intelligence in multiple ways. The platform includes SentinelOne's own threat-intelligence feed, which powers the detection engines. The Threat Landscape widget on the Dashboard (Chapter 2) shows a live feed of threats being observed across the SentinelOne customer base. Integration points (Chapter 11) let you feed third-party threat intelligence from services like MISP, AlienVault, or commercial feeds directly into SentinelOne. Custom detection rules and alerts (Chapter 6) can be written to trigger on indicators from your threat intelligence platform.

SentinelOne does not create threat intelligence; it consumes it. Your organization sources intelligence from your sector peers, from threat-intelligence vendors (CrowdStrike, Mandiant, Recorded Future), and from your incident-response provider.

Implementation Group: IG2. Threat intelligence is most valuable once you have mature detection and response capabilities.

Control 18: Incident Response and Management

Control 18 requires that your organization have a plan for detecting, investigating, and responding to security incidents. The plan should specify roles, responsibilities, communication protocols, evidence preservation, and recovery procedures.

SentinelOne is central to this control. The Incidents interface (Chapter 6) is the hub where all threats and alerts land. Deep Visibility (Chapter 6) allows you to conduct forensic investigation: reconstructing the attack sequence, identifying the initial compromise, and understanding what an attacker accessed. Remote Shell, File Fetch, and Network Disconnect (Chapters 4 and 5) allow you to remediate without physically touching the machine. Activity (Chapter 8) provides the audit trail. Automation (Chapter 10) lets you orchestrate response at scale.

SentinelOne does not write your incident-response plan or manage your SOAR. The platform is the tactical tool that your SOC uses to execute the plan. Chapters 6 and 10 walk incident response in detail.

Implementation Group: IG1. Incident response is required by virtually every compliance framework.

Common Mappings at a Glance

The following summary table groups CIS Controls by which chapters in this book most directly teach the SentinelOne capabilities that support them.

Book Chapter	CIS Controls Supported
Chapter 2: Dashboard	Control 13 (Protective Monitoring), the Dashboard is your real-time view of threats and endpoint health.
Chapter 3: Ranger	Control 1 (Asset Inventory), Control 12 (Network Segmentation), Ranger discovers rogue devices and maps network topology.
Chapter 4: Sentinels	Control 1 (Asset Inventory), Sentinels is where you manage your endpoint fleet and view hardware/software details.
Chapter 5: Policies & Detection	Control 3 (Unauthorized Software), Control 10 (Malware Defenses), Control 13 (Protective Monitoring), the detection engines are the core of your protective capability.
Chapter 6: Incidents & Investigation	Control 13 (Protective Monitoring), Control 18 (Incident Response), threat investigation and forensic hunting.
Chapter 7: Applications	Control 1 (Asset Inventory), Control 2 (Software Asset Management), identifies installed software and vulnerabilities.
Chapter 8: Activity & Audit	Control 8 (Audit Logging), Control 16 (Account Monitoring), the audit trail for compliance and forensics.
Chapter 9: Reports	Control 8 (Audit Logging), Control 18 (Incident Response), reporting for audits and management oversight.
Chapter 10: Automation	Control 18 (Incident Response), orchestrating response at scale.
Chapter 11: Settings & Integration	Control 17 (Threat Intelligence), integrating threat feeds and SIEMs.

References

- CIS Controls v8 Official Documentation: https://www.cisecurity.org/cis-controls

- CIS Critical Security Controls v8.0 PDF: https://www.cisecurity.org/controls
- Center for Internet Security (CIS): https://www.cisecurity.org
- Implementation Groups: https://www.cisecurity.org/controls/v8/#implementation-groups

Operator's Note: Using This Appendix for Compliance

If your organization is adopting the CIS Controls, use this appendix to identify which SentinelOne chapters cover which control.

For each control, this appendix notes whether SentinelOne provides strong, partial, or no direct support. For controls where SentinelOne is partial or absent, you will need to source additional tools.

The Implementation Group levels (IG1, IG2, IG3) indicate maturity stages. Start with IG1 controls; add IG2 and IG3 as your team and budget allow.

Document your evidence collection process. Auditors will want to see how SentinelOne reports, Activity logs, and incident investigations demonstrate compliance with each control.

Mastering SentinelOne

Appendix E, Academic Edition Draft for Review

by Kendrick Washington, Technology Interpreters, Inc.

Appendix E

ISO/IEC 27001:2022 Annex A Controls Mapping

Why ISO 27001 Matters

ISO/IEC 27001 is the international standard for Information Security Management Systems (ISMS). Organizations that implement ISO 27001 establish a comprehensive, documented, and auditable approach to managing information security across people, processes, and technology. Unlike frameworks that provide guidance or checklists, ISO 27001 is a certification standard: an independent auditor verifies that your organization meets the standard, and you receive a certificate valid for three years (subject to annual surveillance audits).

The 2022 revision of ISO 27001 made significant structural changes. It reduced the control set from 114 in ISO 27001:2013 to 93 in the 2022 edition, and reorganized them into four themes: Organizational (A.5), People (A.6), Physical (A.7), and Technological (A.8). This consolidation reflects industry experience: many controls were redundant or rarely used, and the new structure is more intuitive for organizations designing from scratch.

For many global enterprises, financial institutions, and government contractors, ISO 27001 certification is mandatory for doing business. Compliance auditors will review your information security practices against Annex A controls and require evidence that you meet each applicable control. SentinelOne provides critical evidence for the Technological controls (particularly A.8) and contributes to several Organizational controls as well.

ISO 27001:2022 Annex A Structure

Annex A of ISO 27001 contains ninety-three controls organized into four themes:

A.5: Organizational Controls (26 controls) address governance, policies, asset management, and supplier relationships. These are high-level and often owned by senior management or the Chief Information Security Officer.

A.6: People Controls (13 controls) address recruitment, training, discipline, and the management of people as part of your security program. These are typically owned by Human Resources and Security.

A.7: Physical Controls (15 controls) address the security of physical spaces: access to data centers, monitoring, environmental controls (fire, water), and disposal of physical media. These are typically owned by Facilities.

A.8: Technological Controls (39 controls) address the security of systems, networks, and data. These include access control, encryption, incident response, malware defense, and many others. This is the domain where SentinelOne is most relevant.

Every organization must adapt the control set to its risk context. A cloud-native SaaS company might skip physical controls. A traditional bank with on-premise data centers will implement all themes. The ISO 27001 framework is flexible enough to accommodate both.

Theme-by-Theme Mapping

A.5: Organizational Controls

SentinelOne contributes to several A.5 controls through visibility and audit logging. A.5.2 (Information Security Policies and Responsibilities), the Activity log and integration capabilities allow you to audit enforcement of security policies. A.5.8 (Documented Operating Procedures), SentinelOne can generate automated procedures for common tasks (agent deployment, policy updates, incident response) via Automation, covered in Chapter 10. A. 5.15 (Supplier Relationships), if your suppliers are endpoints or integrate with SentinelOne, the agent can monitor their behavior and report back. A. 5.23 (Information Security Incident Management Planning), SentinelOne provides the detection and investigation infrastructure that your incident response plan depends on; Chapter 6 covers this in detail.

A.6: People Controls

SentinelOne's role in A.6 controls is primarily detection and audit. A.6.2 (General Access Control), the Activity log shows administrative access and unusual login patterns. A.6.4 (Access Responsibility), Activity logs audit who accessed what and when, providing evidence for access reviews. A.6.6 (Managing Secret Authentication Information), SentinelOne does not manage passwords (that is a PAM or identity provider function), but can detect if an attacker has obtained credentials and is using them; see Chapter 6. A.6.7 (Periodic Review), the audit trail in Activity (Chapter 8) supports periodic user-access reviews. Detection of credential misuse or privilege escalation supports discipline procedures when a user violates policy.

A.7: Physical Controls

SentinelOne does not directly address physical controls. A.7 covers data-center security, building access, fire suppression, power backup, and environmental monitoring. These are the domain of Facilities, your data-center provider, and (in cloud environments) your cloud provider. SentinelOne does not install or monitor physical infrastructure. However, if your organization manages endpoints in data centers, SentinelOne monitors the security posture of those systems; the physical layer remains out of scope.

A.8: Technological Controls

This is where SentinelOne is most relevant. The following mappings cover the key Technological controls and how SentinelOne capabilities address them. For each control, the mapping references relevant chapters from this book.

A.8.1: User Endpoint Devices

Managing security on user-facing devices (laptops, desktops, smartphones). SentinelOne covers this comprehensively through Sentinels (Chapter 4), where you manage endpoint fleet state, and through Policies (Chapter 5) where you define what behavior is allowed.

A.8.2: Privileged Access Rights

Controlling privileged accounts and preventing privilege escalation. SentinelOne detects privilege-escalation attempts through Behavioral AI (Chapter 4 and 5). The Activity log (Chapter 8) audits administrative actions. For enforcement, use your PAM tool or identity provider in combination with SentinelOne's detection.

A.8.3: Information Access Restriction

Limiting access to information based on need-to-know. SentinelOne does not enforce file permissions (that is your OS and file-share system), but Deep Visibility (Chapter 6) lets you see who accessed what files and when, providing audit evidence.

A.8.4: Access to Cryptographic Keys

Protecting the keys used for encryption. SentinelOne does not manage cryptographic keys (that is handled by key-management services like AWS KMS, Azure Key Vault, or on-premise HSMs), but can detect if someone is trying to steal them; see Chapter 6.

A.8.5: Logical Access Control

Enforcing authentication and authorization. SentinelOne detects when attackers try to bypass access controls (lateral movement, credential reuse). The Identity module (referenced in Chapters 1 and 3) detects credential-based attacks like Kerberoasting.

A.8.6: Boundary Protection

Firewalls, intrusion detection, and network segmentation. SentinelOne supports this through Ranger (Chapter 3, which maps the network), Behavioral AI detection of lateral movement (Chapter 5), and Threat Path analysis (Chapter 1, Identity section).

A.8.7: Protection Against Malware

Detecting and removing malware. SentinelOne is a primary technology for this control. Static AI, Behavioral AI, Script AI, Fileless AI, Anti-Exploitation, and Ransomware detection (all in Chapter 5) provide multi-layered malware defense.

A.8.8: Spam and Phishing Protection

Defending against email and web-based attacks. SentinelOne provides endpoint-level detection (if a phishing email got past your gateway, the Script AI and Behavioral AI can detect malicious code at execution time). However, the primary defense is a secure email gateway, which is external to SentinelOne.

A.8.9: Mobile Device Management

Managing security on mobile devices. SentinelOne supports iOS and Android agents on some enterprise mobile platforms. The Sentinels interface (Chapter 4) can manage these alongside desktop agents, though MDM platforms like Intune or Jamf remain primary.

A.8.10: Information Backup and Recovery

Ensuring data can be recovered after loss or corruption. SentinelOne does not perform backups itself, but Deep Visibility (Chapter 6) helps you understand what data was affected by an incident (ransomware, deletion). Use SentinelOne data to inform your recovery strategy.

A.8.11: Redundancy of Information Systems

High availability and disaster recovery. SentinelOne is deployed on endpoints, not on infrastructure, so this control is primarily about your infrastructure (server clustering, failover, geographic redundancy). SentinelOne supports this by enabling fast incident recovery.

A.8.12: Cryptography

Encrypting sensitive data. SentinelOne does not perform encryption (that is handled by BitLocker, FileVault, third-party encryption tools, or cloud providers), but Deep Visibility (Chapter 6) shows you whether encrypted data is being accessed.

A.8.13: Secure Development Policies and Procedures

Building security into software development. SentinelOne does not develop your code, but can detect when an attacker modifies source code or artifacts during build. Behavioral AI detects unusual compiler or build-tool behavior.

A.8.14: Secure Development Environment

Protecting development infrastructure. SentinelOne agents can be deployed on developer machines and on CI/CD pipeline servers. Chapters 4 and 5 cover managing these endpoints.

A.8.15: Outsourced Development

Managing security in outsourced software development. If your outsourced developers use endpoints running SentinelOne, you can monitor those. This is typically covered under a separate contract and visibility agreement.

A.8.16: Monitoring of Activities

Auditing system and user activities. This is one of SentinelOne's core strengths. Activity logs (Chapter 8) record console actions. Deep Visibility (Chapter 6) logs endpoint telemetry. Reports (Chapter 9) aggregate this for compliance.

A.8.17: Clock Synchronization

Ensuring system clocks are synchronized (for audit timestamps). SentinelOne relies on NTP for time synchronization. Ensure your infrastructure and endpoints are synchronized; Chapter 4 (Sentinels) shows the agent's reported time.

A.8.18: Secure Installation and Maintenance

Securely deploying and updating systems. SentinelOne agent deployment is covered in Chapter 4. Agent updates are coordinated through the Sentinels interface (Chapter 4) and automated through policies or Automation (Chapter 10).

A.8.19: Removal or Deactivation of Access

Deprovisioning accounts and access when people leave. SentinelOne decommissioning is covered in Chapter 4. Activity logs audit deprovisioning actions.

A.8.20: Review of User Access

Periodic access reviews to ensure authorization is still valid. SentinelOne provides the audit trail (Activity, Chapter 8) that shows who accessed what. Use this to support your access-review process.

A.8.21: Network Segmentation

Isolating sensitive systems from the rest of the network. Ranger (Chapter 3) shows network topology and can help validate segmentation. Behavioral AI detects lateral movement across segment boundaries (Chapter 5).

A.8.22: Attack Surface Management

Identifying and prioritizing vulnerabilities. Applications (Chapter 7) identifies vulnerable software on endpoints. Combined with vulnerability scanning and penetration testing, this gives you attack-surface visibility.

A.8.23: Web Filtering

Blocking access to malicious or unauthorized websites. SentinelOne does not proxy web traffic, but can detect when a user visits a malicious site (Behavioral AI, Chapter 5) or downloads malware from one (Script AI, Document AI).

A.8.24: Use of Cryptography

Protecting data in transit and at rest. SentinelOne uses encryption for agent-to-console communication and for protecting sensitive data in transit. For data encryption at rest, use your OS encryption tools.

A.8.25: Secure Authentication

Multi-factor authentication, strong passwords, and credential protection. SentinelOne detects when attackers abuse credentials (Behavioral AI, Chapter 5; Identity module, Chapter 1). Credential enforcement (MFA, password policy) is handled by your identity provider.

A.8.26: Containment of Malware

Isolating compromised systems to prevent spread. Network Disconnect (Chapter 4-5) isolates a compromised endpoint while keeping it manageable. Quarantine and file isolation (Chapter 5) prevent malware from executing.

A.8.27: Handling of Suspected Malware

Collecting evidence and responding to malware. Chapter 6 covers incident response, including evidence collection via File Fetch, forensic investigation via Deep Visibility, and remediation via Remote Shell.

A.8.28: Handling of Incident-Related Improvements

Learning from incidents and updating your controls. SentinelOne provides the raw material (Incidents, Activity, Deep Visibility logs) that you analyze in postmortems. Chapter 6 and Chapter 10 cover postmortem and automation improvements.

A.8.29: Integrity of Logs

Protecting audit logs from tampering. Activity logs (Chapter 8) should be exported regularly and retained in a protected repository (your SIEM or log-archival system). SentinelOne does not itself protect against log tampering, so use log aggregation and SIEM forwarding.

A.8.30: Identification of Risks

Recognizing and documenting security risks. This is a governance and risk-management process, not a technology control. Use SentinelOne data (vulnerability scans from Applications, threat detections from Incidents) to feed your risk register.

A.8.31: Responsibility and Procedures

Documentation and governance around security incident response. This is a policy and training topic. SentinelOne provides the tools; you provide the runbooks. Chapter 6 and Chapter 10 show what SentinelOne enables.

A.8.32: Assessment of and Response to Information Security Incidents

Investigating and responding to security events. SentinelOne is central to this. The Incidents interface (Chapter 6), Deep Visibility forensics (Chapter 6), and remediation actions (Chapters 4-5) are your primary tools for A.8.32.

A.8.33: Collection of Evidence

Gathering forensic evidence during and after incidents. Deep Visibility (Chapter 6) and File Fetch (Chapter 4-5) are your primary evidence-collection tools. Store collected evidence in a protected, time-locked repository.

A.8.34: Information Systems Availability and Resilience

Ensuring systems can recover from incidents and continue operating. SentinelOne contributes through quick incident response and system remediation (Chapters 5-6), reducing downtime.

Compliance Considerations

When an ISO 27001 auditor reviews your organization's security controls, they will ask for evidence that you meet each applicable control in Annex A. For Technological controls, SentinelOne is a primary source of evidence. Here is what an auditor will expect to see:

Policy Documents: You should have documented security policies (incident response, asset management, access control) that reference SentinelOne or EDR as part of your control architecture. Chapters 8-11 help you document these.

Audit Logs: The Activity log (Chapter 8) is your primary evidence of administrative actions. Export these logs regularly and retain them for the auditor. Most auditors expect at least 12 months of retention.

Threat and Incident Records: Incidents (Chapter 6) and Deep Visibility searches should be documented. When you detect and respond to threats, document the detection, the investigation, the remediation, and the lessons learned.

Vulnerability Management: Applications (Chapter 7) provides the evidence that you are identifying vulnerabilities and tracking remediation. Combined with your change log, this shows you have addressed A.8.22 (Attack Surface Management).

Network Asset Inventory: Ranger (Chapter 3) contributes to A.5.8 (Documented Operating Procedures) by providing a live inventory of managed and unmanaged devices. Export this periodically.

Automation Runbooks: If you use Automation (Chapter 10) to orchestrate response, document those runbooks. They are evidence that you have codified your incident-response procedures.

During the audit, the auditor will likely request samples of detected threats, remediation actions, and postmortem analysis. Use the Incidents interface to pull a representative month or quarter of detections, and the postmortem process to show lessons learned. The auditor wants to see that you are not just detecting threats, but learning from them.

References

- ISO/IEC 27001:2022 Standard: https://www.iso.org/standard/27001
- ISO/IEC 27002:2022 Code of Practice (guidance for implementing controls): https://www.iso.org/standard/27002
- ISACA CIS-IEC 27001 Guidance: https://www.isaca.org (search for ISO 27001 implementation guides)
- BSI ISO 27001 Advice: https://www.bsigroup.com/en-GB/iso-27001-information-security-management/

Auditor's Perspective: What They Will Ask

Show me your incident-detection policy and how SentinelOne implements it. (Reference: Chapter 6, Incidents.)

Demonstrate that you have identified a real threat, investigated it, and responded. Provide the Incidents record, Deep Visibility forensic data, and remediation action log.

Walk me through your malware defense strategy. How do the Static AI, Behavioral AI, Script AI, and other engines work together? (Reference: Chapter 5, Policies and Detection.)

How do you make sure that administrative actions are audited? Show me a sample of Activity logs with sensitive events clearly marked. (Reference: Chapter 8, Activity.)

How do you manage software vulnerabilities? Show me your Applications inventory and your remediation workflow. (Reference: Chapter 7, Applications.)

For each A.8 control, document whether you have implemented it, partially implemented it, or determined it is not applicable to your risk context. Provide evidence for each implemented control.

Mastering SentinelOne

Appendix F, CLI and API Quick Reference

by Kendrick Washington, Technology Interpreters, Inc.

Appendix F

CLI and API Quick Reference

About This Reference

This appendix is a working reference, not exhaustive documentation. It provides the most common SentinelOne CLI commands and Management Console REST API endpoints that you will use for scripting, automation, and integration. Commands and API endpoints evolve with each product release; always verify the current syntax and supported parameters against the official SentinelOne documentation for your deployed version. The goal of this reference is to give faculty and students a practical starting point for writing automation scripts, building SIEM integrations, and automating routine endpoint management tasks.

Section 1: Endpoint Agent CLI (Windows / macOS / Linux)

Every SentinelOne agent comes with a command-line interface that allows local administrative users to query and manage the agent directly on the endpoint. The location and name of the command vary by operating system.

Command Locations by OS:

- Windows: sentinelctl.exe (in %ProgramFiles%\SentinelOne\Sentinel or similar)
- macOS: /usr/local/bin/sentinelctl
- Linux: /opt/sentinelone/bin/sentinelctl or /opt/sentinel/bin/sentinelctl

Common sentinelctl Subcommands:

sentinelctl status, Show current agent status (connected/disconnected), threat count, and uptime.

sentinelctl version, Display agent version, build number, and component versions (e.g., threat engine).

sentinelctl management, Show management console URL and connectivity status (connected/unreachable).

sentinelctl reboot_required, Check if agent has a pending reboot after updates or remediation.

sentinelctl uninstall <passphrase>, Uninstall the agent. Requires admin privileges and the uninstall passphrase.

sentinelctl ranger status, Show Ranger module status if deployed; displays asset discovery activity.

sentinelctl log level [debug|info], Set agent logging level for troubleshooting (requires restart).

sentinelctl health, Show agent health status, including memory, CPU, and sensor stability.

Example: Check agent status on Windows

Example: View management console URL on Linux

Advanced sentinelctl: Remote Shell and Script Execution

- Remote shell (if enabled in policy): sentinelctl remote-shell, open an interactive shell to the endpoint via the console (requires RemoteOps license).
- Fetch file from endpoint: sentinelctl fetch-file <path>, retrieve a file from the endpoint for forensic analysis.
- Run remediation: sentinelctl remediate <threat-id>, trigger remediation for a specific threat (advanced users).

> **WARNING: Uninstall Requires Passphrase**
> The uninstall command requires the passphrase set by your administrator. Without the correct passphrase, the uninstall will fail silently. In a lab or proof-of-concept environment, always document the passphrase with the test plan. Never run uninstall commands in production without approval from security leadership and a rollback plan.

Scripting sentinelctl Across Multiple Endpoints

In a Windows domain or Linux environment with SSH access, you can wrap sentinelctl in a loop to query status across multiple machines:

Interpreting sentinelctl Output

- Agent Status: "Connected" means the agent has an active connection to the management console. "Disconnected" or "Unmanaged" means the agent cannot reach the console; check network and proxy settings.
- Threat Count: Shows active threats on the endpoint. If non-zero, investigate in the Incidents section of the console.
- Ranger Status: If enabled, shows network discovery activity. "Active" means Ranger is scanning the local network for unmanaged devices.
- Reboot Required: If true, the endpoint needs a restart (usually after a critical engine update or rollback action). Plan downtime accordingly.

Section 2: Management Console REST API (v2.1)

The SentinelOne Management Console exposes a REST API for programmatic access to agents, threats, policies, users, and Sites. All requests require authentication via an API token and follow standard HTTP methods (GET, POST, PUT, DELETE).

Authentication

- Create an API token in the console under Settings > Users > Service Users. Service users can generate tokens valid for up to 1 year, unlike regular user tokens which expire after 30 days.
- Include the token in every request using the Authorization header:
- Authorization: ApiToken <your-token-here>

Base URL

Common Endpoints by Category

Agents

GET /agents, List all agents in your scope; supports pagination and filters (?limit=100, ?offset=0, ?filters[osType]=windows).

GET /agents/{id}, Get detailed information about a specific agent by ID.

POST /agents/actions/connect, Force an agent to reconnect to the console.

POST /agents/actions/disconnect, Force an agent to disconnect (goes offline; will attempt auto-reconnect).

POST /agents/actions/uninstall, Queue an agent for uninstall; agent remains in console for 90 days.

Threats

GET /threats, List threats in your scope; filter by status (?status=unresolved, ?status=resolved).

GET /threats/{id}, Get threat details including mitigation state and file information.

POST /threats/actions/mitigate/{action}, Mitigate a threat; actions include: kill, quarantine, remediate, isolate.

POST /threats/actions/resolve, Mark a threat as resolved (analyst verdict: resolved).

POST /threats/actions/unmark, Reverse an earlier mitigation or analyst verdict.

Activities & Audit Log

GET /activities, List all activities in your scope (logins, policy changes, agent updates, etc.); highly filterable.

GET /audit/logins, Get audit trail of user logins (who logged in, from where, when).

Sites, Groups & Organizational

GET /sites, List all Sites (customers) in your Account.

GET /sites/{id}/groups, List all Groups within a Site.

GET /sites/{id}/policies, List policies configured for a Site.

GET /users, List all users with console access in your Account or Site.

API Documentation Subject to Change

SentinelOne updates endpoints and response schemas with each major release. Always check the API swagger/OpenAPI documentation in your console (typically at /api/swagger) or against the vendor documentation for your deployed version. Endpoints and parameters in this reference reflect v2.1; older versions (v2.0) and newer versions (v3.0+) may differ.

Additional Useful Endpoints

GET /events, List raw events captured by agents; used for advanced threat hunting and forensic analysis.

GET /processes, Query processes observed on endpoints; useful for investigating suspicious activity.

GET /network-connections, List network connections made by endpoints; helps identify command-and-control communication.

GET /registry-keys, Retrieve registry key values from Windows endpoints (if Deep Visibility is enabled).

POST /agents/actions/scan, Trigger a full scan on specified endpoints.

GET /exclusions, List current exclusions (file hashes, paths, processes) for this Site or Group.

POST /exclusions, Create a new exclusion (requires threat analyst or admin role).

DELETE /exclusions/{id}, Remove an exclusion; commonly done when the issue causing the exclusion is remediated.

Request and Response Structure

Most API endpoints follow a consistent structure for requests and responses. Here is a typical response from a GET request:

For POST/PUT requests that create or modify resources, the response typically includes the created/updated object and a success message.

Common HTTP Status Codes

200 OK, Request succeeded. Response body contains the requested data or confirmation of action.

201 Created, Resource was successfully created (typically for POST requests that create new objects).

400 Bad Request, Malformed request. Check JSON syntax, required fields, and parameter types.

401 Unauthorized, Authentication failed. Verify your API token is correct, not expired, and included in the Authorization header.

403 Forbidden, Authenticated, but you lack permissions for this action. Check RBAC settings for your service user.

404 Not Found, The requested resource (agent, threat, site) does not exist or has been deleted.

429 Too Many Requests, Rate limit exceeded. Implement backoff and retry logic.

500 Internal Server Error, Server error. Retry after a short delay; if persistent, contact SentinelOne support.

Section 3: Common Automation Patterns (Python Examples)

The following code patterns show how to accomplish routine analyst tasks using Python and the requests library. Each pattern includes error handling guidance and production considerations.

Pattern 1: Export Active Agents to CSV

Use this to generate an inventory snapshot for reporting or compliance audits.

Before running in production: Test with a small limit parameter (?limit=10) to verify column names match your API version.

Handle pagination: For large environments, use limit=1000 and check resp.json()["pagination"]["nextCursor"] to fetch all agents.

Error handling: Always check resp.status_code and log failures; token expiration returns 401.

Pattern 2: Isolate Endpoints in Response to Threat

Quarantine endpoints that have a specific threat. Requires approval workflow in production.

Before running: Verify endpoint list is correct; use a dry-run filter if available to confirm targets.

Isolation vs. uninstall: disconnect() isolates the endpoint from the console; use with caution as it may break remediation workflows.

Approval: In production, send isolation requests to a ticketing system and require human approval before posting to the API.

Pattern 3: Pull Last 24 Hours of Threats and Email Summary

Fetch recent threats and send a summary to security leadership.

Timestamp format: Use ISO 8601 (2024-04-24T12:00:00Z); check API docs for your server timezone.

HTML formatting: Wrap body in HTML tags for better email formatting; consider using a template.

Delivery reliability: Use an organization-managed SMTP relay, not a personal email account.

Pattern 4: Compare Current Ranger Devices Against Baseline

Find new or missing devices on the network since your last inventory snapshot.

Baseline management: Run once a month to establish a clean baseline; document the baseline date.

False positives: Some devices (mobile, guest wifi) are expected to be transient; filter by device type.

Integration: Export new_devs to a ticketing system for onboarding review or security team approval.

Pattern 5: Deploy a STAR Rule (Automation) from JSON Definition

Automate the deployment of a response rule across your environment.

Testing: Deploy to a pilot group first; monitor for 7 days before production rollout.

Scope: Always specify groupId to limit rule scope; never deploy at Account level without testing.

Guardrails: STAR rules include built-in rate limiting to prevent runaway automation; verify endpoint online status before action.

Section 4: SIEM/SOAR Integration Quick Reference

Most SIEM and SOAR platforms can ingest SentinelOne data via Syslog, webhooks, or native connectors. Configuration typically occurs in the console under Settings > Integrations.

Common Integrations

Splunk, Syslog or HTTP Event Collector (HEC) via webhook. Configure Syslog in Settings > Notifications > Syslog or use Splunk TA (Technical Add-on) for native integration.

Elastic Stack (ELK), Syslog forwarding or Beats integration. Use Syslog receiver on Logstash port 514.

QRadar, Syslog or OPSEC/LEA protocol. Requires QRadar to accept Syslog on port 514 (or configured alternate).

Azure Sentinel, Native connector available via Azure Marketplace. Maps threat and activity data to Microsoft Sentinel incidents.

Phantom / XSOAR, Webhook or API-driven playbooks. Phantom playbooks can call SentinelOne REST API endpoints directly.

Sample Webhook Payload (Threat Detection)

When SentinelOne detects a threat and notifications are configured, it sends a JSON payload to your webhook URL.

Authentication & Transport

- Syslog: Typically unencrypted UDP 514 or TLS port 6514. For production, use TLS encryption.
- Webhooks: SentinelOne sends HTTP POST with threat data. Your SIEM must have a public IP and port open to receive webhooks.
- API Key for SOAR: Generate a service user token with appropriate permissions (read-only for queries, read-write for response actions).

Integration Planning Note

Most SIEM and SOAR integrations are configured in the console UI (Settings > Integrations), not via direct API. Test in a lab environment first with a small group of endpoints to verify data flow before enabling for production.

Monitor volume: A busy environment can generate thousands of Syslog messages per day. Ensure your SIEM has adequate ingestion capacity.

Sample Code: Consuming Syslog from SentinelOne

If you are building a custom intake for threat data, here is a minimal Python Syslog server that listens for SentinelOne events:

Security Note for Syslog Integration

By default, Syslog is unencrypted UDP. In production, use TLS encryption (port 6514) and restrict which IPs can send to your Syslog server. Never expose Syslog to the internet; use a bastion host or VPN if sending across networks.

Syslog events can contain sensitive information (file paths, usernames, threat hashes). Treat Syslog infrastructure with the same security controls as your SIEM backend.

Query Parameters and Filters

Most API endpoints support filtering, pagination, and sorting. Use these to reduce response size and focus on relevant data.

?limit=100, Set the number of results per page (default often 10 or 20). Max limit typically 1000.

?offset=100, Skip the first 100 results; used for pagination alongside limit.

?sort=createdAt&sortOrder=asc, Sort results by a field in ascending or descending order.

?threatStatus=unresolved, Filter threats by status: unresolved, resolved, mitigated, etc.

?osType=windows, Filter agents by OS: windows, macos, linux.

?status=online, Filter agents by connectivity status: online, offline, disconnected.

?createdAt__gt=2024-04-20T00:00:00Z, Filter by date range using comparison operators: __gt (greater than), __lt (less than), __gte, __lte.

Example: Fetch recent unresolved threats from Windows endpoints only

Section 5: Troubleshooting Cheat Sheet

Quick reference for common issues and their most likely causes. Always check the SentinelOne Activity log (Settings > Activity) for recent actions related to the problem.

Issue	First Steps
Agent shows "Disconnected"	Check console URL setting, network egress (port 443), certificate trust, and agent logs (/opt/sentinelone/logs on Linux). If agent is behind proxy, configure proxy settings in policy.
API returns 401 Unauthorized	Token expired (30 days for user tokens, 1 year for service tokens) or incorrect format. Regenerate token in Settings > Users. Check Authorization header format: "ApiToken <token>"
Mitigation did not take effect	Verify agent is online; offline agents queue actions. Check policy permissions at Group level. Confirm user has "Threat Mitigation" RBAC permission. Review threat status in Incidents.
Storyline shows incomplete data	Known limitation with offline endpoints. Recheck endpoint when it comes online. Behavioral AI relies on continuous telemetry; gaps create incomplete timelines.
Syslog integration stopped working	Verify Syslog server is accepting connections on configured port. Check Settings > Integrations for errors. Verify firewall rules allow outbound from console to Syslog server.
High agent CPU usage	May indicate over-aggressive scan policy. Reduce scan frequency or disable non-critical detection engines at Group level. Check recent policy changes in Activity log.

Section 6: Best Practices for Automation and Integration

Rate Limiting and Backoff

The SentinelOne API has rate limits (typically 600 requests per minute for most endpoints). Implement exponential backoff to avoid overwhelming the API:

Error Handling and Logging

- Always log API responses: Capture status codes, request IDs (if provided), and error messages for troubleshooting.
- Validate inputs: Before posting to the API, validate agent IDs, threat IDs, and JSON payloads to catch errors early.
- Use try-except blocks: Wrap API calls in exception handlers to catch connection errors, timeouts, and JSON parse errors.
- Alerting: Set up alerting if automation scripts fail (e.g., send email or Slack notification if isolation script encounters repeated 401 errors).

Testing and Validation

Always test automation in a non-production environment first:

- Use a test Site with a small number of endpoints (5-10).
- Verify API calls with curl or Postman before writing full automation scripts.
- Run isolation or remediation scripts on a pilot Group for 7 days before rolling to production.
- Document expected behavior and success/failure criteria for each automation rule.

Audit and Compliance

- Service user tokens: Assign appropriate RBAC permissions (read-only for queries, read-write for response actions). Document the purpose of each service user.
- Activity logging: All API actions are logged in Settings > Activity. Periodically review Activity logs for unexpected changes.
- Change control: For production automation, require peer review and approval before deployment. Document the business justification.
- Retention: Keep logs and automation scripts for at least 90 days (or per your organization policy) for audit and forensic purposes.

Documentation and Runbooks

Maintain documentation for all custom integrations and automation:

API endpoints used and their purpose.

Service user account names and permissions.

Error handling and escalation procedures.

Test results and deployment dates.

Contacts for support if the automation fails.

Automation Guardrails

SentinelOne includes safeguards to prevent runaway automation: rate limiting, action queueing on offline endpoints, and approval workflows for high-impact actions. However, these are not substitutes for careful design and testing. Always scope automation to the narrowest set of endpoints and threat classifications.

A poorly designed STAR rule or API loop can impact thousands of endpoints in minutes. Test thoroughly, monitor closely, and have a rollback plan.

Section 7: Quick Reference for Common Tasks

When to Use CLI vs. API

Use sentinelctl when, You have local administrative access to the endpoint. You want to quickly check agent status without logging into the console. You are troubleshooting a single endpoint.

Use REST API when, You need to operate on multiple endpoints at once. You are building integration with SIEM, SOAR, or ticketing systems. You want to automate routine tasks. You need audit trail (all API calls are logged).

Service User Permissions Guide

When creating a service user for integration, request the minimum required permissions:

Read-only access, For SIEM integration, threat hunting queries, inventory reports. Service user needs: Threat Read, Agent Read, Activity Read.

Response access, For SOAR playbooks that mitigate threats. Add: Threat Write, Threat Mitigation.

Full Admin, Only for internal tools and high-trust integrations. Not recommended for third-party SaaS integrations.

Debugging Automation Scripts

If your automation is not working as expected, use these debugging steps:

- Enable verbose logging: Add print() statements or logging.debug() calls to log every API request and response.
- Test with curl: Before running a full script, test the exact URL and headers with curl to isolate network/auth issues.

- Check Activity log: Log into the console and review Settings > Activity for any related API calls. Errors often appear there.
- Verify token: Confirm your service user token has not expired. Tokens are valid 1 year from creation; regenerate if unsure.
- Validate JSON: Use a JSON validator to check request payloads for syntax errors (missing quotes, commas, etc.).
- Check scope filters: Verify your filter queries match your data (e.g., ?osType=windows will return zero results if all endpoints are Linux).
- Review rate limits: If you get 429 errors, you may be hitting rate limits. Implement backoff as shown in Section 6.

Key Takeaways

- sentinelctl is your endpoint-side tool; know the OS-specific path and always require admin privileges. Use it for quick status checks and troubleshooting.
- The REST API (v2.1) uses service user tokens for long-lived integrations; regular user tokens expire after 30 days.
- Create service users with minimal required permissions; do not grant unnecessary access to third-party integrations.
- Common patterns: fetch agents for inventory, isolate endpoints, query threats, compare Ranger baselines, deploy STAR rules.
- Integration: Most SIEMs can ingest Syslog; SOAR platforms can call the API directly via orchestration workflows.
- Troubleshooting: Always check Activity logs, verify network connectivity and certificate trust, and consult the current API docs for your deployed version.
- Test automation in non-production first, then monitor closely during production rollout. Have a rollback plan.

Always Verify Against Current Documentation

This reference is current as of SentinelOne v24.x. API versions, endpoint names, and parameters change with major releases. Before deploying any script or integration to production, verify the command or endpoint syntax against your deployed version documentation and test in a non-production environment. Use the Swagger/OpenAPI docs available at your console URL (/api/swagger) as the authoritative source.

Section 8: Comprehensive sentinelctl and API Reference

Complete sentinelctl Command Index

The following table lists all commonly documented sentinelctl subcommands. Note: Some commands may be unavailable depending on your license tier and agent version.

status, Display current agent status (online/offline), threat count, last check-in time.

version, Show agent version, build number, OS, and installed modules (e.g., Ranger, DeepVisibility).

management, Display management console URL, connection status, and last communication timestamp.

reboot_required, Check if endpoint has a pending reboot after agent updates or system changes.

uninstall <passphrase>, Uninstall the agent using the passphrase set by administrator. Requires admin privileges.

ranger status, Show Ranger module status if deployed; includes asset discovery counts.

log level <level>, Set agent logging verbosity: debug, info, warning, error. Useful for troubleshooting.

log fetch, Download agent logs for diagnostic purposes.

health, Display agent health metrics: memory usage, CPU, event queue depth, sensor stability.

network-status, Show network connectivity details, including proxy configuration if applicable.

policy-info, Display the effective policy applied to this endpoint.

threats, List threats detected on this endpoint (local command; does not require console).

exclude-hash <hash>, Exclude a file hash from detection (requires local admin).

device-control status, Show device control module status if USB/ Bluetooth controls are enabled.

asr-status, Display Attack Surface Reduction (ASR) rules status if available.

REST API Endpoint Index by Use Case

Incident Investigation

- GET /threats, fetch threats (supports filters by status, classification, agent)

- GET /threats/{id}, get full details on a specific threat including file hashes, IOCs
- GET /processes, query processes observed on endpoints (requires Deep Visibility)
- GET /network-connections, list C2 communication or suspicious network activity
- GET /events, raw telemetry events (most granular data available)

Endpoint Management

- GET /agents, list all endpoints with filters (status, os, group, policy)
- GET /agents/{id}, detailed endpoint info (installed software, IP, last seen, policy)
- POST /agents/actions/connect, force endpoint to reconnect to console
- POST /agents/actions/disconnect, isolate endpoint (breaks console connection)
- POST /agents/actions/scan, trigger full system scan on endpoint(s)
- POST /agents/actions/remediate, remediate a specific threat on targeted endpoints

Configuration & Policy

- GET /sites/{id}/policies, list policies at Site level
- POST /sites/{id}/policies, create new policy
- PUT /sites/{id}/policies/{id}, update an existing policy
- GET /exclusions, list all exclusions (by hash, path, process)
- POST /exclusions, create new exclusion after resolving threat

Organizational & Reporting

- GET /sites, list all Sites (customers) in your Account
- GET /users, list all users with console access
- GET /activities, audit log of all console and agent actions
- GET /audit/logins, login history and failed authentication attempts
- POST /reports, schedule automated report generation

Common Filter and Parameter Examples

Build complex queries by chaining parameters. URL encode special characters.

Filter by multiple statusesGET /threats?threatStatus=unresolved&threatStatus=suspicious

Combine date range and OSGET /agents?createdAt__gte=2024-04-01T00:00:00Z&createdAt__lt=2024-05-01T00:00:00Z&osType=windows

Paginate large result setsGET /threats?limit=500&offset=0; then &offset=500 for next page

Sort by creation dateGET /agents?sort=createdAt&sortOrder=desc

Filter offline endpointsGET /agents?agentStatus=disconnected

Find high-risk threatsGET /threats?threatSeverity=critical&threatSeverity=high

Mastering SentinelOne

Academic Edition Glossary

by Kendrick Washington, Technology Interpreters, Inc.

This glossary defines technical and operational terms encountered throughout Mastering SentinelOne. Terms are organized alphabetically with cross-references where appropriate. SentinelOne trademarks are noted on first occurrence.

A

Account, The second level of the SentinelOne console hierarchy, representing a tenant or organization. An Account sits between Global and Site and contains all Sites and endpoints for that customer or business unit. In MSSP environments, policies at Account level propagate to all Sites within that Account.

Active Directory (AD), Microsoft's identity and access management service. SentinelOne integrates with AD for user management, deception, and lateral-movement detection through specialized modules like AD Secure EP and Ranger AD.

Active Scanning, Network discovery technique where Ranger probes devices by sending packets (ICMP ping, SNMP queries, SMB enumeration, DNS resolution, TCP/UDP port scans) to identify and fingerprint network assets. See also: Passive Discovery.

Alert, A detection triggered by a custom query rule (PowerQuery) defined by the security team, as opposed to an AI engine detection. Alerts appear in Incidents and can be automatically acted upon via STAR rules. See also: Threat.

API Key, A token used for programmatic access to the SentinelOne API, typically created for Service Users integrating external systems (SIEM, SOAR, ticketing). Keys can be set to expire after a period (90 days recommended) to limit exposure if compromised. See also: Service User.

Application Insights, A SentinelOne report template that inventories installed software and cross-references against the National Vulnerability Database, providing vulnerability scoring and remediation guidance. See also: CVSS Score.

ARP (Address Resolution Protocol), Layer 2 protocol mapping IP addresses to MAC addresses. Ranger uses ARP observation to discover and fingerprint devices on local network segments.

B

Behavioral AI, A SentinelOne detection engine that analyzes runtime process and system behavior, injection, privilege escalation, persistence mechanisms, rather than file signatures. Behavioral AI typically produces high-confidence detections with low false positive rates. See also: Static AI.

Block List, A list of file hashes, process names, or other indicators that SentinelOne automatically blocks or quarantines at detection time. Different from an exclusion, which suppresses detection entirely. See also: Exclusion.

C

C2 (Command and Control), A server or infrastructure used by an attacker to remotely command compromised endpoints. Network isolation and threat hunting focus on breaking C2 communication channels.

CVSS (Common Vulnerability Scoring System), The standard metric for measuring vulnerability severity on a scale of 0-10, with bands: Critical (9-10), High (7-8.9), Medium (4-6.9), Low (0.1-3.9). SentinelOne Applications cross-references CVSS scores from the National Vulnerability Database. See also: National Vulnerability Database.

D

Dashboard, The primary status-awareness surface in SentinelOne showing threat counts, endpoint health, detection engine activity, Ranger device classification, and application vulnerability risk. Filterable by Scope and time window. See Chapter 2.

Decommissioning, The automatic or manual process of hiding an offline endpoint from the active console inventory after a configured period (default 21 days). Decommissioned endpoints are not uninstalled; they remain hidden until they check back in and re-commission. See also: Uninstall.

Deep Visibility, SentinelOne's query-driven threat-hunting surface where operators write structured queries against endpoint telemetry (process trees, file activity, network connections, user behavior) to follow attack chains and proactively hunt. Requires appropriate license tier and user training. See Chapter 6.

Detect Only, A policy mode where SentinelOne detects and alerts on threats but does not take automatic remediation action (kill, quarantine, remediate). Often used in pilot groups or for sensitive environments requiring human approval before response. See also: Full Enforcement.

Detection Engine, An AI or behavioral subsystem in SentinelOne that analyzes telemetry and produces threat detections. Examples: Static AI, Behavioral AI, Document AI, Script AI, Anti-Exploitation, Ransomware, Intrusion Detection. Each engine can be enabled or disabled per policy.

Device Review Status, A Ranger classification field indicating whether a discovered device has been reviewed and approved. Values: Not Reviewed (default), Under Analysis, or Allowed. Helps operators track network inventory review progress. See also: Ranger.

DHCP (Dynamic Host Configuration Protocol), Protocol for assigning IP addresses to network devices. Ranger observes DHCP activity to discover devices and correlates against DHCP logs for inventory verification.

Disconnect, An action that breaks all network connectivity from an endpoint, including to the SentinelOne console. Distinct from isolate; used when containment must be absolute. See also: Isolate.

DNS (Domain Name System), Network service translating domain names to IP addresses. Ranger uses DNS observation and queries for device discovery; SentinelOne detections flag suspicious DNS behavior.

Document AI, A SentinelOne detection engine analyzing suspicious behaviors in office documents (Word, Excel, PowerShell scripts, etc.), including macros, embedded executables, and obfuscation patterns.

E

EDR (Endpoint Detection and Response), Category of cybersecurity products that deploy agents to endpoints for continuous telemetry collection, threat detection, incident investigation, and response capabilities. SentinelOne is a leading EDR platform. See also: Sentinel.

Emotet, A banking trojan and botnet that spreads across networks through phishing and exploit chains. Frequently referenced in the book as an example of high-confidence malware detection warranting auto-isolation. See Chapter 10.

Endpoint, Any device (laptop, server, workstation, mobile device) running a SentinelOne agent and reporting to the console.

Exclusion, A narrow carve-out allowing a specific process, file hash, file path, or executable to bypass SentinelOne detection and remediation. Exclusions suppress detection entirely and must be governed strictly due to insider-risk implications. See Chapter 11; See also: Policy Override.

Extensive Vulnerability Scan, An optional SentinelOne Applications policy setting that improves fidelity of vulnerability detection at modest cost to agent resource consumption.

F

False Positive, A detection of legitimate software or activity incorrectly classified as malicious by a detection engine or alert rule. Tracking false positive rates is critical to tuning detections and building analyst confidence. See also: Verdict.

File Fetch, A remote action allowing an analyst to download files directly from an endpoint to the console for analysis, typically malware samples, logs, or forensic artifacts. See Chapter 4.

Fileless (Fileless Malware), A SentinelOne detection engine targeting malware that resides in memory or exploits system tools (PowerShell, WMI, registry) without leaving executable files on disk.

Full Enforcement, A policy mode where SentinelOne automatically kills processes, quarantines files, and remediates changes without analyst intervention. Used in production groups with high confidence in detection tuning. See also: Detect Only.

G

Global, The top level of the SentinelOne console hierarchy, accessible only to the entity holding the direct SentinelOne contract. Policies at Global level propagate to all Accounts and Sites below.

Group, The leaf level of the SentinelOne hierarchy, sitting below a Site. Groups subdivide endpoints within a Site for granular policy enforcement. Common patterns: Monitoring Only, Full Enforcement, Pilot, Servers, Workstations, Critical Assets. See Chapter 1.

Group Policy, A policy assigned to a specific Group, overriding the Site-level policy for all endpoints in that Group. See also: Site Policy; See Chapter 11.

H

Hash (File Hash), A cryptographic fingerprint (MD5, SHA1, SHA256) uniquely identifying a file content. Used in exclusions, block lists, and threat indicators. Hash-based exclusions are safer than path-based because they identify specific file versions.

I

ICMP (Internet Control Message Protocol), Network protocol used for ping and traceroute. Ranger uses ICMP probes as a lightweight active discovery method to confirm device reachability and estimate response times.

Incident, A threat or alert that has been opened for investigation and response in the SentinelOne Incidents interface. Incidents track the analysis verdict and operational status (New, In-Progress, Resolved, Unresolved). See Chapter 6.

Indicator of Compromise (IOC), Evidence of a successful or attempted attack, including malicious file hashes, IP addresses, domains, and behavioral patterns. IOCs inform threat hunting and inform block lists. See also: MITRE ATT&CK.

Intrusion Detection, A SentinelOne detection engine identifying network-based or exploitation-based attack patterns, including protocol anomalies and known CVE exploitation signatures.

Isolate, An action where the SentinelOne agent enforces network isolation (via firewall rules or kernel-level filters) blocking all outbound connections except to the SentinelOne console. Distinct from disconnect; allows remediation to continue. See also: Disconnect.

K

Kill, A remediation action terminating a malicious running process immediately. Stops active damage but does not remove the binary from disk; persistence mechanisms can restart the process.

L

Location, A logical grouping of endpoints based on network criteria (IP range, DNS configuration, interface type, registry keys, connection state) used to apply location-aware policies. See Chapter 11.

M

MAC Address (Media Access Control), A hardware-level network address identifying devices on a local network segment. Used by Ranger for device fingerprinting and deduplication.

Malware, Software designed to harm or exploit a device, including trojans, worms, and ransomware. SentinelOne detects malware via multiple engines and classifies it accordingly.

mDNS (Multicast DNS), Local network discovery protocol used by printers, smart home devices, and Bonjour services to advertise themselves. Ranger listens for mDNS announcements to classify IoT and networked peripherals.

Mitigation, Any action taken to contain or remediate a threat, including killing a process, quarantining a file, isolating an endpoint, or rolling back system changes. See also: Kill, Quarantine, Remediate, Rollback.

MITRE ATT&CK, A comprehensive framework documenting adversary tactics (what attackers are trying to accomplish) and techniques (how they accomplish it). SentinelOne maps threat indicators to MITRE ATT&CK classifications for context and threat hunting. See Chapter 6.

MSSP (Managed Security Service Provider), An organization providing security services (monitoring, incident response, vulnerability management) to customers. SentinelOne's multi-tenant architecture supports MSSP deployments at scale.

MTTR (Mean Time to Respond), Average time from detection to analyst acknowledgment or remediation action. A key performance indicator for SOC efficiency; must be measured carefully to avoid gaming (see Chapter 9).

N

National Vulnerability Database (NVD), U.S. government repository of vulnerability information maintained by NIST. SentinelOne Applications cross-references application versions against NVD to produce CVSS scores and patch guidance.

Notification, An automated message sent to operators or external systems (SIEM, SOAR) when a SentinelOne event occurs (threat detection, policy change, user login, etc.). Delivered via email or Syslog. See Chapter 11.

O

Offline, Status indicating an endpoint has not checked in with the SentinelOne console within the policy-defined timeout window (typically 12-24 hours). Distinct from online and disconnected; may indicate power-off, network loss, or dormancy.

Online, Status indicating an endpoint has checked in with the console within the last few minutes (typically within the 5-minute telemetry reporting interval). Online endpoints are actively monitored and responsive to remote actions.

P

Passive Discovery, Ranger's primary network discovery method, listening to broadcasts, DNS queries, and DHCP handshakes without sending probes. Low-overhead, real-time detection of new network devices. See also: Active Scanning.

Passphrase, A security token protecting SentinelOne agent uninstallation, preventing unauthorized removal of security software. Generated at install time and stored in agent configuration.

Policy, A ruleset defining endpoint security posture: which detection engines are enabled, whether automatic remediation is allowed, behavioral controls (USB, network, process), and response actions. Policies cascade down the hierarchy and can be overridden at lower levels. See Chapter 1; Chapter 5.

Policy Override, A surgical exception rule telling a specific detection engine not to act on a specific behavior pattern. More dangerous than exclusions; requires peer review and rollback planning. See Chapter 1; Chapter 11.

Potentially Unwanted Application (PUA), Software that is not malicious but may be unwanted in a corporate environment (games, personal productivity tools, browser toolbars). SentinelOne detects PUAs separately from malware, giving analysts granular control over response.

PowerQuery, SentinelOne's query language for writing custom detection rules and threat-hunting queries against endpoint telemetry. Supports complex Boolean logic, pattern matching, and time-based analysis.

Q

Quarantine, A remediation action moving a malicious file to a protected vault on the endpoint where it cannot execute or be accessed. Preserves the file for forensics and can be reversed if detection was wrong.

Query (Deep Visibility Query), A structured search against endpoint telemetry in the Deep Visibility surface. Analysts write queries to extract process trees, network connections, file activity, and user behavior for hunting and incident investigation.

R

Ranger, SentinelOne's network asset discovery product, leveraging existing agents as sensors to passively and actively discover all devices on the network and classify them as Secured, Unsecured, Unsupported, or Unknown. See Chapter 3.

Ransomware, Malware encrypting victim files and demanding payment for decryption. SentinelOne includes a dedicated Ransomware detection engine and supports auto-isolation playbooks for high-confidence detections.

RBAC (Role-Based Access Control), A permission model where users are assigned roles (Global Admin, Account Admin, Site Admin, Operator, Analyst, etc.) determining what console actions they can perform. Enforces principle of least privilege. See Chapter 11.

Remediate (Remediation), A suite of corrective actions: disabling malicious services, removing registry persistence, deleting malware binaries, clearing tasks. Different from kill (stops process) or quarantine (isolates file). See Chapter 5.

Remote Shell, An interactive command prompt (PowerShell on Windows, bash/sh on Mac/Linux) allowing an analyst to execute commands directly on an endpoint through the SentinelOne agent tunnel. Foundational for incident response and evidence collection. See Chapter 4.

RemoteOps, SentinelOne's capability to upload and execute PowerShell, shell, or Python scripts at scale across endpoint groups. Used for custom remediation, evidence collection, and infrastructure changes. See Chapter 10.

Rogue (Rogue Device), An unauthorized or unexpected device on the network. Ranger identifies rogues by classifying all devices as Secured (has SentinelOne agent), Unsecured (manageable but no agent), Unsupported (cannot have agent), or Unknown (unclassified, likely rogue). See Chapter 3.

Rollback, The most disruptive remediation action, restoring an endpoint to a pre-infection snapshot using Volume Shadow Copy (Windows) or equivalent mechanism (macOS, Linux). Undoes all malware and legitimate changes since snapshot; typically requires endpoint restart. See Chapter 5.

S

SAM (Software Asset Management), Discipline of inventorying and managing organizational software licenses and installations. SentinelOne Applications provides complementary SAM visibility alongside dedicated SAM tools.

SAML (Security Assertion Markup Language), Single Sign-On protocol used by SentinelOne to integrate with identity providers (Okta, Entra ID, Ping). Allows users to authenticate via corporate credentials instead of separate SentinelOne passwords.

Sandbox, Isolated testing environment for safely executing and analyzing suspicious files or testing automation rules before production deployment.

Script AI, A SentinelOne detection engine analyzing scripting language behavior (PowerShell, VBScript, shell scripts, Python) for obfuscation, payload staging, and command-and-control communication patterns.

Secured (Device Classification), A Ranger classification for devices running a SentinelOne agent and actively participating in network discovery. Represents the primary enforcement boundary.

Sentinel, A SentinelOne agent deployed on an endpoint. "Sentinels" is also the name of the endpoint-management console section where you view, filter, tag, and administer all deployed agents. See Chapter 4.

SentinelOne™, A leading endpoint detection and response (EDR) platform. Trademark of SentinelOne, Inc. Throughout this book, the platform and console are referred to as "SentinelOne."

Service User, A non-human user account representing an external system (SIEM, SOAR, script) integrating with SentinelOne via API. Service Users can have API keys with extended expiration (up to 1 year) vs. regular users (30 days). See Chapter 11.

Shadow IT, Unapproved software running in an organization without formal procurement or management. SentinelOne Applications reveals shadow IT by inventorying installed software, helping organizations manage security and licensing risk.

Site, The third level of the SentinelOne hierarchy, representing a customer (in MSSP model) or business unit (in enterprise model). A Site has its own license pool, policies, and Site Key. Sits below Account and above Group.

Site Key, A unique identifier for a Site used by the SentinelOne agent installer to register agents into the correct Site. Loss or misconfiguration of a Site Key causes agents to register into wrong Sites or Accounts. See Chapter 11.

Site Policy, A policy assigned to a Site that flows down to all Groups in that Site unless a Group overrides it. Usually left as a baseline; Group policies provide granular enforcement. See also: Group Policy; See Chapter 11.

SMB (Server Message Block), Protocol used by Windows systems to share files and printers. Ranger uses SMB queries to identify and enumerate Windows-like devices on the network.

SNMP (Simple Network Management Protocol), Network management protocol used to query network devices (switches, routers) for inventory and status information. Ranger uses SNMP enumeration to discover and classify network infrastructure.

SOAR (Security Orchestration, Automation, and Response), Platform automating security incident response by integrating multiple tools and enabling workflow orchestration. SentinelOne can forward alerts and threat data to SOAR platforms via API and webhooks.

SOC (Security Operations Center), The team (or function) monitoring and responding to security incidents 24/7. SentinelOne is a primary tool for SOC teams, providing visibility and response capabilities.

SSO (Single Sign-On), Authentication method allowing users to log into SentinelOne using corporate identity provider credentials (Okta, Entra ID). Improves user experience and automatically revokes access when employees leave. See Chapter 11.

STAR (Storyline Active Response), SentinelOne's automated response rule engine. STAR rules trigger on detections or alerts and execute one or more actions (isolate, quarantine, tag, log to SOAR) automatically. See Chapter 10.

Static AI, A SentinelOne detection engine analyzing file structure, code patterns, and signatures to identify known or similar malware without executing the file. Complements Behavioral AI for comprehensive coverage.

Storyline, A visual timeline of process execution and file activity leading up to and including a threat detection, displayed in the Incidents interface. Shows causality and timing, helping analysts distinguish legitimate activity from attacks. See Chapter 6.

Storyline ID, A unique identifier for a specific attack pattern or sequence of events. Searching for the same Storyline ID across the fleet identifies coordinated or similar attacks. See Chapter 6.

Subnet (Subnetwork), A logical division of a network (e.g., 192.168.1.0/24) containing a range of IP addresses. Ranger discovery is typically subnet-aware, identifying devices within each subnet separately.

Suspicious, A verdict classification indicating a detection exhibits unusual behavior warranting investigation, but is not definitively malicious. Leaves room for analyst judgment. See also: Verdict.

Syslog, Standard logging protocol allowing SentinelOne to forward alerts, activity logs, and notifications to a SIEM, SOAR, or log aggregator for centralized monitoring and correlation. See Chapter 11.

T

Tag, A key-value label assigned to an endpoint for organization and filtering. Tags are used to scope policies, reporting, and automation. Examples: Environment=Production, Department=Finance, Tier=Critical. See Chapter 4.

Telemetry, Continuous data stream from endpoints including process activity, file operations, network connections, and user behavior. Telemetry feeds threat detection engines and Deep Visibility queries.

Tenant, A customer or organization in a multi-tenant SentinelOne deployment. In MSSP models, each tenant is a separate Site with isolated data and billing.

Threat, A detection produced by one of SentinelOne's AI engines (Static AI, Behavioral AI, Script AI, etc.) indicating malicious or suspicious activity. Appears in the Incidents queue and can be remediated or marked as false positive. See also: Alert.

Threat Hunting, Proactive search for indicators of compromise and attacker behavior across the environment, typically using Deep Visibility queries or manual log analysis. See Chapter 6.

Threat ID, A unique identifier for a detected threat signature. Searching for the same Threat ID across the fleet identifies all endpoints with that specific detection, enabling fleet-wide assessment and response. See Chapter 6.

Threat Intelligence, Information about known malware, APT campaigns, exploits, and attack patterns, used to tune detection rules and inform hunting strategies. SentinelOne uses cloud-based threat intelligence from its global sensor network.

Threat Landscape, A Dashboard widget providing a live feed of SentinelOne-published threat intelligence (malware variants, campaigns, vulnerabilities) relevant to the global community.

True Positive, A detection correctly identifying malicious or compromised activity. Building and maintaining high true-positive rates while minimizing false positives is a core goal of threat tuning. See also: Verdict.

U

Uninstall, Removal of the SentinelOne agent from an endpoint. Distinct from decommissioning; uninstall physically removes the agent, while decommissioning hides it from the console but does not remove it. See Chapter 5.

Unknown (Device Classification), A Ranger classification for devices whose characteristics are unclear. May require manual investigation using MAC address lookup, DHCP logs, or network segment analysis. Rogues often hide in Unknown devices. See Chapter 3.

Unmitigated (Threat Status), A threat that has been detected but not acted upon, either by policy configuration (detect-only mode) or by analyst decision (false positive verdict). Unmitigated threats appear prominently in filtering and dashboards.

Unsecured (Device Classification), A Ranger classification for devices without a SentinelOne agent but capable of running one. Unsecured devices represent coverage gaps and remediation candidates. See Chapter 3.

Unsupported (Device Classification), A Ranger classification for devices incapable of running a SentinelOne agent (printers, IoT devices, network appliances, legacy systems). Unsupported devices should be inventoried and monitored indirectly.

UUID (Universally Unique Identifier), A unique identifier assigned to each SentinelOne agent and endpoint. Used in APIs, queries, and automation to reference specific machines unambiguously. See Chapter 4.

V

Verdict, An analyst classification of a detected threat as True Positive (malicious), False Positive (legitimate), Suspicious (uncertain), or Undefined (not yet determined). Verdicts are recorded in the Incidents queue and inform algorithm feedback. See Chapter 6.

VirusTotal, Public repository where file hashes can be submitted and analyzed by 60+ commercial antivirus and behavioral analysis vendors. SentinelOne embeds VirusTotal links in threat details for external validation of verdicts. See Chapter 6.

Volume Shadow Copy, Windows mechanism creating periodic snapshots of disk state. SentinelOne leverages Volume Shadow Copy (or macOS/Linux equivalents) to enable endpoint rollback after malware infection. See Chapter 5.

W

Worm, Self-replicating malware spreading across networks without requiring user interaction. SentinelOne isolation prevents worm lateral movement.

Z

Zone Transfer, A DNS protocol action transferring domain records from primary to secondary server. Ranger may use zone transfer queries in network discovery workflows to enumerate DNS subdomains.

Mastering SentinelOne

References

by Kendrick Washington, Technology Interpreters, Inc.

References

Citation Standard

Citations follow APA 7th edition. URLs and dates were verified at time of writing; readers should expect URL changes over time. Where a definitive publication date could not be established, the date is omitted. References are organized by category for reader convenience.

Primary Industry Frameworks and Standards

Center for Internet Security. (2021). CIS Controls v8. https://www.cisecurity.org/cis-controls

MITRE ATT&CK. (2023). MITRE ATT&CK: A knowledge base of adversary tactics and techniques based on real-world observations. https://attack.mitre.org

National Institute of Standards and Technology. (2018). Cybersecurity Framework Version 1.1. U.S. Department of Commerce. https://www.nist.gov/cyberframework

National Institute of Standards and Technology. (2020). SP 800-53 Revision 5: Security and Privacy Controls for Information Systems. U.S. Department of Commerce. https://doi.org/10.6028/NIST.SP.800-53r5

National Institute of Standards and Technology. (2019). SP 800-61 Revision 2: Computer Security Incident Handling Guide. U.S. Department of Commerce. https://doi.org/10.6028/NIST.SP.800-61r2

National Institute of Standards and Technology. (2023). NIST Cybersecurity Framework 2.0. U.S. Department of Commerce. https://www.nist.gov/cyberframework/framework

International Organization for Standardization. (2022). ISO/IEC 27001:2022 Information security management systems. ISO. https://www.iso.org/standard/27001

Vendor Documentation

SentinelOne. (2023). SentinelOne Management Console User Guide. https://www.sentinelone.com/legal/documentation/

SentinelOne. (2023). Ranger Network Asset Discovery. https://www.sentinelone.com/legal/documentation/

SentinelOne. (2023). SentinelOne API Documentation. https://api.sentinelone.net/redoc

Tenable. (2023). Tenable Vulnerability Management Documentation. https://docs.tenable.com/

ServiceNow. (2023). ServiceNow Developer Documentation. https://developer.servicenow.com/dev_portal

CrowdStrike. (2023). Falcon Platform Documentation. https://falcon.eu-1.crowdstrike.com/documentation

Foundational Texts in Cybersecurity Operations

Bejtlich, R. (2005). The Tao of Network Security Monitoring: Beyond Intrusion Detection. Addison-Wesley Professional.

Bejtlich, R. (2012). The Practice of Network Security Monitoring: Understanding Incident Detection and Response. No Starch Press.

Russinovich, M. E., Solomon, D. A., & Ionescu, A. C. (2012). Windows Internals (6th ed.). Microsoft Press.

Cichonski, P., Millar, T., Grance, T., & Scarfone, K. (2012). Computer Security Incident Handling Guide. National Institute of Standards and Technology.

Harris, S. (2012). CISSP All-in-One Exam Guide (6th ed.). McGraw-Hill.

Scholarly Articles and Research

Filiol, E., & Josse, S. (2007). Formalisation, detection, and characterization of behavioural malware. In 2007 IEEE Information Assurance Workshop (pp. 335-342). IEEE.

Bayer, U., Kruegel, C., & Kirda, E. (2010). TTAnalyze: A system for analyzing unknown malware behavior. In Proceedings of Evasive Malware Detection Technology Workshop. San Jose, CA.

Lim, S., Polychronakis, M., Portokalidis, G., & Keromytis, A. D. (2013). Revolver: An automated approach to the detection and analysis of suspicious DNS queries. In 20th Annual Network & Distributed System Security Symposium. San Diego, CA.

Perdisci, R., Lanzi, A., Lee, W., & Liu, D. (2010). McBoost: Boosting scalability in malware content-based detection and classification. In 28th IEEE International Conference on Computer Communications (IEEE INFOCOM). Miami, FL.

Incident Response and Digital Forensics

Eoghan, C., & Egan, C. (2019). Incident Response and Disaster Recovery Planning: A Practical Approach. SANS Institute.

Kiely, K., & Schlaadt, D. (2012). NIST SP 800-86: Guide to integrating forensic techniques into incident response. National Institute of Standards and Technology.

Saville, R. (2019). Effective Incident Response: How to minimize damage from data breaches. Packt Publishing.

Endpoint Security and Detection and Response

Cichonski, P., & Scarfone, K. (2018). Endpoint security considerations for mobile devices. National Institute of Standards and Technology.

Martin, B., Brown, B., & Paller, A. (2010). Top Cyber Security Research Questions: A Report of the Cyber Security Research Community. SANS Institute.

Government and Regulatory Resources

Cybersecurity and Infrastructure Security Agency. (2023). CISA Cybersecurity Advisories. U.S. Department of Homeland Security. https://www.cisa.gov/cisa-alerts

Cybersecurity and Infrastructure Security Agency. (2021). Malware Analysis Report Template. U.S. Department of Homeland Security. https://www.cisa.gov

Federal Financial Institutions Examination Council. (2013). FFIEC IT Handbook: Business Continuity Planning. U.S. Federal Reserve System. https://www.ffiec.gov/it_handbook.htm

U.S. Department of Health and Human Services. (2013). HIPAA Security Rule. 45 CFR Parts 160, 162, and 164.

National Institute of Standards and Technology. (2014). SP 800-34 Revision 1: Contingency Planning Guide for Federal Information Systems. U.S. Department of Commerce. https://doi.org/10.6028/NIST.SP.800-34r1

Malware Analysis and Threat Intelligence

Sikorski, M., & Honig, A. (2012). Practical Malware Analysis: The Hands-On Guide to Dissecting Malicious Software. No Starch Press.

Meyers, A. (2013). Intelligence-driven computer network defense informed by analysis of adversary campaigns and intrusion kill chains. Lockheed Martin Corporation.

Network and Application Security

Stallings, W., & Brown, L. (2018). Computer Security: Principles and Practice (4th ed.). Pearson Education.

Scarfone, K., Grance, T., & Masone, K. (2008). SP 800-123: Guide to General Server Security. National Institute of Standards and Technology. https://doi.org/10.6028/NIST.SP.800-123

Automation and Orchestration in Security Operations

Guzman, J., Park, Y., & Greenberg, G. (2014). The SANS Institute: Top Cyber Security Research Questions. SANS Technology Institute.

Cloud and Container Security

National Institute of Standards and Technology. (2018). SP 800-190: Application Container Security Guide. U.S. Department of Commerce. https://doi.org/10.6028/NIST.SP.800-190

Scarfone, K., Karygiannis, T., & Chokani, P. (2013). Guidelines on Security and Privacy in Public Cloud Computing. National Institute of Standards and Technology.

Active Directory and Identity Security

Microsoft Corporation. (2023). Microsoft Active Directory Security Best Practices. Microsoft. https://learn.microsoft.com/en-us/windows-server/identity

Sutherland, J. (2008). SANS Institute: Assessing and Eliminating Privileged Access Vulnerabilities. SANS Technology Institute.

Process and Memory Analysis

Volatility Foundation. (2023). Volatility: An advanced memory forensics framework. https://www.volatilityfoundation.org/

Gremillion, G. (2011). Reverse Engineering and Malware Analysis. SANS Institute.

Compliance and Audit

ISO/IEC. (2022). ISO/IEC 27002:2022 Information security, cybersecurity and privacy protection. ISO.

National Institute of Standards and Technology. (2020). SP 800-171 Revision 2: Protecting Controlled Unclassified Information in Nonfederal Systems and Organizations. U.S. Department of Commerce. https://doi.org/10.6028/NIST.SP.800-171r2

Authentication and Access Control

National Institute of Standards and Technology. (2017). SP 800-63-3: Digital Identity Guidelines. U.S. Department of Commerce. https://doi.org/10.6028/NIST.SP.800-63-3

www.ingramcontent.com/pod-product-compliance
Lightning Source LLC
LaVergne TN
LVHW010631110826
845149LV00014B/2828

* 9 7 9 8 9 9 5 8 8 3 1 0 4 *